Microsoft® Windows® 6-in-1

Written by Jane Calabria and Dorthy Burke

with

Laurie Ann Ulrich and Susan Trost

A Division of Macmillan Computer Publishing
201 West 103rd Street, Indianapolis, Indiana 46290 USA

To the thousands of students we have met during hundreds of classes over many years. Thank you for all you have taught us.

Library of Congress Catalog Card Number: 97-69184

International Standard Book Number: 0-7897-1385-3

99 98 97   8 7 6 5 4 3

Interpretation of the printing code: the rightmost double-digit number is the year of the book's first printing; the rightmost single-digit number is the number of the book's printing. For example, a printing code of 97-1 shows that this copy of the book was printed during the first printing of the book in 1997.

Printed in the United States of America

Screen reproductions in this book were created by means of the program Collage Complete from Inner Media, Inc., Hollis, NH.

Publisher
Roland Elgey

Senior Vice President/Publishing
Don Fowley

Publisher
Joseph B. Wikert

Publishing Director
Brad R. Koch

Manager of Publishing Operations
Linda H. Buehler

General Manager
Joe Muldoon

Director of Editorial Services
Carla Hall

Managing Editor
Thomas Hayes

Director of Acquisitions
Cheryl Willoughby

Acquisitions Editor
Angie Wethington

Senior Product Director
Lisa D. Wagner

Product Development Specialist
Stephen L. Miller

Production Editor
Kate Givens

Editors
Elizabeth Barrett
San Dee Phillips

Product Marketing Manager
Kourtnaye Sturgeon

Assistant Product Marketing Manager
Gretchen Schlesinger

Technical Editors
John Purdum
Nadeem Muhammed
Christopher Lawrence
Rob Kirkland

Media Devlopment Specialist
David Garratt

Acquisitions Coordinator
Michelle R. Newcomb

Software Relations Coordinator
Susan D. Gallagher

Editorial Assistant
Jennifer L. Chisolm

Book Designers
Glenn Larsen
Kim Scott

Cover Designer
Dan Armstrong

Production Team
Jenny Earhart
Bryan Flores
Julie Geeting
Laura A. Knox

Indexer
Craig Small

Composed in **Palatino** and **Helvetica** by Que Corporation.

Trademarks

Acknowledgments

To Angie Wethington for presenting this opportunity to us, and to Brad Koch for siding with her! We thank you whole heartedly for your belief in us and for this wonderful and fun project. We think Angie and Brad make an ace team and look forward to an opportunity to work with them again and again!

To John Purdum for his expert technical editing and his warm and wonderful sense of humor. It was John's job to catch technical errors, and we wish we could say that John was not kept busy enough. Congratulations, John, on a great job.

To Steve Miller, our Development Editor, and Kate Givens, our Production Editor. This was our first time working with Steve and Kate, and we'd do it again, any time, any place. Thanks, Steve for your invaluable input, your decisiveness, and your ability to get things done quickly! And thank you, Kate, for putting and keeping it together for all of us.

We'd Like to Hear from You!

As part of our continuing effort to produce books of the highest possible quality, Que would like to hear your comments. To stay competitive, we *really* want you, as a computer book reader and user, to let us know what you like or dislike most about this book or other Que products.

You can mail comments, ideas, or suggestions for improving future editions to the address below, or send us a fax at (317) 581-4663. The address of our Internet site is **http://www.mcp.com/que** (World Wide Web).

In addition to exploring our forum, please feel free to contact me personally to discuss your opinions of this book. My e-mail address is **lwagner@que.mcp.com**.

Thanks in advance—your comments will help us to continue publishing the best books available on computer topics in today's market.

Lisa D. Wagner
Senior Product Development Specialist
Que Corporation
201 W. 103rd Street
Indianapolis, Indiana 46290
USA

Contents

Part I: Windows 95 Essentials

Part II: Customizing Windows 95

Part III: Using Windows 95 on a Network

Part IV: Communications and the Internet

Part V: Active Desktop Essentials

Part VI: Real World Solutions

Part VII: Appendixes

Introduction

Whether you are using a computer at home or at work, odds are good that you are using—or you're about to use—Microsoft Windows 95. A powerful and flexible operating system, Windows 95 offers multitasking (the ability to work with many applications open at one time), a consistent look and feel across programs designed to run in Windows, the ability to integrate a variety of servers, 16- and 32-bit applications, and easy network access to other computers files, printers, and the Internet. Windows is designed to make computing easier, and this introduction is designed to help you decide if this book can make Windows 95 easier for you to work with and understand.

Who Should Use this Book

Microsoft Windows 95 6-in-1 is for anyone who:

- Is new to Windows 95.
- Is new to Internet Explorer 4.
- Is new to the Internet.
- Is new to computers.
- Wants to expand his Windows 95 skills.
- Wants to learn about Active Desktop.
- Wants to learn or reference tasks in short, 10 minute spurts.
- Wants real world solutions to using Windows 95 in the real world!

Why *This* Book?

We present to you, in a reasonable and concise method, the tools and information you need to understand the most powerful software installed on your computer—your operating system. We help you to make Windows work for you—not against you. We've dedicated an entire section to "Real World Solutions" with suggestions and information about living with and working with computers.

This book is written using the Que "Ten Minute Guide" formula, a proven and popular format. Over 4 million 10 Minute Guides have been sold around the world. The authors have taught computer applications, operating systems, hardware, networking, and programming classes for many years. As consultants they have worked with companies all over the country providing systems, software, and education solutions.

How This Book Is Organized

Windows 95 6-in-1 has lessons ranging from basics to some more advanced features. Each lesson is intended to take 10 minutes or less of your time. You can work through the book lesson by lesson, building upon your skills, or you can use the book as a quick reference when you want to perform a new task.

Following is a brief description of each part of *Microsoft Windows 95 6-in-1:*

- **Part I, Windows 95 Essentials**   The book begins with an overview of Windows 95 and its capabilities. You'll learn how to work with multiple windows, manage files, use multimedia features, print, backup, and more.

- **Part II, Customizing Windows 95**   Here, you learn how to use the Control Panel, customize your desktop and Start menu, and install new hardware and software.

- **Part III, Using Windows 95 on a Network**   If you're new to networks, you'll gain some important skills from Part III. Learn how to attach to a network, map drives, share printers and files, use dial-up networking, and use Network Neighborhood.

- **Part IV, Communications and the Internet**   Internet Explorer 4 (IE4) is introduced in this section, from installing to configuring to surfing the Net. Learn about the new capabilities of IE4 and even learn the basics of the Internet and the Web.

- **Part V, Active Desktop Essentials**   Once installed, Internet Explorer 4 changes your desktop and the look of My Computer and Explorer. Learn how to *explore* your computer with Internet Explorer 4.

- **Part VI, Real World Solutions**   This section is developed to provide solutions to computer and computer related problems and questions. Information found here is generally not operating-system related; rather it is information that you need to successfully work in a computing world. You will find suggestions for: organizing a hard drive, preparing to call a help desk, e-mail etiquette, traveling with a laptop or notebook, and working in a safe computer environment at home, just to name a few.

- **Appendix A: Installing and Using Microsoft Plus!**   Learn how to install Microsoft Plus! and select from the great screensavers and themes that Plus! provides.

- **Appendix B: About Installing Windows OSR2**   OSR2 is a software release meant for installation by computer hardware suppliers. If you want to have some of the features of OSR2, this appendix tells you where to find information on upgrading to OSR2 and precautions you should take if you decide to upgrade yourself.

- **Inside Cover**   Check out the inside front cover, which contains Windows shortcut keystrokes and a sample figure of a window. Soon, you'll be navigating through Windows quickly and efficiently.

Conventions Used in This Book

All of the short lessons in this book include step-by-step instructions for performing specific tasks. The following *icons* (small graphic representations) are included to help you quickly identify particular types of information.

These icons indicate ways for you to save time when performing a task.

TIP

These icons point out definitions of words you'll need to know in order to understand how to use a program or system.

TERM

These icons will help you avoid making mistakes.

CAUTION

If you are working with Internet Explorer, your screen will probably look different in some instances, and you may have to follow different steps. These tips will let you be aware of those situations.

 Many of the tasks you learn in this book can be applied globally to Microsoft programs. These tips will tell you when you can use a task that you are learning in some other situation.

In addition to the icons, the following conventions are also used:

`On-Screen text`	On-screen text will appear monospaced.
What you type	Information that you type appears in bold type.
Items you select	Items you select, buttons you click, or keys you press appear in bold type.

About the Authors

Jane Calabria has authored or contributed to no less than 12 Que books, which include the *Professional Developers Guide to Domino 4.5*. She has been an independent consultant since 1990 and used her first computer in 1981—a hand-held 16K Radio Shack special. She became hooked on that little computer when, within a week, she was teaching herself Basic and writing programs. Since 1992, she has been training, consulting, and developing applications. Jane teaches Windows, Windows NT, a variety of databases, word processing, electronic mail, and the Internet. She is heard weekly in the Philadelphia area on KYW News Radio 1060 AM, giving reports on computing and computer news as "JC on PCs." Her reports are also found on AOL. She can be reached at **74754.3360@compuserve.com**.

Dorothy Burke started life as a technical magazine editor. She has been an independent consultant and trainer for many years. She has contributed to several Que books, including *Special Edition, Using PowerPoint*. As a trainer, Dorothy teaches desktop publishing, operating systems, spreadsheets and graphics programs, as well as Lotus Notes and Domino. As a consultant, Dorothy works with Lotus Notes and Domino, developing applications. Dorothy can be reached at **70161.364@compuserve.com**.

Jane and Dorothy have teamed up successfully on several Que books, including the *10 Minute Guide to Lotus Notes Mail 4.5, Lotus Notes and the Internet 6-in-1* and *Microsoft Works 6-in-1*. Both are independent consultants, trainers, and authors who are certified in several products including Lotus Notes and Domino, and travel the United States teaching and consulting.

Laurie Ann Ulrich has been working with computers since 1981, and teaching computer skills to people of all ages and backgrounds since 1990. Currently, she teaches continuing education courses at colleges and computer training organizations throughout the Pennsylvania, New Jersey, and New York areas. In addition, Laurie is president of Limehat & Company, Inc., a consulting firm in Huntingdon Valley, PA, that specializes in technical documentation, desktop publishing, presentations, and graphics design. She can be reached at **Limehat@aol.com**.

Susan Trost is an independent software consultant who has worked internationally for Andersen Consulting and Lotus Development. Her areas of expertise include groupware application design and development, heterogeneous systems integration, and messaging. She used her first Microsoft application back in 1989. This is the fourth book she has worked on for Que Corporation. Susan holds a B.S. from Towson State University, and an M.S. in Telecommunications from the University of Colorado, Boulder. She is currently pursuing a Ph.D. in Information Systems at the University of Salford in Manchester, England. She can be reached via e-mail at **Susan_Trost@Compuserve.com**.

Windows 95
Essentials

Navigating the
Windows 95
Desktop

In this lesson, you learn to start and shut down Windows, work with the parts of the Windows desktop, and use a mouse to manipulate items on the desktop.

What Is Windows 95?

Windows 95 is an *operating system*. It controls the hardware of your computer and interprets the instructions from your software and operating systems to the hardware. When you use a menu command such as **File**, **Save**, Windows 95 is the driving force that writes the file to your disk or hard drive.

Windows 95 includes such features as *multitasking*, or the ability to run more than one program at a time. It uses a *graphical user interface* (GUI), which allows you to get up and running through the use of pictures and graphics, instead of having to type out long commands to the operating system. Programs designed to run under Windows 95 (such as Word or Lotus) use similar keyboard and mouse operations to select objects and choose commands. Video and graphics applications run smoothly on Windows 95, enabling multimedia programs to run quickly and efficiently.

Starting Windows 95

To start Windows 95, you simply turn on your computer and monitor. As your computer *boots*, Windows loads the files it needs to run. You'll notice the Windows 95 logo screen and several black screens with white type.

After the operating system is loaded, a password dialog box appears asking for your *user name* and your *password*. If you are a member of a network, you must use the exact user name and password assigned to you by your network administrator; if you are not sure of what to enter in this dialog box, ask your administrator. You should use the same user name and password each time you *log on* to Windows so that your desktop, applications, and customization settings will always be the same. By default, Windows displays the Log On dialog box if you're on a network. If you don't see a Log On dialog box, you don't have to enter a user name or password to work in Windows.

Boot   A term used to describe a computer's starting up process, during which the operating system and configuration files are loaded into the computer's memory.

User Name and Password   Identifies you to your computer or to the network server, and protects your computer from illegal entry.

Log On   Attaching to the network so you can use its resources—files, printers, and so on.

Follow these steps to open the Windows program if you're on a network:

1. Enter the following information:

   - **User Name**   The name by which you are identified to your computer or the network.
   - **Password**   Your personal watchword for logging in to the computer or network.

2. Press **Enter** or click **OK** to start Windows.

Error Message!   Many different errors could occur at this point. For example, a message might appear on your screen telling you a connection could not be restored or that you're not a valid user. First, make sure you've typed your password correctly and used the appropriate case when typing. If you still have a problem connecting to the network, see your network administrator for help.

For more information on working with Windows in a networked environment, see Part III, "Using Windows 95 on a Network."

Should I Press Enter or Click OK? Pressing **Enter** in a dialog or message box is the same as choosing the **OK** button; pressing the **Escape** key is the same as choosing the **Cancel** button.

Understanding the Windows Desktop

After Windows 95 starts, you will see various items on the screen, as shown in Figure 1.1. The items you see enable you to open applications, manage files, send and receive mail, and perform many other tasks throughout your work day. Depending on your installation, you may or may not see all of the items shown in the following figure.

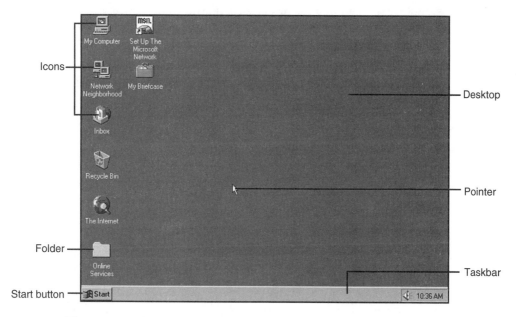

Figure 1.1 Common components of the Windows screen.

 With IE4 and Active Desktop Running... If Internet Explorer 4 is installed on your computer, your desktop may look different. See Part V, Lesson 1 "Navigating Active Desktop" for more information.

The components of the Windows screen include:

- **Desktop**   This is the background on which all other elements appear. You can think of the Windows desktop like the top of your own traditional office desk. Just as you can move papers around, hide certain items in drawers, and add and remove things on your desk, you can manipulate items on your Windows desktop.

- **Icons**   Icons are pictures that represent programs (the Internet, Word for Windows, Excel, and so on), folders, files, printer information, computer information, and so on, in both Windows 95 and Windows applications. Most often, you use icons to open folders and files.

- **My Computer**   The My Computer icon represents the contents of your computer, including the hard drive, floppy and CD drives, applications, folders, files, and so on. Double-click an icon to open it and view its contents.

- **Network Neighborhood**   This icon displays other computers connected to your computer on a Microsoft or other type of network, such as NT or NetWare.

- **Inbox**   The Inbox represents Microsoft Exchange, a program you can use to fax and e-mail other computers.

- **The Internet**   If you have access to an Internet Service Provider, you can use the Internet Explorer to access the Net, including Web pages and e-mail.

- **Recycle Bin**   The Recycle Bin is a place in which deleted objects remain until you empty the trash. You can retrieve items—files, programs, pictures, and so on—from the Recycle Bin after you delete them. Once you empty the trash, however, you can no longer retrieve items from the bin.

- **My Briefcase**   My Briefcase is a feature you can use for copying and transferring files from your computer to a notebook or other computer. My Briefcase enables you to easily transfer and update your files.

- **Online Services**   This folder icon enables you to quickly and easily sign up for any of the online services it contains, including America Online, AT&T WorldNet, and CompuServe. You must have a modem connected to your computer and configured before using one of these services.

- **Set Up The Microsoft Network**   A step-by-step guide to configuring your computer and connecting to Microsoft's special Internet network. Again, you need a modem to use this feature.

- **Taskbar** The taskbar contains the Start button, any open application or window buttons, and the time. You can click a taskbar button to open the window or application it represents. Use the Start button to open programs, documents, help, and so on.

- **Start Button** The Start button displays a menu from which you can choose to open an application, open a document, customize Windows, find a file or folder, get help, or shut down the Windows 95 program.

- **Folder** A folder contains files, programs, or other folders on your computer; for example, the Online Services folder contains programs that let you sign up for an online service like CompuServe. A folder is the same thing as a directory.

- **Pointer** The pointer is an on-screen icon (usually an arrow) that represents your mouse, trackball, touchpad, or other selecting device. You use it to select items and choose commands. You move the pointer by moving the mouse or other device across your desk or mouse pad. You learn how to use the mouse in the next section.

Using the Mouse

You use the mouse to perform many actions in Windows and in Windows applications. With the mouse, you can easily select an icon, folder, or window, among other things. Selecting involves two steps: pointing and clicking. You also can open icons and folders by double-clicking them, and you can move an item by clicking and dragging that particular article.

To *point* to an object (icon, taskbar, Start button, and so on) move the mouse across your desk or mouse pad until the on-screen mouse pointer touches the object. You can pick up the mouse and reposition it if you run out of room on your desk. To *click*, point the mouse pointer at the object you want to select, and then press and release the left mouse button. If the object is an icon or window, it becomes highlighted. When following steps in this book, click the left mouse button unless the directions specify otherwise.

The right mouse button can be used when you want to display a shortcut, or a quick menu. To *right-click*, point the mouse pointer at an object—folder, taskbar, desktop, and so on—and click the right mouse button. A shortcut menu that presents common commands relating to the object appears. If, for example, you right-click a folder, the menu might offer these commands: Open, Explore, Create Shortcut, and Properties. The items on the menu depend on the object you're right-clicking.

When you *double-click* an item, you point to the item and press and release the left mouse button twice quickly. Double-clicking is often a shortcut to performing a task. For example, you can open a folder or window by double-clicking its icon.

You can use the mouse to move an object (usually a window, dialog box, or icon) to a new position on-screen. You do this by *clicking and dragging* the object. To drag an object to a new location on-screen, point to the object, press and hold the left mouse button, move the mouse to a new location, and release the mouse button. The object moves with the mouse cursor as you drag it. If you want some practice with the mouse, open the Solitaire game and play a round or two; choose **Start**, **Programs**, **Accessories**, **Games**, and then **Solitaire**.

You also can perform certain actions, such as selecting multiple items or copying items, by performing two additional mouse operations. *Shift+click* means to press and hold the Shift key and then click the left mouse button while pointing to various objects; *Ctrl+click* means to press and hold the Ctrl key, and then click the left mouse button. The result of either of these actions depends upon where you are in Windows.

Using the Start Button

The Windows Start button provides access to programs and documents, the help feature, find feature, and many other elements in Windows 95. You use the Start button to perform most tasks in Windows.

To use the Start button, follow these steps:

1. Point the mouse at the **Start** button, located on the taskbar, and click the button. The **Start menu** appears (see Figure 1.2). Your Start menu may display more options than the one in the figure, depending on what is installed on your computer.

2. Click the task or command you want to display, as follows:

   - **Programs**   Displays a submenu (also called a "cascading" or "secondary" menu) that includes Windows Accessory programs, Online Services, the Internet Explorer, and other programs on your computer.

   - **Documents**   Displays up to 15 of the most recently opened documents; for quick and easy access, click the document name and the application. The document opens, ready to work.

- **Settings** Displays a secondary menu that includes the Control Panel and Printers folders, and the taskbar command for customizing your Windows setup. For more information, see Part II, "Customizing Windows 95."

- **Find** Enables you to search for specific files, folders, or computers. You can search your own hard drive or the network drive.

- **Help** Displays help for performing tasks and procedures in Windows. For more information, see Lesson 5.

- **Run** Enables you to enter a command line (such as a:\install) to run a program from hard, floppy, or CD disks.

- **Shut Down** Displays the Shut Down dialog box in which you prepare your computer before turning it off.

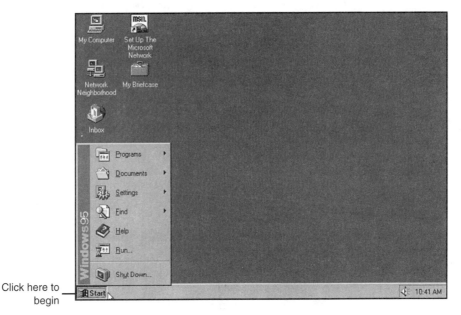

Click here to begin

Figure 1.2 The Start menu provides easy access to programs.

Submenu An arrow after any menu command designates another menu, called a submenu (or sometimes a "cascading" or "secondary" menu). It will appear if you choose that command. Windows supplies as many as four submenus starting from the Start menu.

For more information abou using menus, see Lesson 3. To learn how to customize the Start Menu see Part II, Lesson 5, "Customizing the Start Menu."

Using the Taskbar

In addition to the Start button, the taskbar displays buttons representing open windows and applications. You can quickly switch between open windows by clicking the button on the taskbar. Figure 1.3 shows the taskbar with two buttons representing open and minimized programs—Microsoft Word and Microsoft Excel.

Figure 1.3   Open and minimized windows are represented on the taskbar by buttons and the window's name.

You can move the taskbar to the top, left, or right side of the screen to customize your workspace. Additionally, you can hide the taskbar until you need it.

To move the taskbar, click the mouse anywhere on the bar—except on a button—and drag the taskbar to the right, the left, or the top of the screen. As you drag, the taskbar relocates to that area. You can easily drag the taskbar back to the bottom if you prefer it there.

To hide the taskbar, follow these steps:

1. Click the **Start** button.
2. From the **Start** menu, click **Settings** and then click **Taskbar**.
3. Choose the **Auto Hide** check box by clicking that box; then press **Enter** to close the dialog box. The taskbar slides off of the screen.

When you need the taskbar, move the mouse to where the taskbar was; you may have to slide the mouse off of the screen. The taskbar reappears.

I Can't Display the Taskbar!   If you move the mouse to where the taskbar should be and the taskbar doesn't display, press **Ctrl+Esc** to display the taskbar and open **Start** menu.

CAUTION

To show the taskbar all the time, click **Start**, **Settings**, **Taskbar** and click the **Auto Hide** check box so no check mark appears. Press **Enter** to close the dialog box. For more on working with the taskbar, see Part II, Lesson 4 "Customizing the Taskbar."

Shutting Down Windows 95

Before you turn off your computer, you must shut down Windows to ensure you don't lose any data or configuration. You also can shut down Windows and restart the computer, in MS-DOS mode, for example, or to log onto the network under a different name. Following are the Shut Down options available to you in the Shut Down Windows dialog box:

- **Shut Down the Computer**   Choose this option when you're finished using your computer for the day. When Windows displays a message telling you to shut off your computer, you can safely turn off the machine.

- **Restart the Computer**   Choose this option to shut down and then restart the computer in Windows mode. You use this option when you've changed configuration in the Control Panel, for example, and you want that configuration to take effect.

- **Restart the Computer in MS-DOS Mode**   This option shuts down Windows and starts the computer back in DOS mode, with a black screen, white type, and a C-prompt, or command prompt. From the command prompt, you can enter many familiar DOS commands or install DOS applications.

- **Close All Programs and Log On as a Different User**   Choose this option when you're sharing a computer with someone and they are already logged onto the network. When you choose this option, the network logon dialog box appears in which you can enter your user name and password.

To shut down Windows, follow these steps:

1. From the Desktop, click **Start**, **Shut Down**.
2. When the **Shut Down Windows** dialog box appears, choose one of the options previously described. To quit working on the computer, choose **Shut Down the Computer**. Then choose **Yes**.
3. Do not turn the computer off until Windows displays the message telling you that it's okay to turn off your computer (some computers turn off automatically, so this message isn't displayed).

In this lesson, you learned to start and shut down Windows, work with the parts of the Windows desktop, and use a mouse to manipulate items on the desktop. In the next lesson, you learn to work with windows.

Working with a Window

In this lesson, you learn to open, resize, move, view, and close a window, and how to use scroll bars to view more of a window.

What Is a Window?

A *window* is a boxed area in which you view files, folders, drives, hardware icons, or other elements. Figure 2.1 shows the components that make up a window. Many of these components are the same for all windows in Windows 95 and Windows applications, which makes it easy for you to manage your work. Keep in mind that although most windows are similar, some will not have all of the following components.

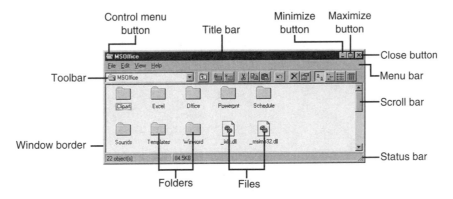

Figure 2.1 The elements of a typical window.

You can open and close a window, reduce and enlarge a window, and move a window around—which is what this lesson is all about. In addition, you can open more than one window at a time, stack one window on top of another, and otherwise manipulate windows, as explained later in Lesson 7. Table 2.1 briefly describes the common elements of a window.

Table 2.1 Window Elements

Element	Description
Title bar	Contains the window's name, the Control menu, and the Minimize, Maximize or Restore, and the Close buttons.
Menu bar	Contains menus with related commands and options that help you control the window and its contents. See additional information about menus in Lesson 3.
Control menu button	Contains commands that help you manage the window itself.
Toolbar	Graphic tool buttons that represent shortcuts to various menu commands you use in your work.
Minimize button	A button that reduces the window to a button on the taskbar.
Maximize button	A button that enlarges the window to fill the screen.
Close button	A button that closes the window.
Folders	Icons within windows that represent directories; folders can hold other folders and files.
Files	Document, spreadsheet, database, program, and other components stored in folders on a drive in your computer.
Windows border	A rim around a restored window that you can use to resize the window.
Status bar	A bar across the bottom of the window that describes the contents of the window, such as free space, number of objects or files in a window, and so on.
Scroll bar	A vertical or horizontal bar that enables you to view hidden areas of a window.

 TIP **No Toolbar or Status Bar Showing?** If a window doesn't display the toolbar, choose the **View** menu, and the **Toolbar** command; to display the Status bar, choose **View**, **Status Bar**.

Windows Contents

Windows 95 is made up of a series of windows that often contain different items. When opened, each icon on your desktop, for example, displays different contents just as various folders, files, and applications display various contents. Additionally, after you open a window, you can usually open items within the window, such as icons, folders, programs, and documents. Often, you can open a window within a window within a window, and so on, until your desktop is filled with windows. Be aware, however, that having a lot of windows open (especially program windows) may slow down the operation of your computer.

Following is an example of a set of windows you can open from the My Computer icon:

- **My Computer window** Displays hard drive icons, floppy disk and CD icons, Control Panel folder and the Printers folder; often this window also includes the Dial-Up Networking icon.

- **Hard drive icon** Displays all folders (or directories) on that drive, plus any files found on the root directory (usually C).

- **Program Files folder** Displays folders representing programs included with Windows, such as the Accessories, Internet Explorer, Online Services, and so on.

- **Internet Explorer folder** Includes the Internet Explorer program and files needed to run the program, plus several text files you can read to get more information about the Internet Explorer.

Opening a Window

To open a window from an icon, double-click the icon. For example, point at the **My Computer** icon and double-click. If you do it correctly, the My Computer icon opens into the My Computer window.

CAUTION

Having Double-Click Trouble? If you have trouble opening a window by double-clicking, you need to practice the double-click movement. You can also change the speed of the double-click to better suit your "trigger" finger. See Part II, Lesson 8 for more information on customizing your mouse.

There is another method you can use to open a window. Just point to the icon and right-click once, and a shortcut menu appears. Select **Open** from the menu to open the window.

Sizing a Window with Maximize, Minimize, and Restore

You may want to increase the size of a window to see its full contents, or you may want to decrease a window to a button on the taskbar in order to make room for other windows. One way to resize a window is to use the Maximize, Minimize, and Restore commands found on the Control menu. If you use the mouse, you will use the Maximize, Minimize, and Restore buttons located at the right end of the window's title bar (see Figure 2.1). The buttons and commands work as described here.

Select the **Maximize** button, or command, to enlarge the window. A maximized hard drive window, for example, fills your entire screen, thus hiding any of the desktop in the background. Clicking the Maximize button of a program, document, or other window enlarges that window to fill the screen.

Select the **Minimize** button, or command, to reduce the window to a button on the taskbar.

Select the **Restore** button, or command, to return a window to the size it was before it was maximized. (The Restore button and command are available only after a window has been maximized; the Restore button replaces the Maximize button in a maximized window.)

Figure 2.2 shows the hard drive window (opened from My Computer) maximized; it fills the entire desktop. At full size, the hard drive window's Restore button is available. When the window is at any other size, you see the Maximize button instead of the Restore button.

 With IE4 and Active Desktop Running... If Internet Explorer 4 is installed on your PC, the My Computer window may look differently. Refer to Part V, "Active Desktop Essentials" for more information on My Computer.

To maximize, minimize, or restore a window with the mouse, click the appropriate button in the title bar of the window. To maximize, minimize, or restore a window using the Control menu, follow these steps:

1. Click the **Control menu** button to open the window's Control menu; alternatively, press **Alt+Spacebar**.

2. Click the command (**Restore**, **Minimize**, or **Maximize**) you want to initiate. Alternatively, use the down arrow to move to and highlight the command, and then press **Enter**.

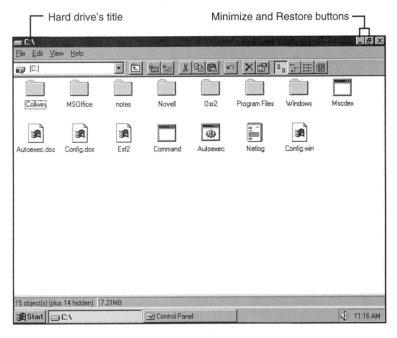

Figure 2.2 The hard drive window enlarges to fill the screen.

Sizing a Window's Borders

At some point, you'll need a window to be a particular size to suit your needs. For example, you might want to fit two or more windows on-screen at the same time. You can drag the window's frame, or border, to change the size of the window. A window's border appears only on a restored window, not on a maximized or minimized window.

To use the mouse to size a window's borders, follow these steps:

1. Place the mouse pointer on the portion of the border that you want to resize: left or right side, top or bottom. When the mouse is positioned correctly, it changes shape to a double-headed arrow.

Use the vertical double-headed arrow (on the top or bottom of the window border) to resize the window's height by dragging the frame up or down.

Use the horizontal double-headed arrow (on the left or right window border) to resize the window's width by dragging the frame left or right.

Use the diagonal double-headed arrow (on any of the four corners of the window border) to resize the window's height and width proportionally by dragging the corner diagonally.

2. Click and drag the border toward the center of the window to reduce the size of the window, or away from the center to enlarge the window.

3. When the border reaches the desired size, release the mouse button.

Using Scroll Bars

Scroll bars appear along the bottom or the right edge of a window when the window contains more text, graphics, or icons than it can display.

Using scroll bars, you can move up, down, left, or right in a window (see Figure 2.3.) Because all of the hard drive window's contents are not fully visible in the window, the scroll bars are present on the right side and the bottom of the window.

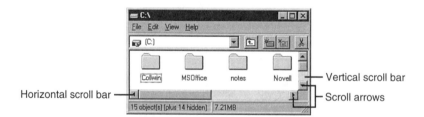

Figure 2.3 Use scroll bars to move within the window.

  What Is a Scroll Bar? A scroll bar is a bar that contains three items: two scroll arrows and a scroll box. You use the scroll arrows and the scroll box to move around in the window, scrolling a line at a time, or even a page at a time.

The following steps teach you how to use the scroll bars to view items not visible in the window:

1. To see an object that is down and to the right of the viewable area of the window, point at the down arrow located on the bottom of the vertical scroll bar.

2. Click the arrow, and the window's contents move up.

3. Click the scroll arrow on the right side of the horizontal scroll bar, and the window's contents shift to the left.

By its placement within the scroll bar, the scroll box depicts how much of a window is not visible. If you know approximately where something is in a window, you can drag the scroll box to get there quickly. To drag the scroll box and move quickly to a distant area of the window (top or bottom, left or right), use this technique:

1. Point to the scroll box in the scroll bar and press and hold the left mouse button.

2. Drag the scroll box to the new location.

3. Release the mouse button.

On the other hand, sometimes you may need to move slowly through a window (to scan for a particular icon, for example). You can move through the contents of a window one screen at a time by clicking inside the scroll bar on either side of the scroll box.

Empty Windows? Don't worry if text, graphics, or icons don't appear in a window. Use the scroll bar to bring them into view. Items in any window appear first in the upper-left corner.

CAUTION

Moving a Window

When you start working with multiple windows, moving a window becomes as important as resizing one. For example, you may need to move one or more windows to make room for other work on your desktop, or you may need to move one window to see another window's contents. You can move a window easily with the mouse.

Don't Lose the Title Bar! Be very careful that you do not move a window so far off the screen that you cannot see the title bar. If you lose the title bar, you may never be able to move the window back into full view.

CAUTION

To move a window, point at the window's title bar, press and hold the left mouse button, and drag the window to its new location.

Viewing a Window's Contents

Windows displays the contents of a window in icon form; for example, the elements in the My Computer window are represented by pictures of a hard drive, floppy drive, and folders. Other windows, such as your hard drive window, display elements as folders and files.

You can display the contents of any window in various ways so you can better see the contents. The default, or standard, view in most windows is by Large Icons (refer to Figure 2.3). Large icons help you quickly identify the contents. You also can view the contents of a window as follows:

- **Small Icons**   Contents are displayed with a small icon next to the file or folder name; small icons represent the application in which a file was created, folder, or executable program.

- **List**   Similar to small icons but the icons are even smaller.

- **Details**   Lists icon, file or folder name, file size, file type, and last date modified. When in Details view, you can click the heading button—Name, Size, Type, or Modified—to automatically sort the contents by that heading. For example, click **Name** and folders list in alphabetical order followed by file names listed alphabetically.

Figure 2.4 shows four windows, each with a different view of the window's contents: Large Icons, Small Icons, Details, and List.

To change views of the window's contents, choose **View**, and then select **Large Icons**, **Small Icons**, **List**, or **Details**.

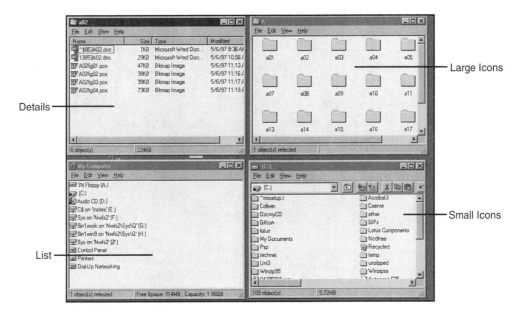

Figure 2.4 Display the contents of a window in a different view so you can easily identify files or folders.

Closing a Window

When you're finished working with a window, you should close it. This often helps speed up Windows, conserve memory, and keep your desktop from becoming cluttered.

To close a window, you can do any of the following:

- Click the **Control menu** button and choose **Close**.
- Click the **Close** button in the title bar.
- Press **Alt+F4**.
- Choose **File, Close**.
- Double-click the window's **Control menu** button.

 TIP   Quickie Close   To quickly close several related open windows, hold the **Shift** key while clicking the **Close** button on the last window you opened.

Closing Windows in Applications   These methods of closing Windows apply when you close other programs such as Word or Lotus 1-2-3 with some small differences. File, Close will close a file or document, keeping the program opened. All of the other keystrokes described will close the actual application.

In this lesson, you learned to open, resize, move, view, and close a window, and how to use scroll bars to view more of a window. In the next lesson, you learn to use menus and toolbar buttons.

Using Menus

In this lesson, you learn how to use toolbar buttons, select menus, open menus, choose menu commands, and use menu shortcuts.

Using Toolbar Buttons

Most windows and applications offer a toolbar containing various buttons you can use as shortcuts. Toolbar buttons represent common commands you often use in Windows, such as cut, copy, undo, and so on. The tools that are available to you depend on the window or application you're using. Figure 3.1 shows the toolbar for the My Computer window.

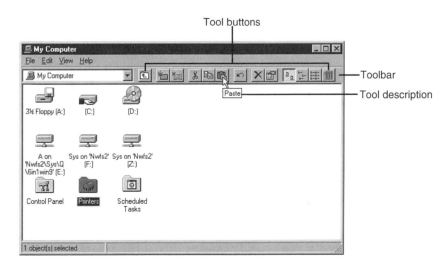

Figure 3.1 Use tool buttons to speed up your work.

My Toolbar Doesn't Look Like this If Internet Explorer 4 is installed on your PC, the My Computer window toolbar will appear differently. To learn how to use the new toolbar using Internet Explorer 4, refer to Part V, "Active Desktop Essentials."

What Does That Button Do? Most Windows applications provide helpful descriptions of the tools on a toolbar. Position the mouse pointer over any tool button and wait a second or two. A small box or bubble containing the button's name or a description of its function appears. When you move the mouse pointer, the description disappears. To activate the tool button, click it with the mouse.

To use a tool button, click it. Just like commands, any of a variety of results may occur. If, for example, you select a folder or file and choose the Copy tool button, a duplicate of the folder or file moves to the Windows Clipboard for pasting to another area later. If you choose the Undo tool button, the last action you performed is reversed.

What Is a Menu?

A menu is a list of related commands that you use to perform tasks in Windows and in Windows applications (tasks such as copying or deleting selected items in a window). Menu commands are organized in logical groups. For example, all the commands related to arranging and opening windows are located on the Windows menu. The names of the available menus appear below the Title bar of any window or application that uses menus.

CAUTION

Lost with No Idea of What to Do? Any time you're not sure what to do next or how to perform a specific task, click each menu in the application and read each command. Generally, you can find what you want in this way; if not, you can always choose the Help menu (described in Lesson 5).

In this book, I will use the format *menu title, menu command* to tell you to choose a command from a pull-down menu. For example, the sentence "choose File, Properties" means to "open the File menu and select the Properties command."

Pull-Down Menu A menu that appears to "pull-down" from the menu bar. You access the menu by clicking its name in the menu bar. You then have several options to choose from within the pull-down menu.

Choosing Menu Commands

To choose a menu command with the mouse, follow these steps:

1. Click the menu title in the menu bar. The menu opens to display the available commands.

2. To choose a particular command, simply click it. For example, to see the View commands available for the My Computer window, click the **View** menu in the menu bar. The **View** menu appears (see Figure 3.2).

Click here to display the menu

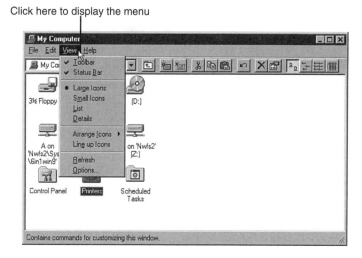

Figure 3.2 Click any menu to view its contents.

3. To make the menu disappear, click anywhere outside the menu.

To choose a command on the menu, move the mouse to that command and click. What happens next depends on the menu and the command.

TIP **Want to Use the Keyboard?** If you want to use the keyboard to choose menu commands, press the **Alt** key to activate the menu bar of the active window. Use the left and right arrow keys to highlight the menu you want; then use the up and down arrows to highlight the command you want. Press **Enter** to activate the highlighted command. You could, alternatively, press **Alt+** the underlined letter to activate a menu; press **Alt+F**, for example, to open the **File** menu and then press the underlined letter in the command you want to activate.

Reading a Menu

Windows menus contain a number of common elements that indicate what will happen when you choose a command, provide a shortcut, or limit your choice of commands. Some menus, for example, may contain commands that are dimmed or grayed-out. However, most commands perform some sort of task when you select them.

CAUTION

Unavailable Commands If a command appears grayed-out, you cannot currently use that command. Grayed-out commands are only available for use under certain circumstances. For example, you cannot choose the Copy command or the Delete command if you have not first selected an object to copy or delete.

Depending on the type of command you select, one of four things will happen:

- An action will take place. For example, choosing File, Delete erases the selected icon or file.
- A dialog box will appear. Any command followed by an ellipsis (…) displays a dialog box containing related options (see Lesson 4 for more information).
- A submenu will appear. A command followed by an arrow displays a second menu offering related commands.
- A feature will be turned on. A check mark or bullet appears to the left of the option on the menu and that option remains active until you either select a different bulleted option in the same menu or deselect the checked option by clicking it a second time.

TIP **Separator Lines Give You a Clue** Commands on most menus are grouped together and divided by separator lines. When bulleted option commands are grouped, you can select only one option in the group, for example. When checked commands are grouped, you can choose as many or as few options as you want.

Figure 3.3 shows common menu elements: the ellipsis, the check mark, and option bullet, an arrow with submenu, and separator lines.

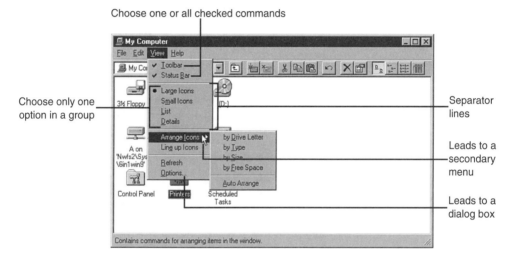

Figure 3.3 Indicators let you know what will happen before you select the command.

To practice using menu commands, follow these steps:

1. In the My Computer window, choose **View**, **Toolbar**. The Toolbar displays, if it was not already displayed.
2. Choose **View**, **Options** (notice the ellipsis after the Option command). A dialog box appears.
3. To cancel the dialog box, choose the **Cancel** button.

Using Shortcut Keys Instead of Menus

Until you become familiar with Windows and your various Windows applications, you'll need to use the menus to view and select commands. However, after you've worked in Windows for a while, you'll probably want to use shortcut keys for commands you use often. Shortcut keys enable you to select commands without using the menus. Shortcut keys generally combine the Alt, Ctrl, or Shift key with a letter key (such as W). If a shortcut key is available, it is listed on the pull-down menu to the right of the command.

For example, Figure 3.4 shows the Edit menu from the hard drive window on My Computer. As you can see, the shortcut key for Cut is Ctrl+X. You cannot use the shortcut key while the menu is open; you must either choose a command or cancel the menu. You can, however, remember the shortcut key and use it instead of opening the menu the next time you need to cut a file or folder.

Shortcut keys

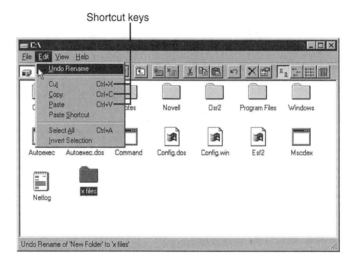

Figure 3.4 Use shortcut keys to save time.

Using Shortcut Menus

Windows supplies a variety of shortcut, or quick, menus that contain common commands you often use. You can display a shortcut menu by right-clicking an object—the desktop, a window, a folder or file, and so on. The commands that a shortcut menu displays depend on the item and its location.

To display and use a shortcut menu, point the mouse at the object you want to explore, cut, open, or otherwise manipulate, and right-click the mouse. The shortcut menu appears; move the mouse to the command and click again. Cancel a shortcut menu by clicking the mouse anywhere besides on the menu.

Figure 3.5 displays a shortcut menu resulting from right-clicking a hard drive icon.

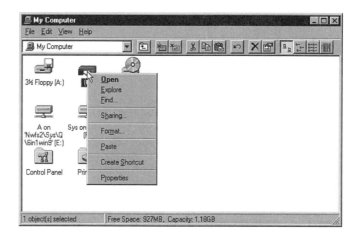

Figure 3.5 Quickly access a command with a right-click.

In this lesson, you learned how to use toolbar buttons, select menus, open menus, choose menu commands, and use menu shortcuts. In the next lesson, you learn to use dialog boxes.

Using Dialog Boxes

In this lesson, you learn how to use the various dialog box components.

What Is a Dialog Box?

Windows and Windows applications use dialog boxes to exchange information with you. As you learned in Lesson 3, a menu command followed by an ellipsis (…) indicates that a dialog box will appear. A dialog box asks for related information the program needs in order to complete the operation.

Windows also displays dialog boxes to give you information. For example, Windows might display a dialog box to warn you about a problem (as in `File already exists, Overwrite?`) or to confirm that an operation should take place (to confirm you want to delete a file, for example).

CAUTION

Why Is My Computer Beeping at Me? If a dialog box won't go away and your computer beeps at you when you try to continue your work, don't worry. That beep is Windows' way of telling you that you must always respond to a dialog box before you can continue. You can press **Enter** or choose **OK** to accept the message or changes in the dialog box, or you can press the **Esc** key or choose **Cancel** to cancel the message or changes in the box.

Using the Components of a Dialog Box

Dialog boxes vary in complexity depending on the program, the procedure, and the number of options in the actual box. Some simply ask you to confirm an operation before it is executed; others ask you to choose, for example, a drive, folder, file name, file type, network path, or any of numerous other options.

The following list briefly explains the components of a dialog box. Not all dialog boxes contain all components, so don't be afraid to tackle a dialog box.

- **Text box**   A text box provides a place to type an entry, such as a file name, path (drive and directory), font, or measurement.

- **List box**   A list box presents a slate of possible options from which you can choose. Scroll bars often accompany a list box so you can view the items on the list. In addition, a text box is sometimes associated with a list box; you can either choose from the list or type the selection yourself.

- **Drop-down list box**   This box is a single-line list box with a drop-down arrow button to the right of it. When you click the arrow, the drop-down list box opens to display a list of choices. You can often scroll through a drop-down list as you do a list box.

- **Option buttons**   Option buttons present a group of related choices from which you can choose only one. Click the option button you want to select and all others become deselected.

- **Check box**   A check box enables you to turn an option on or off. You might find a single check box or a group of related check boxes. A check mark appears in the box next to any option that is active (turned on). In a group of check boxes, you can choose none, one, or any number of the options.

 Dialog Box Options   Round circles, such as those found in Option buttons, are often referred to as *radio buttons*. When a dialog box presents radio buttons, you can select only one choice. Check boxes are square and when they appear in dialog boxes, you may choose none, any, or all of the selections. This applies to all of Windows 95 and programs designed to run under Windows.

- **Command button**   When selected, a command button carries out the command displayed on the button (Open, Help, Quit, Cancel, or OK, for example). If there is an ellipsis on the button (as in Option…), choosing it will open another dialog box.

- **Tabs** Tabs represent multiple sections, or pages, of a dialog box. Only one tab is displayed at a time, and each tab contains related options. Choosing a tab changes the options that appear in the dialog box.

Using Text Boxes

You use a text box to enter the information that Windows or a Windows application needs in order to complete a command. This information is usually a file name, folder name, measurement, style or font name, or other information related to the original menu and command. Figure 4.1 shows a text box and list boxes in the Open dialog box (accessed from the Windows WordPad File menu).

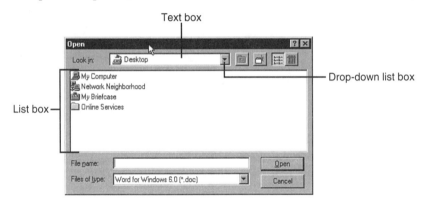

Figure 4.1 Use text boxes and list boxes to specify your preferences.

TIP **Save Time and Trouble** If you want to replace text that's already in a text box, drag your mouse I-beam over the text (to highlight text) and start typing. When you type the first character, the original text is deleted. Often when you first open a dialog box containing a text box, there is already text present and highlighted; if you start typing, you automatically delete the current text.

To activate a text box using the mouse, position the mouse over the text box (the mouse pointer changes to an I-beam) and click. The I-beam pointer shape indicates that the area you're pointing to will accept text. Look for the I-beam when you want to enter text in a dialog box. Notice that the insertion point (a flashing vertical line) appears in the active text box.

To activate a text box using the keyboard, press **Alt+selection letter** (The selection letter is the underlined letter in a menu, command, or option name. The combination of Alt+selection letter is called a *hotkey*.). After you have activated a text box and typed text into it, you can use several keys to edit the text. Table 4.1 outlines these keys.

Table 4.1 Editing Keys for Text Boxes and Other Text

Key	*Description*
Delete	Deletes the character to the right of the insertion point
Backspace	Erases the character to the left of the insertion point
End	Moves the insertion point to the end of the line
Home	Moves the insertion point to the beginning of the line
Arrow keys	Moves the insertion point one character in the direction of the arrow
Shift+End	Selects the text from the insertion point to the end of the line
Shift+Home	Selects the text from the insertion point to the beginning of the line
Shift+Arrow key	Selects the next character in the direction of the arrow
Ctrl+C	Copies the selected text to the Clipboard
Ctrl+V	Pastes the selected text from the Clipboard

 Clipboard The Clipboard is a tool provided by Windows that holds any cut or copied text for you so you can paste it to another location, document, or application. For more information, see Lesson 9, "Understanding Files and Folders."

Using List Boxes

You use a list box to select from multiple available options. For example, you use the Look In list box in the Open dialog box (refer to Figure 4.1) to select the drive that contains the file you want to open.

To select an item from a list box using the mouse, click the appropriate list item and click **OK**. You can also select more than one item in many list boxes by holding the Shift key as you click. The item you select automatically appears in the linked box above the list box.

 TIP   **Quick Close**   Double-click an item in a list box to select the item and close the dialog box as if you had clicked **OK**.

To select an item from a drop-down list box, open the list box by clicking the down-arrow, and then click the appropriate item.

Using Option Buttons

Option buttons enable you to make a single choice from a group of possible command options. For example, the Print Range options displayed in Figure 4.2 enable you to choose which pages of your document you want to print. The active option (the All option in Figure 4.2) has a filled-in circle. The figure is from WordPad using the File, Print command.

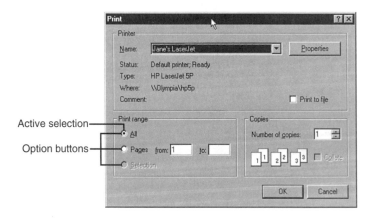

Figure 4.2   You can choose only one option in a group.

To select an option button, click the circle for the option you want. (If you have trouble pointing into the circle, click the accompanying text instead.)

Using Check Boxes

For options that you can select (activate) or deselect (deactivate), Windows and Windows applications usually provide check boxes. When a check box is selected, an **X** or a check mark appears in the box, indicating the associated option is active (see Figure 4.3); this figure is from WordPad using the Format, Font command.

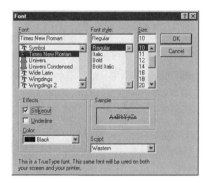

Figure 4.3 A check mark indicates the active, or selected, option.

To select or deselect a check box, click the box.

Using Command Buttons

You use command buttons to either accept or reject the changes you've made in a dialog box, to get help, or to access another related dialog box. To select a command button, simply click it.

Figure 4.4 shows the two most common command buttons: OK and Cancel. Select the **OK** command button to accept the information you have entered or to verify an action and close the dialog box. Select the **Cancel** command button to leave the dialog box without putting into effect the changes you made in the dialog box.

TIP **Quick and Easy** You can press the **Enter** key in a dialog box to quickly accept the changes and close the dialog box. Similarly, you can press the **Esc** key to cancel the changes made to the dialog box and close the box at the same time.

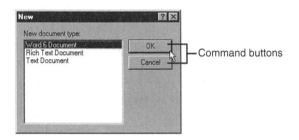

Command buttons

Figure 4.4 Use command buttons to control the dialog box.

CAUTION

Look Before You Click If you accidentally select the **Cancel** command button in a dialog box, don't worry. You can always reenter the changes to the dialog box and continue. However, you need to be more careful when you select OK in a dialog box. The instructions you enter in the dialog box will be executed and changing them back may be a bit harder than canceling changes.

TIP **Close means Cancel** Choosing the Close button in a dialog box is the same thing as canceling it.

Using Property Sheets and Tabs

As noted previously, property sheets are similar to dialog boxes in the components they contain: check boxes, list boxes, text boxes, command buttons, and so on. Figure 4.5 shows the Taskbar Properties sheet.

In a property sheet containing more than one tab, choose options within the sheet and then click the **Apply** button to accept the changes. You can then select the other tabs and make other changes. Once you've chosen the Apply button, however, you cannot cancel those changes using the Cancel command button; you must go back to the tab and change the options.

To select a tab, click the tab with the mouse pointer.

Tabs—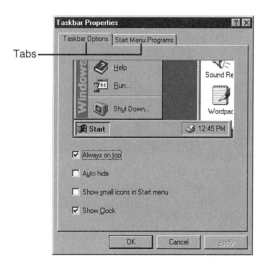

Figure 4.5 Choose a tab that represents the options you want to change.

In this lesson, you learned how to use the various dialog box components. In the next lesson, you learn how to use Windows help.

Using Windows 95 Help

In this lesson, you learn how to get help, use the Help feature's shortcut buttons, and use the What's This? feature.

Getting Help in Windows 95

Windows offers several ways to get online help—instant on-screen help for menu commands, procedures, features, and other items. Online help is information that appears in its own window whenever you request it. Windows' Help feature offers three types of help: contents features, index, and find.

The Contents feature displays a list of topics (such as Introducing Windows and Tips and Tricks) as well as a 10 minute tour of using Windows. The Index feature enables you to access specific categories of topics—such as adapters, disk configuration, copying, and so on. Find lets you search for specific words and phrases—such as About, Mem, Printing, and so on.

 TIP   **Setting Up Help**   The first time you choose Find in Windows Help, Windows runs a Find Setup Wizard that compiles every word from the Help files into a database you will use to find subjects. Follow the directions and the Wizard will guide you.

 Fast Help   Most dialog boxes, including Help dialog boxes, have a Help button (a question mark in the title bar) that enables you to get help on items within the dialog box. Click the question mark and point the mouse at an area you have a question about. Windows displays a box with a definition or other information relating to your question. When you're finished reading the help, click the mouse to hide the information box.

Using the Contents Feature

You can get help with common procedures using Help's Contents feature. The Contents feature displays the top level groups of information covered in Help, such as How To and Troubleshooting. When you select a major group, a list of related topics appears, as shown in Figure 5.1.

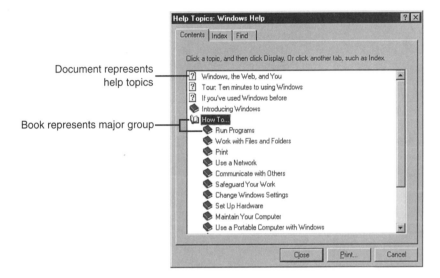

Figure 5.1 Choose from the listed topics for task-specific help.

Follow these steps to use Help's Contents feature:

1. Choose the **Start** button and then choose **Help**. The **Help Topics: Windows Help** dialog box appears; select the **Contents** tab if it is not already selected.

TIP **Pick a Tab** The last tab in the Help Topics window that you accessed is the one that appears the next time you open Help.

2. In the Contents list, double-click the book icon in front of the topic you want to view. The book opens and related topics appear either in a list of books or documents.

3. Double-click a document icon to view information about that topic (see Figure 5.2).

Figure 5.2 A Help window tells you what you need to know when you have trouble printing, for example.

4. When you finish with the Help topic, you can choose one of the following buttons:

- **Close (X)** To close the Help window and return to the Desktop.
- **Help Topics** To return to the Contents tab of the Help Topics window and select another topic.
- **Back** To display the previously viewed Help window.
- **Options** To copy, print, or otherwise set preferences for the Help window.

Using the Index Feature

Help's Index feature provides a list of Help topics arranged alphabetically on the Index tab of the Help Topics window. Either you can enter a word for which you are searching, or you can scroll through the list to find a topic. Figure 5.3 shows the Index tab of the Help Topics: Windows Help dialog box.

To use the Help Index, follow these steps:

1. In the Help Topics window, choose the **Index** tab.
2. Click the text box with the number **1** above it and type a topic you want to know about. As you type, Windows moves to the topics beginning with the first letters you enter.

Figure 5.3 Use the Index tab to find specific words and phrases in Help.

 TIP **Browse the List** You can scroll through the index list to see what other topics are available.

3. In the list of topics, select the topic you want to view and choose **Display**, or simply double-click the topic. The Help topic window appears.

4. When you're finished with the Help topic, you can choose another option, or you can close the Help window by pressing **Alt+F4**.

Using the Find Feature

You can search for specific words and phrases in a Help topic instead of searching for a Help topic by category. The first time you use the Find feature, however, you have to instruct Windows to create a list that contains the words from your Help files. (You only create this list once.)

The Find feature is especially useful when you cannot find a particular Help topic in Help Contents or on the Index tab's list of topics.

To use the Find feature, follow these steps:

1. In the Help Topics window, choose the **Find** tab. If you have used Find before, skip down to the next set of steps. If you haven't previously set up the Help topics, the **Find Setup Wizard** dialog box appears. Continue with these steps.

2. In the **Find Setup Wizard** dialog box, choose one of the following:

   - **Minimize Database Size**   Creates a short, limited word list (recommended because it takes less hard disk space).

   - **Maximize Search Capabilities**   Creates a long, detailed word list.

   - **Customize Search Capabilities**   Enables you to create a shorter word list, including only the Help files you want to use. Use this option if you have limited disk space. If you select this option, choose **Next**, and then choose the topics you want to include.

3. Click the **Finish** button to create the word list.

When Windows finishes creating the word list, the **Find** tab contains a text box, a word list, and a topic list as shown in Figure 5.4.

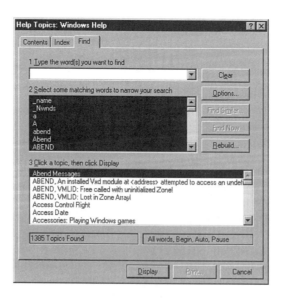

Figure 5.4   Windows now has a word list to search through.

To search for words or a phrase in the **Find** tab, follow these steps:

1. Type the word or phrase you want to find in the first text box at the top of the dialog box. This enters the word for which you want to search, and Windows displays forms of the word in the word list in the middle of the **Find** tab.

2. If you see a word that applies to your topic, select that word to narrow your search. If you do not want to narrow the search, move on to step 3.

TIP **Topic List** Instead of typing something in the text box, you can scroll through the word list and select the word you want from the list. If you want to find words similar to the words in a Help topic, click the **Find Similar** button.

3. Click one or more topics in the topic list, and then click the **Display** button. Windows displays the selected Help topic information in a Windows Help window.

4. When you finish with the Help topic, you can close the Help window or select another option, as described in the next section, "Using Help Windows."

CAUTION **Rebuild the List** If you don't want to use the first list that Windows creates, you're not stuck with it. You can rebuild the list to include more words or to exclude words. Click the **Rebuild** button and choose a word list option to recreate the word list.

Using Help Windows

When you access a Windows Help topic window, a toolbar appears at the top of the Help window and always remains visible. This toolbar includes three buttons: Help Topics, Back, and Options. Table 5.1 describes each button in the toolbar of a Windows Help window as well as the Options menu.

Table 5.1 Windows Help Toolbar Buttons and Menu

Button	Description
Help Topics	Opens the Help Topics: Windows Help window containing the Contents, Index, and Find tabs.
Back	Displays the previous Help topic window you viewed during the current session.
Options	Displays a menu containing the following commands: Annotate, Copy, Print Topic, Font, Keep Help on Top, and Use System Colors.

The following list describes the Options menu commands in more detail:

- **Annotate**   Enables you to mark any text or topic in a Help window so you can easily find the topic later. A paper clip icon appears beside any annotated text in Help.

- **Copy**   Places a copy of the text in the Help window on the Windows Clipboard for pasting to another document, application, or window.

- **Print Topic**   Sends the text in the Help window to the printer for a hard copy.

- **Font**   Select from Small, Normal, or Large type to view the help text; Normal is the default.

- **Keep Help on Top**   Choose whether to always display the Help window on top of all documents and windows so you can easily follow directions as you work.

- **Use System Colors**   Choose this option to restart the Help feature and change the colors in the Help box.

Using the What's This? Feature

The What's This? feature provides a handy way for you to get more information about dialog box options. You activate this feature by selecting the **?** icon that appears at the right end of the title bar in some (but not all) Windows dialog boxes. Figure 5.5 shows a window with the What's This icon and a description you might see if you clicked that icon.

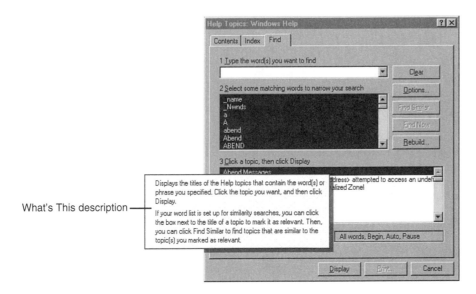

What's This description ⎯

Figure 5.5 Use the What's This? feature to get help on certain dialog box elements.

The following steps tell you how to use the What's This? feature to display a description of most options in a Windows dialog box:

1. Click the **?** icon in the upper-right corner of the Windows dialog box. A large question mark appears next to the mouse pointer.

2. Click any option in the dialog box, and Windows displays a box containing a short description of the item you selected.

3. When you finish reading the Help information, click anywhere on the screen to close the Help box.

TIP   **Quick Description**   If you right-click an option in a dialog box, a shortcut menu appears displaying one menu command: **What's This?** Click **What's This?** to view a description of the option. Note, however, that this only works if the dialog box contains a question mark in its title bar.

In this lesson, you learned how to get help, use the Help feature's shortcut buttons, and use the What's This? feature. In the next lesson, you learn to start and exit applications in Windows.

Starting and Exiting Applications in Windows 95

In this lesson, you learn to start and exit a Windows 95 application as well as how to view the common elements of Windows applications' screens.

Opening a Windows Application

Windows provides a Start menu from which you can perform many tasks, including starting Windows programs. To display the Start menu, click the **Start** button on the Windows taskbar. You can open the Help feature from the Start menu; you also can open various applications from the Start menu by choosing the Programs command. The menus you see stemming from the Programs menu will vary depending on your system setup (see Figure 6.1).

To open an application, follow these steps:

1. Choose the **Start** button.
2. Select **Programs** to display the Programs menu.
3. Choose the application you want to open, if it's listed on the Programs menu; alternatively, select the group containing the application you want to open and then choose the application from the submenu.

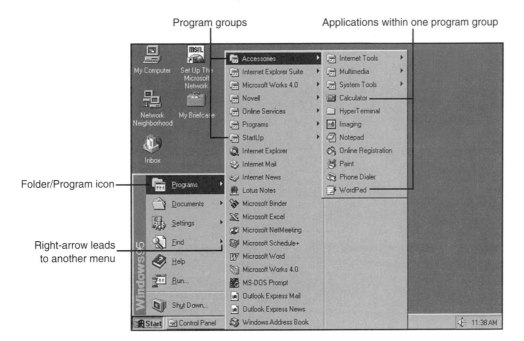

Figure 6.1 Access applications or other program's menus from the Programs menu.

 Program Groups The Programs menu displays various group names—such as Accessories, Online Services, Startup, and so on—that display a menu of related applications when selected. You can identify a program group by the Folder/Program icon in front of it and the right-arrow following the command. Accessories, Online Services, and StartUp are installed when you install Windows. You may also have program groups for Microsoft Office, Lotus SmartSuite, or other applications you've installed on your computer.

 Open Documents If you have a specific document you want to open and you've recently worked on that document, you can click the **Documents** command on the **Start** menu to display a list; click the document you want to open and the source application opens with the document, ready for you to work on.

Viewing an Application's Screen

Depending on the application you open—whether it's a word processor, database, spreadsheet, or other program—the screen will include elements particular to the tasks and procedures used for that application. For example, the mouse may appear as an I-beam (for typing), an arrow (for pointing), or a cross (for selecting cells in a spreadsheet program); the "document" area may appear as a blank sheet of paper or a table with many cells.

Most applications, however, display the following elements: Title bar, Menu bar, Toolbars, Ruler, Scroll bars, a Document area, and a Status bar. Figure 6.2 shows the screen you see when you open the Windows accessory, WordPad.

 There's Always Help   If you need help with any applications, you can click the **Help** menu in that application and select a help topic. You can also press the **F1** key in many applications to activate the Help screens.

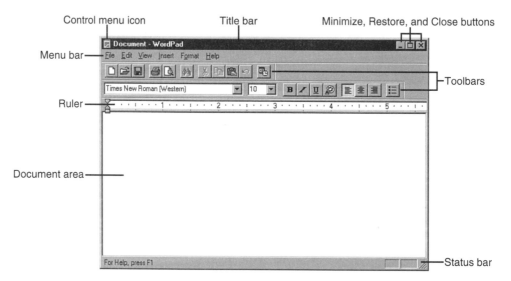

Figure 6.2   Most application screens contain similar elements.

Exiting an Application

You should always exit an application when you're done with it to ensure that your documents are saved before Windows shuts down. You can exit most Windows applications in one of the following ways:

- Choose the **File**, **Exit** command.
- Click the **Close** button (**X**).
- Choose **Close** from the **Control** menu.
- Double-click the application's Control menu icon.
- Press **Alt+F4**.

CAUTION

If You Get a Message Before Closing   If the application displays a message asking you to save the document before you close the program, choose **Yes** to save, **No** to close the application without saving the changes, or **Cancel** to return to the application. If you choose Yes, the application might display the Save As dialog box in which you assign the document a name and location on your computer's drive.

In this lesson, you learned to start and exit a Windows 95 application as well as how to view the common elements of Windows applications' screens. In the next lesson, you learn to work with multiple windows.

Working with Multiple Windows

In this lesson, you learn how to arrange windows, switch between windows in the same application, and switch between applications.

In Windows, you can have more than one application open at a time, and in each Windows application, you can work with multiple document windows. As you can imagine, opening multiple applications with multiple windows can make your desktop pretty cluttered. That's why it's important that you know how to manipulate and switch between windows. The following sections explain how to do just that.

Arranging Windows on the Desktop

When you have multiple windows open, some windows or parts of windows are inevitably hidden by others, which makes the screen confusing. You can use various commands to arrange your open windows. To access the cascade and tile windows commands, right-click the mouse in any open area of the taskbar and then select the command from the shortcut menu.

 TIP **Quick! Clean the Desktop**   You can minimize all windows by choosing one command to quickly clear the desktop of open windows. Right-click the taskbar and choose **Minimize All Windows**. All open windows then become buttons on the taskbar.

Cascading Windows

A good way to get control of a confusing desktop is to open the taskbar's shortcut menu and choose the **Cascade** command. When you choose this command, Windows lays all the open windows on top of each other so that the title bar of each is visible. Figure 7.1 shows a cascaded window arrangement using WordPad, Solitaire, and Notepad. To access any window that's not on the top, simply click its title bar. That window then becomes the active window.

Active Window The active window is the one in which you are working. You activate a window by clicking its title bar, anywhere inside the window, or by clicking its button on the taskbar. The active window's title bar becomes highlighted, and the active window comes to the front.

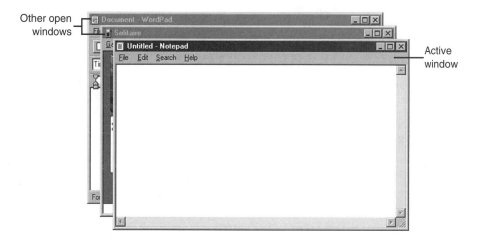

Figure 7.1 With cascaded windows, you can easily access the one you need.

You can still click and drag the title bar of any window to another location on the desktop and you can use the mouse to resize the window borders of any open window, even when it is cascaded with other windows.

Tiling Windows

If you need to see all open windows at the same time, open the taskbar's short-cut menu and select either the **Tile Horizontally** or the **Tile Vertically** command. When you choose to tile, Windows resizes and moves each open window so that they all appear side by side (vertically) or one on top of the other (horizontally), as shown in Figure 7.2.

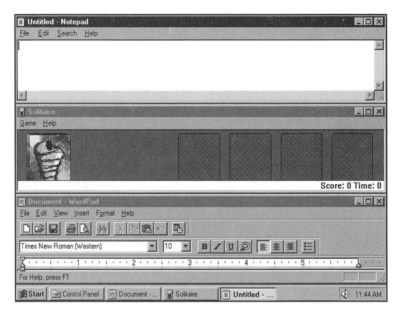

Figure 7.2   Tile windows so you can see a part of each window at the same time.

Moving Between Applications

Windows enables you to have multiple applications open at the same time. If the open application windows are not maximized, you might be able to see all of those open windows overlapped, on-screen. In this case, you can click any window to bring it forward. Often, however, it's easier to work in a single application by maximizing the application's window. Switching between applications then requires a different procedure. You'll most likely use the taskbar to switch from application to application by clicking the minimized application button on the taskbar.

After opening several applications—such as WordPad, Paint, and Solitaire, for example—you can use the taskbar by following these steps:

1. On the taskbar, click the button representing the application you want to bring forward (see Figure 7.3).

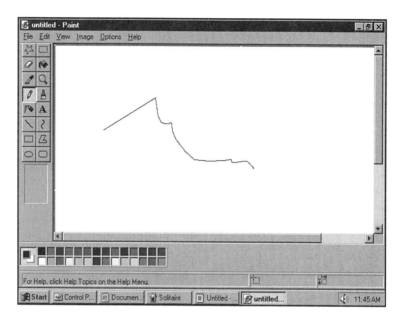

Figure 7.3 All open and minimized application windows appear on the taskbar.

2. To switch to another open application, click its button on the taskbar. The open window minimizes back to the taskbar and is replaced by the next application you select.

Moving Between Windows in the Same Application

In addition to working in multiple applications in Windows, you also can open multiple windows within an application. Moving to a new window means you are changing the window that is active. If you are using a mouse, you can move to a window by clicking any part of it. When you do, the title bar becomes highlighted, and that particular window comes to the front so you can work in it.

Figure 7.4 shows multiple document windows open in Microsoft Word. You can switch between the windows, arrange windows, and open and close windows within the application, just as you can manipulate windows within the Windows 95 program.

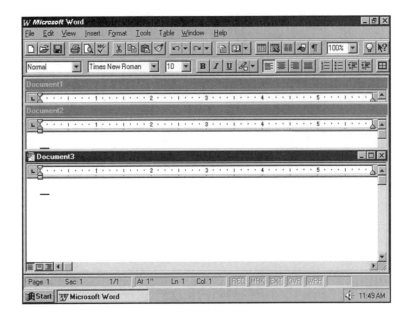

Figure 7.4 Three document windows are open within the program.

Open multiple document windows using the **File**, **Open** command. By default, each window is maximized within the document area. To switch between open, maximized windows, click the Window menu and select the document from the list at the bottom of the menu. Alternatively, you can press **Ctrl+F6** to cycle through open windows.

To view multiple document windows on-screen, follow these steps:

1. Restore the document window by clicking the document's **Restore** button. The open document windows cascade in the document area. The Restore button replaces the Maximize button.

2. To activate an open document window, click in the window's title bar or press **Ctrl+F6**.

3. To tile the windows, choose **Window**, **Arrange All**. Windows reduces each open document window and tiles them (horizontally) in the document area.

 TIP **They're All Just Windows** You can use the window frames to resize each window. Likewise, you can minimize, maximize, open, and close the windows as you would any window. (See Lesson 2 for instructions.)

In this lesson, you learned how to arrange windows, switch between windows in the same application, and switch between applications. In the next lesson, you learn to copy and move information between windows.

Copying and Moving Information Between Windows

8

In this lesson, you learn about the Clipboard and how to copy and move information between windows.

What Is the Clipboard?

One of the handiest features of the Windows environment is its capability to copy or move information (text, graphics, and files) from one location to another. This feature enables you to share information between document windows, applications, and other computers on your network.

When you cut or copy data from an application, Windows places the data on the Clipboard; it remains there until you cut or copy again. You can paste the data from the Clipboard to a document or application. Note, however, that you don't have to open the Clipboard to use it—and 99 percent of the time, you won't. You simply cut or copy your data, and then paste it to a new location.

 TERM **Copy, Cut, and Paste** When you copy information, the application copies it to the Clipboard without disturbing the original. When you cut information, the application removes it from its original location and places it on the Clipboard. When you paste information, the application inserts the information that's on the Clipboard to the location you specify. (The copy on the Clipboard remains intact, so you can paste it again and again, if necessary.)

You can view the information on the Clipboard viewer by choosing **Start**, **Programs**, **Accessories**, and **Clipboard Viewer** (see Figure 8.1). In the Viewer, you can save the contents to a file name, add or remove text, edit the text, and open saved Clipboard files.

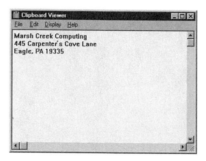

Figure 8.1 View and even save the contents of the Clipboard.

Without a Trace When you turn off your computer or exit Windows, the contents of the Clipboard disappear. Be sure you save the contents of the Clipboard if you want to use the text or graphics later.

Selecting Text for Copying or Moving

Before you can copy or cut text, you must identify the text by selecting it. Selected text appears in reverse video (highlighted). Figure 8.2 shows selected text in a WordPad document.

To select text, follow these steps:

1. Position the mouse pointer just before the first character you want to select.
2. Press and hold the left mouse button, and drag the mouse pointer to the last character you want selected.
3. Release the mouse button, and the selected text appears highlighted.

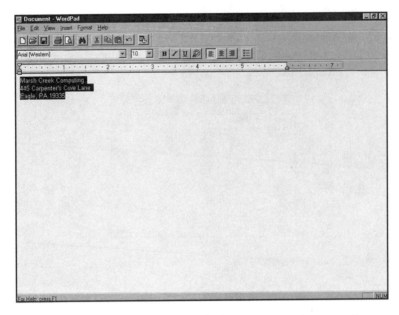

Figure 8.2 You must first select text before you can cut or copy it.

TIP **Quick One-Word Selection** Quickly select one word of text by double-clicking the word.

CAUTION

Where's My Selected Text? If you press an alphanumeric key (a letter, number, or any other character) while text is highlighted, Windows deletes the selected text and replaces it with the character you typed. Choose **Edit**, **Undo** or press **Ctrl+Z** (in most applications) to reverse the action.

Selecting Graphics

The procedure for selecting graphics depends on the Windows application you use. In a word processing program such as WordPad or Microsoft Word, you select a graphic by clicking the object. In a program such as Paint, however, there are special tools for selecting shapes. Because the procedure may vary, you should refer to the instructions for each application. However, no matter how you select a graphic, small *handles* appear on the corners and sides of the graphic frame to indicate it is ready to copy or move.

Copying Information Between Windows

After you select text or graphics, the procedures for copying and pasting are the same in all Windows applications. To copy and paste information between windows of the same application, as well as between windows of different applications, follow these steps:

1. Select the text or graphic you want to copy.

2. Click the **Copy** button on the toolbar, or choose **Edit**, **Copy**. You can, alternatively, use a keyboard shortcut, such as **Ctrl+C** for copy. A copy of the selected material appears on the Clipboard; the original selection remains in place.

3. Click to position the insertion point where you want to insert the selection. You can switch between document windows or between applications as learned in Lesson 7.

4. Click the **Paste** button, choose **Edit**, **Paste**, or press **Ctrl+V**. Windows copies the selection from the Clipboard to the insertion point.

Multiple Copies Because the selected item remains on the Clipboard until you copy or cut again, you can paste the same information from the Clipboard multiple times.*

Moving Information Between Windows

In all Windows applications, you can use a similar procedure to move selected text or graphics with cut and paste. To cut and paste information between windows of the same application or windows of different applications, follow these steps:

1. Select the text or graphic.

2. Click the **Cut** button; choose **Edit**, **Cut**; or press **Ctrl+X.** Windows removes the selection from its original location and places it on the Clipboard.

3. Place the insertion point where you want the selection to appear.

4. Click the **Paste** button, choose **Edit**, **Paste**, or press **Ctrl+V**. Windows copies the selection from the Clipboard to your document. (A copy remains on the Clipboard until you cut or copy something else.)

In this lesson, you learned about the Clipboard and how to copy and move information between windows. In the next lesson, you learn to view files, folders, and drives in the Windows Explorer.

Understanding Files and Folders

In this lesson, you get a basic overview of files, folders, and drives.

What Is a File?

When you create a letter in your word processor, a worksheet in your spreadsheet program, a drawing in your graphics program, or a mailing list in your database program, the only way you can keep your work is to save it. You save it as a file.

Files can be documents created by applications, the pieces of the program itself, or parts of the Windows 95 operating system. They are the basic storage unit of your computer; everything is stored in files.

When you save a file, you must give the file a name. Otherwise, you won't be able to identify it when you want to use it again. The name of the file can be up to 255 characters long, including spaces.

I Can't Save My File   When you name a file you cannot use any of the following characters: **\, /, :, ", ", *, ?, <, >,** or **I**. Remove them from the file name and try saving again.

TIP **File Names**   Just because you can use 255 characters doesn't mean you should. Keep the file name short but descriptive. Also, keep in mind that you will look for this file later. If you call it **A Letter to Joe** it will appear under **A** in a list of files. Call it **Joe Vacation Letter** so you know who it's addressed to and what it's about.

If you learned computing in the MS-DOS days, this means you're no longer confined by the 8-letter file name rule. But what about the extensions? Well, they're still there, but most of the time you won't see them. Except when you want to be specific, you won't need to use them. Your programs will add them to your file names automatically.

How will you tell what program a file was created by? Windows uses different icons for every type of file, so you can see immediately if a file was created in Microsoft Word or Lotus 1-2-3 (see Figure 9.1).

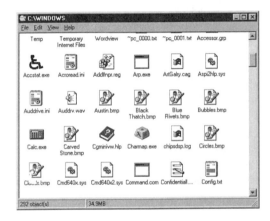

Figure 9.1 Files listed in My Computer.

What Is a Folder?

You don't want to scatter your files about anywhere on your computer. When you have many files, you won't be able to find anything.

Instead, organize your files into folders. Folders are like manila folders (the icon even looks like one). Just as you might put several letters to the same person in the same manila folder, you can group similar files in the same folder. Don't you throw documents on the same topic or project in the same folder at your office? A computer folder works the same way.

Many of the folders on your computer were created by your programs as they were installed. One called **My Documents** comes with Windows 95 (see Figure 9.2). You can put all your files there if you want, or you can create your own folders. You can also store folders within folders (called *subfolders*) as well as files.

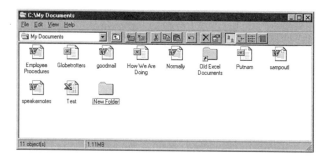

Figure 9.2   Sample contents of a "My Documents" folder.

The contents of My Documents depends on the user of the computer. The window in Figure 9.2 shows you the contents of one person's My Documents folder. There are several files there. Some of them are PowerPoint presentations, some are Word documents, and some are Excel spreadsheets. There is also a folder called New Folder because it was just created. (For more information on creating folders, see Lesson 11 "Managing Files with My Computer".)

What Is a Drive?

A *drive* holds some type of storage media. It's a place to store files and folders.

On most computers there are at least two drives. One is the *hard disk* that represents the largest storage area on your computer. You can retrieve data from your hard drive faster than the other drives. This drive also stores your program files. Every drive is assigned a letter, and the letter for your hard drive is **C** (see Figure 9.3).

Figure 9.3   My Computer shows the drives on your computer.

Your computer probably has a *floppy disk* too. Today that's normally a $3^1/_2$ inch drive named **A**. (The floppy disks that use that drive are $3^1/_2$ inches wide.) You can store files and folders on a floppy disk, but the size is limited. If you use high-density disks, they only hold 1.44 MB. The benefit of these smaller disks is that they're portable. You can remove them from your disk drive and take them to another computer.

 MB (Megabytes)   All storage media (hard disks, floppy disks, CDs) measure their capacity in bytes. A *byte* is approximately the size of one character (without getting technical). A thousand bytes is a *kilobyte* (abbreviated K or KB), a million bytes is a *megabyte* (abbreviated MB, nicknamed "Meg"), and a billion bytes is a *gigabyte* (abbreviated GB, nicknamed "Gig").

You may have a second floppy drive, called **B**. This may be a 5$\frac{1}{2}$ -inch floppy (named for its size). A high-density disk in this size holds 1.2 MB of data.

The computer shown in Figure 9.3 also has a CD-ROM drive (**D**). The CDs that go into this drive look just like your music CDs—in fact, you may be able to put your music CDs in here to play music. Most programs today are available in CD format as are most games. CDs can hold several hundred megabytes of data, but you can't use them to store data. You can only read the files on the CDs. That's why the drive is called a CD-ROM; ROM means Read Only Memory. You can read but not write to this drive.

You may also have a tape drive, which holds a tape cassette and can store a large amount of data. Tape drives are generally used for backing up the folders and files on your hard disk.

For more information on backing up files, see Lesson 16 "Using Backup." For more information on organizing your hard drive, see Part VI, "Real World Solutions," Lesson 1, "How to Organize a Hard Drive."

In this lesson, you learned about files, folders, and drives. In the next lesson, you learn how to start and exit applications and how to save documents.

Using My Computer

In this lesson, you learn about My Computer: what it is, how
to browse files, what's on the menu, how to use the toolbar,
how to open drives and folders, and how to work with more
than one window open at a time.

Active Desktop? This lesson describes using My Computer without Shell
Integration active. Shell Integration can be installed with Internet Explorer 4 and
makes your system's desktop function like a Web browser. If you have Shell
Integration active, please go to Part V to learn how to use My Computer with
this feature.

What Is My Computer?

My Computer is a way to quickly see everything on your computer—files,
folders, and drives—and how it's organized.

Before computers, when an office worker typed a letter, a carbon copy of that
document was also created to store in the office for reference. That carbon copy
was placed into a manila file folder, and the folder was stored in a filing cabinet.
In a larger company with a central filing room, an index of the files was made to
help all the employees find documents.

This same type of system was carried over to computers. When you create a
document in a word processor, for instance, you save it as a *file* so you can
retrieve the same document later, like a carbon copy. You store that file in a
folder that may contain other similar files, like a manila folder. The folder is kept
on a disk drive, which resembles a filing cabinet in the way it's used. My Computer serves as your "index" to find your folders and files.

To open My Computer, double-click its icon on the desktop (see Figure 10.1).

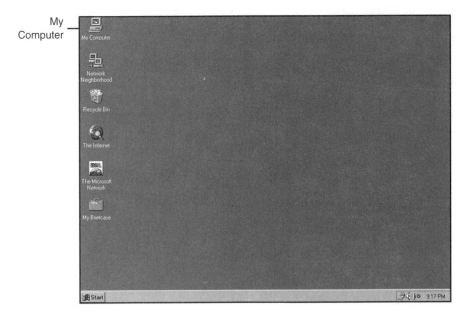

My Computer

Figure 10.1 The My Computer icon on the desktop.

The My Computer Window

When you double-click the My Computer icon, the My Computer window appears (see Figure 10.2).

CAUTION

My Window Doesn't Have All Those Things! The icons that appear in the My Computer window vary from computer to computer. Depending on what components are installed on your computer, you may see different icons than those shown in Figure 10.2.

With Internet Explorer 4 and Active Desktop Running... My Computer may look different than it does here. Refer to Part V, Active Desktop Essentials, for more information.

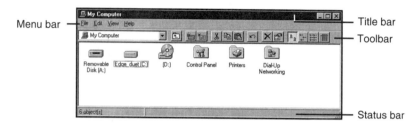

Menu bar

Title bar

Toolbar

Status bar

Figure 10.2 The My Computer window.

Some of the icons in the My Computer window represent drives, such as a floppy drive (A:), your hard drive (C:), or your CD-ROM drive (D:). If you have a tape drive or an additional floppy drive, icons for those items will also appear in this window.

There are also icons within folders. The Control Panel icon opens the Control Panel window. You use the icons in that window to configure your computer. For more information on using the Control Panel, see Part II, "Customizing Windows;" Lesson 1 "Understanding the Control Panel".

The Printers icon opens the Printers window. Use the icons in that window to control print jobs and set up new printers. For information on installing printers, see Part II, "Customizing Windows 95;" Lesson 9 "Installing a Printer".

In Figure 10.2 you also see a Dial-Up Networking folder icon. Use that icon when you want to connect one computer to another using a modem.

At the top of the window is the *title bar*, which tells you the name of the window you currently have open. You can move the window by dragging the title bar.

Beneath the title bar is the *menu bar*, which contains commands that you may give to the program.

Below the Menu Bar is the *toolbar*. If your Toolbar is not showing, choose **View, Toolbar** from the menu.

At the bottom of the screen is the *status bar*. In My Computer, the Status Bar displays the number of objects (files and folders) in the window and the number of bytes they take up in memory space. If you select one or more files, the status bar changes to display the number of selected files and how many bytes of memory they total. If you don't see the status bar on your window, choose **View, Status Bar** from the menu.

When you double-click one of the drive icons, another window appears showing a listing of folders and files for that drive (see Figure 10.3). The My Computer window remains open but the new window is the active window.

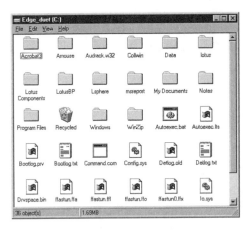

Figure 10.3 The window for the hard drive (C:).

You can view the icons in the window a number of ways (available as choices on the View menu) as shown in Figure 10.4. The. available views are:

- **Large icons** show the icons scattered in the window. Only the names of the files or folders appear below the icons.
- **Small icons** show the icons in reduced size, lined up in a rows alphabetically.
- **List** looks like small icons except that it's organized vertically.
- With **Details**, the small icons are listed vertically, with each row providing information on the size (in kilobytes) of the file, the type of file or folder, and the date and time last modified .You can click the column headers to sort the files by the information in that column. Click once for ascending order (A–Z) and again for descending order (Z–A).

The icons are generally shown in alphabetical order, but you can change the order by choosing **View**, **Arrange Icons** and then selecting the order you want: **By Drive Letter**, **By Name**, **By Type** (file type), **By Size** for files (in kilobytes), by **Free Space** for drives, **By Date**, or **Auto Arrange** to let Windows 95 arrange them for you.

Large
Icons

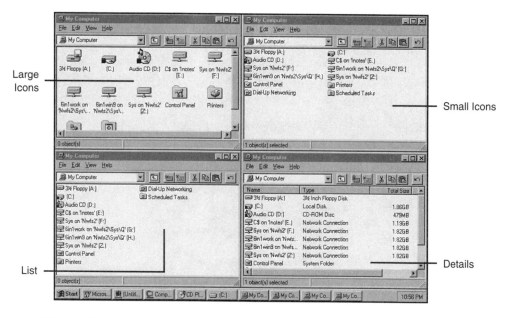

Small Icons

List

Details

Figure 10.4 The four ways to view My Computer icons.

If you accidentally move the icons around and you want them put in straight lines again (especially in the large icon view), choose **View, Line Up Icons**. This option is only available for the Large Icon and Small Icon views.

If you make changes to the folder you're viewing and they haven't appeared yet, choose **View, Refresh** to bring the window up to date.

TIP **Starting Programs** All programs have executable files that start the program. You will find icons representing those executable files in My Computer. You can start programs by double-clicking these file icons.

Opening Files Files saved by applications (such as word processing documents or spreadsheets) also bear a program icon with a piece of paper behind it. If you double-click one of these files, you'll start up the program with that document opened and ready for work.

Using Folder Browsing Options

Double-click a folder to see what folders and files it contains. Another window opens to show you the contents of the folder. Each time you want to look at the contents of a folder, you get another window. After exploring folders and looking for files, your desktop will get cluttered with open windows.

My Computer gives you another option for viewing folders:

1. Choose **View**, **Options**. The Options dialog box opens (see Figure 10.5).

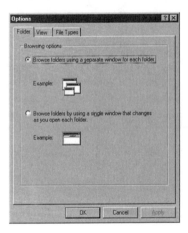

Figure 10.5 The Options dialog box with the Folder tab selected.

2. You see two folder viewing options: **Browse Folders Using a Separate Window for each Folder** (the default setting) and **Browse Folders by Using a Single Window that Changes as You Open Each Folder**. Select the option you prefer.
3. Click **OK**.

Using File Viewing Options

Not all files are displayed when you open a folder. Some system files are hidden. Also, you may have noticed that no file extensions appear in Windows 95.

To change how and what files My Computer displays:

1. Choose **View**, **Options**. The Options dialog box opens.
2. Click the **View** tab to select it (see Figure 10.6).

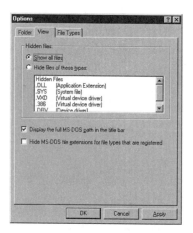

Figure 10.6 The Options dialog box with the View tab selected.

3. Under **Hidden** files, select **Show All Files** to see hidden and system files when you open a folder. To selectively hide files of certain types, select **Hide Files of These Types** and then click the type of file you want to hide.

4. Check **Display the Full MS-DOS Path in the Title Bar** if you want a folder Title Bar to show **C:\Data\Student** instead of displaying just **Student**.

5. If you don't want file extensions to appear with every file name, check **Hide MS-DOS File Extensions For File Types that are Registered**.

6. Click **OK**.

Registered   Similar to association in Windows 3.1, registration of a file links it to a particular program. When you double-click the file, it opens in that program. For example, a file with the extension TXT opens in the Notepad or WordPad because it's a text file. Registration also controls which program prints the file. Files are registered by file type, which is often based on the file extension.

The My Computer Menu

The menu bar on the My Computer window offers four choices: File, Edit, View, and Help.

The **File** menu changes depending on what you may have selected. In the File menu are commands pertaining to file management, such as creating new folders, creating shortcuts, deleting and renaming files or folders, checking file and folder properties, and closing the window.

The **Edit** menu provides an Undo command (to undo your last action), Cut to remove a file or folder and store it in the Clipboard, Copy to store a duplicate of a file or folder and store it in the Clipboard, Paste to put the contents of the Clipboard in the selected window, Select All to select all the files and folders in the window, and Invert Selection to select all the files and folders not selected while de-selecting the currently selected files.

Under the **View** menu are a series of options (discussed in "The My Computer Window" section) for looking at the files and folders with differently sized icons or in a different order.

The **Help** menu offers a way to open the Help Topics window, as well as open the About Windows dialog box. About Windows tells you the version of Windows you're using, its copyright date, the name of the licensee, the amount of memory available to Windows 95, and the percentage of system resources that are available.

The My Computer Toolbar

To see the My Computer toolbar (see Figure 10.7), choose **View**, **Toolbar** from the menu. Table 10.1 lists the buttons and what they do.

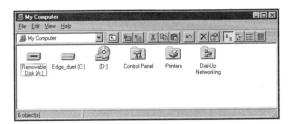

Figure 10.7 The My Computer toolbar buttons.

Table 10.1 The Toolbar Buttons

Button	Name	Use
My Computer	Go to a Different Folder	This drop-down list shows the drives and folders on your computer. Click one to open a window of that drive or folder.
	Up One Level	If the window you are in is a folder on a drive or a folder within another folder, click this button to move up one level to the drive or folder that is the "parent" of the one you have open.
	Map Network Drive	When you work on a network, you have drives and resources available to you on other computers. Mapping the drives allows you to assign a drive letter to that drive, folder, or resource.
	Disconnect Net Drive	Click to disconnect your computer from a specific drive on the network.
	Cut	Click to remove a selected file or folder from the window and store it in the Clipboard.
	Copy	Click to duplicate a selected file or folder from the window and store the copy in the Clipboard.
	Paste	Click to insert the contents of the Clipboard into the active window.
	Undo	Click to undo the last action you performed.
	Delete	Click to delete a selected file or folder.
	Properties	Click to bring up the Properties window for the selected drive, folder, or file.
	Large Icons	Click to see the large icons view of the window.
	Small Icons	Click to see the small icons view of the window.

Table 10.1   Continued

Button	Name	Use
	List	Click to see the list view of the window.
	Details	Click to see the details view of the window

Opening Drives and Folders

There are several ways to open the drives or folders displayed in My Computer:

- Double-click the drive or folder icon.
- Select the drive or folder icon by clicking it or using the arrow keys to move around the window to highlight the icon you want. Press **Enter** to open the highlighted drive or folder.
- Select the drive or folder icon by clicking it or using the arrow keys to move around the window to highlight the icon you want. Choose **File, Open**.
- Point at the drive or folder icon and click the right mouse button. From the pop-up menu, select **Open**.

Working with Multiple Windows

As you look through different drives and folders with My Computer, you will open a number of windows.

To switch between open windows:

- To switch quickly to another window, click whatever portion of it you can see to make it the active window and bring it to the top.
- Each open window is represented by an icon on the taskbar. Click the icon for the window you want to see.
- Hold down the **Alt** key and press **Tab** to bring up the switching window (see Figure 10.8). Each time you press **Tab,** it cycles to the next window. Release the **Alt** key when the title of the window you want to see appears in the switching window.

Figure 10.8   The switching window.

To reduce the clutter of windows on your screen, try one of these strategies:

- Close any unnecessary windows by choosing **File**, **Close** or by clicking the **Close** button on the title bar.

- Minimize any windows you don't need immediately but don't want to close by clicking the **Minimize** button on the title bar. The minimized windows are represented by icons on the taskbar, and you can click the appropriate icon to open the window again.

- To see more than one window at the same time, point at a blank area of the taskbar and click the right mouse button. From the pop-up menu, choose **Cascade** to see the all the open windows piled on top of each other with the title bar of each window visible; choose **Tile Horizontally** to have all the open windows divide up the screen with the windows showing one below the other; or **Tile Vertically** to have all the open windows divide up the screen with each window beside the other.

In this lesson, you learned how to open My Computer and view its contents in different ways. You also explored the My Computer window and its components. In the next lesson, you learn how to manage your files using My Computer.

Managing Files with My Computer

In this lesson, you learn how to manage your files and folders by creating new folders and by moving, copying, renaming, and deleting files and folders. You also discover how to find files and folders.

 This lesson describes using My Computer without Shell Integration active. Shell Integration can be installed with Internet Explorer 4 and makes your system's desktop function like a Web browser. If you have Shell Integration active, please go to Part V to learn how to use My Computer with this feature.

Creating Folders

To organize your files, you need to sort them out into folders such as Correspondence, Memos, Accounts, and so forth. Windows 95 does provide you with a "My Documents" folder for your documents, but you must create other folders for yourself.

1. Open the window for the drive or folder where you want to put the new folder.

2. Choose **File**, **New**, **Folder** from the menu or click in the window with the right mouse button and choose **New**, **Folder** from the pop-up menu.

 TIP **New Isn't a Selection on My File Menu** Check to make sure you don't have a drive, folder, or file selected. If you do, click the white space in the window and open the **File** menu again.

3. A new folder appears in the window with the name **New Folder** in a box and highlighted (see Figure 11.1). Enter a name for the folder (because "New Folder" is highlighted it will automatically disappear as you begin typing the new name, so you don't need to backspace or delete the text first). The name of the folder can be up to 255 characters long, including spaces. You cannot use any of the following characters: \, /, :, ", ", *, ?, <, >, or |.

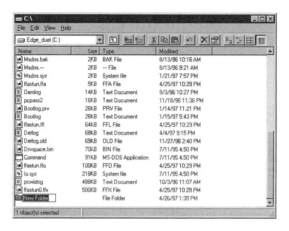

Figure 11.1   Creating a new folder.

4. Press **Enter**.

 TIP   **Folder Names**   Although you can use up to 255 characters, you should avoid doing so. Keep your file names short and simple, but descriptive. The names won't take up as much room in the window, and it'll be easier to find the folder (and remember its name) later. Also, be careful in naming to put the most important word first. As you look through a set of folders listed in alphabetical order, it'll help you find the folder faster.

Selecting Files and Folders

Before you can perform an operation on a file or folder, you must select (or highlight) the item so Windows knows which one you want to use.

To select files or folders:

- **Single file or folder**   Click the file or folder icon, or use the arrow keys to move the highlighting to the file or folder icon you want to select.

77

- **Several files or folders that are together** Click the first file or folder icon, hold down the **Shift** key, and click the last file or folder icon. This method selects all the files between. You can also hold down the **Shift** key and use an arrow key to move down to the final icon in the group you want.

- **Several files or folders that are not together** Click the first file or folder icon, hold down the **Ctrl** key, and click each of the additional file or folder icons you want.

- All the file or folder icons in the window Choose **Edit**, **Select All** from the menu.

- All except the file or folder icons you have currently selected Choose **Edit**, **Invert Selection** from the menu.

Moving Files and Folders

You can move files and folders to different folders or different drives. To do this using the drag-and-drop method:

1. Open the drive or folder window where the file or folder is stored. This is the source window.

2. Open the drive or folder window where you want to put the file or folder. This is the destination window.

3. If the windows you have open are for folders on the same drive, you can just drag the file or folder icon from the source window to the destination window.

   Dragging from a window on one drive to a window on another copies the file, so you have to delete the original icon in the source window if you do this.

CAUTION

My Icon Disappeared When I Released the Mouse Button Be careful as you drag the icon into the destination window that you do not drop it over a folder icon. When you do this, the icon gets moved into that folder and not into the destination window. To fix it, choose **Edit**, **Undo** from the menu and redo the drag and drop, or open the folder you dropped the icon into and then drag the icon to the original destination window.

To move files or folders using the cut and paste method:

1. Open the drive or folder window where the file or folder is stored.

2. Select the files or folders you want to move.

3. Choose **Edit**, **Cut** from the menu or click the **Cut** button on the toolbar. This removes the icon(s) from the current window.

4. Open the drive or folder window where you want to put the file or folder.

5. Choose **Edit, Paste** from the menu or click the **Paste** button on the toolbar.

Copying Files and Folders

You can copy files and folders to different folders or different drives. To do this using the drag and drop method:

1. Open the drive or folder window where the file or folder is stored. This is the source window.

2. Open the drive or folder window where you want to put the file or folder. This is the destination window.

3. If the windows you have open are for folders on different drives, you can just drag the file or folder icon from the source window to the destination window.

Dragging from a window on a drive to another window on the same drive moves the icon. You need to hold down the **Ctrl** key as you drag to copy the icon.

To copy files and folders using the cut and paste method:

1. Open the drive or folder window where the file or folder is stored.

2. Select the files or folders you want to copy.

3. Choose **Edit, Copy** from the menu or click the **Copy** button on the toolbar. This places a duplicate of the selected files or folders in the Clipboard.

4. Open the drive or folder window where you want to put the file or folder.

5. Choose **Edit, Paste** from the menu or click the **Paste** button on the toolbar.

 TIP   **Copying to the Floppy Disk**   If you want to copy selected files or folders from one of your drives to your floppy disk, click the selected icons with the right mouse button. Choose **Send To, 3½ Floppy (A)** from the pop-up menu.

Deleting Files and Folders

When you delete files or folders from your hard disk or a network drive, they are removed from their current window and placed in the Recycle Bin. If necessary, you can recover them from the Recycle Bin (see the next lesson for more information on the Recycle Bin). However, if the file is on a floppy disk it doesn't go to the Recycle Bin, so be very sure you want to delete files from a floppy disk.

CAUTION **I Lost All the Files in that Folder!** Be careful, too, when deleting folders. If you delete a folder, you're also deleting the contents of the folder. The folder doesn't have to be empty before you delete it, as in MS-DOS. Be sure you move any valuable files or folders to other locations before deleting a folder.

To delete a file or folder:

1. Select the files or folders to be deleted.

2. Press the **Delete** key, click the **Delete** button on the toolbar, or choose **File, Delete** from the menu.

3. A Windows 95 alert box appears asking if you are sure you want to send the selected files or folders to the Recycle Bin. If you are certain, select **Yes**. If not, select **No** and the operation will cease.

TIP **A Quick Way to Delete Files or Folders** Drag the file or folder icon from the My Computer window to the Recycle Bin. When Windows 95 highlights the Recycle Bin, release the mouse button.

Renaming Files and Folders

To give a different name to a file or folder:

1. Select the file or folder you want to rename.

2. Choose **File, Rename** from the menu, or click on the icon with the right mouse button and choose **Rename** from the pop-up menu, or click once on the name. The name gets a box around it and the text is highlighted (see Figure 11.2).

3. Enter the text for the new name.

4. Press **Enter**.

Figure 11.2   The file name when ready for renaming.

Creating Shortcuts

Shortcuts provide you with easy access to files and programs. Once you place a shortcut on the desktop, you can double-click that icon to start up a program or open a file or folder.

To create a shortcut from My Computer:

1. Open My Computer.
2. Select the drive, folder, or file for which you want to create the shortcut.
3. Choose **File**, **Create Shortcut**.
4. A copy of the icon appears in the window with the words **Shortcut To** in front of the name. Drag that icon onto the desktop.

Finding Files

You can search a drive with My Computer to find a file.

1. Open the My Computer window.
2. Select the drive you want to search.
3. Choose **File**, **Find** from the menu. The Find: All Files dialog box appears (see Figure 11.3).
4. In the **Named** box, enter the name of the file you want to find. If you don't know the complete name, use an asterisk (*) to substitute for the beginning or end of the name (such as "*97" to find all file names that end in "97"). Choose **Options**, **Case Sensitive** from the menu if you want to find a file

that's in uppercase but not find a file with the same name that's in lower-case.

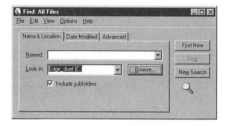

Figure 11.3 The Find: All Files dialog box.

5. The Look In box should already show the name of the drive you selected.

6. To search through all the folders in the specified drive, check **Include Subfolders**.

7. If you want to look in a specific folder, click **Browse** to open the Browse for Folder dialog box (see Figure 11.4) and select the folder you want to search.

Figure 11.4 The Browse for Folder dialog box.

8. Click **Find Now**.

9. When the search is complete, a list of files or folders matching your search criteria appears at the bottom of the dialog box (see Figure 11.5). Double-click the file that you want to open.

10. Click **New Search** to clear the search criteria so you can search for another file.

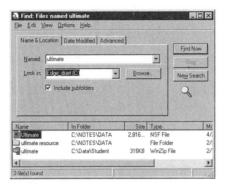

Figure 11.5 The search results appear at the bottom of the Find window.

You can also search for files based on the created or last modified date:

1. Follow steps 1 through 7 of finding a file, except you don't need to enter a file name in the **Named** box.

2. Click the **Date Modified** tab of the Find dialog box (see Figure 11.6).

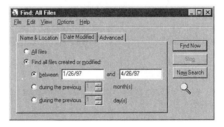

Figure 11.6 The Find dialog box with the Date Modified tab selected.

3. Select **Find All Files Created or Modified**.

4. Then choose one of the three options: **Between** (and enter the starting and ending dates) to look for all files created or modified between those dates, **During the Previous** *x* **Month(s)** (where *x* is the number of months) to return a list of files created or modified in the specified number of previous months, or **During the Previous** *x* **Day(s)** (where *x* is the number of days).

5. Click **Find Now.**

Use the advanced options of search to look for files by type, files that contain text strings, or files that are of a particular size.

83

1. Follow steps 1 through 7 of finding a file, except you don't need to enter a file name in the **Named** box.

2. Click the **Advanced** tab of the Find dialog box (see Figure 11.7).

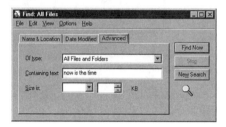

Figure 11.7 The Find dialog box with the Advanced tab selected.

3. From the Of Type drop-down list, select the type of file or folder you are seeking. The list depends on the types of applications or other programs you have loaded on your computer.

4. If you are searching for files containing specific text, enter all or a portion of that text in the **Containing Text** box.

5. To search for files of a particular size, choose **At Least** or **At Most** from the Size Is drop-down list and enter the number of kilobytes in the KB box.

6. Click **Find Now**.

In this lesson, you learned how to move your files around to organize your computer, how to copy them to other folders or drives, and how to rename and delete them. You also learned how to find files. In the next lesson, you explore the Recycle Bin.

The Recycle Bin

In this lesson, you look at the Recycle Bin and find out what it is, how to open it, how to empty it, how to restore files from it, and how to look at its properties.

What Is the Recycle Bin?

The Recycle Bin is a temporary storage area on your hard disk. When you delete a file or folder (as described in the previous lesson), Windows 95 moves it into the Recycle Bin. However, the file or folder still takes up space on the hard disk. You must empty the Recycle Bin to remove the file or folder from the drive.

This means that you still have a second chance to get that file or folder back before it's gone forever. You can restore it back to its former position from the Recycle Bin.

Opening the Recycle Bin

The Recycle Bin icon on the desktop differs slightly depending on whether it is empty as in Figure 12.1, or if files have been placed in the Recycle Bin and the bin appears full as in Figure 12.2.

Figure 12.1   The Recycle Bin icon (empty).

Figure 12.2   The Recycle Bin icon (with files in it).

To open the Recycle Bin, double-click the **Recycle Bin** icon on the desktop, select it using the arrow keys and then press **Enter,** or right-click the icon and choose **Open** from the pop-up menu.

The Recycle Bin window then opens (see Figure 12.3). The Recycle Bin window has the same look and much of the functionality as My Computer (see Lesson 11). Except for the network buttons, the toolbar is the same (if you can't see your toolbar choose **View**, **Toolbar** from the menu). The Status bar at the bottom of the screen shows the number of objects in the window or the number of selected items and the total amount of disk space they use.

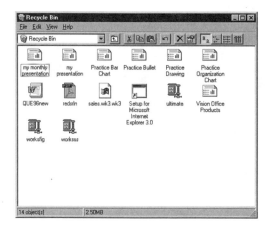

Figure 12.3 The Recycle Bin Window.

Emptying the Recycle Bin

To keep your hard disk drive "lean and mean," you're going to have to empty the Recycle Bin from time to time, especially if you get an error message when you try to save a file saying that there is insufficient disk space.

CAUTION

Do You Have Enough Room? You should check your hard disk space occasionally to make sure you have enough room to add more files. If you don't have much space left on the drive, then you should empty your recycle bin. To check your available disk space, open the My Computer window, click the hard drive icon to select it, and then check the amount of free space listed on the status bar.

Selected Files

You may not want to remove all the files from the Recycle Bin, especially if you think you might need some of them again.

To remove only specified files from the Recycle Bin:

1. Select the files you want to delete (see Lesson 2 to learn how to select files).

2. Press the **Delete** key, click the **Delete** button on the toolbar, or choose **File, Delete** from the menu.

All Files

To remove all the files from the Recycle Bin, choose **File, Empty Recycle Bin** from the menu.

If you don't have the Recycle Bin window open, you can empty the Recycle Bin from the desktop by clicking the icon with the right mouse button and selecting **Empty Recycle Bin** from the pop-up menu.

Restoring Files

Once you have put a file or folder into the Recycle Bin, how do you get it out?

1. Select the file(s) or folder(s) that you want to restore.

2. Choose **File, Restore** from the menu. The file or folder is returned to the location on your computer where it was before it was deleted.

Recycle Bin Properties

To customize your Recycle Bin and how files are deleted on your system, you need to open the Recycle Bin Properties box (see Figure 12.4).

To open the Recycle Bin Properties box, click the **Recycle Bin** icon with the right mouse button and choose **Properties** from the pop-up menu.

You can choose to make your Recycle Bin settings work for all the drives on your computer by selecting **Use One Setting For All Drives**. Otherwise, select **Configure Drives Independently**. If you choose the latter, you have to click each of the other tabs in the Properties box that bear the names of your drives and make the settings on each one.

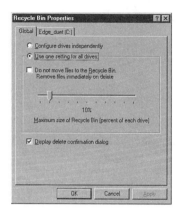

Figure 12.4   The Recycle Bin Properties Box.

There are three properties to set for the Recycle Bin:

> **Do Not Move Files to the Recycle Bin. Remove Immediately on
> Delete**   If you check this option, your deleted files will not be stored in
> the Recycle Bin but will disappear from the drive. This means you won't be
> able to restore the files. However, if you're tight on disk space, you may
> want to do this rather than buying a second or larger disk drive.
>
> **Maximum Size of Recycle Bin (Percentage of Each Drive)**   Use the slide
> indicator to set the maximum size to which the Recycle Bin can grow.
> Making it smaller will conserve disk space.
>
> **Display Delete Confirmation Dialog**   Check this if you want to be asked
> if you really want to delete the files every time you do a deletion. If you're
> tired of seeing the dialog box and having to click Yes every time you want
> to delete files, remove the check mark from this option. Just be sure if you
> check this future that you really want to delete the files, because you'll no
> longer be getting a warning.

Once you've selected your options in the Property box, click **OK**.

In this lesson, you learned what the Recycle Bin is and how to use it to remove
and restore files to your drives. In the next lesson, you learn what the Windows
Explorer is and how it differs from My Computer.

Understanding the Windows Explorer

In this lesson, you find out what the Windows Explorer is, how to open the Explorer, what the features of the Windows Explorer window are, and what the file viewing options are.

 This lesson describes using My Computer without Shell Integration active. Shell Integration can be installed with Internet Explorer 4 and makes your system's desktop function like a Web browser. If you have Shell Integration active, please go to Part V to learn how to use My Computer with this feature.

What Is the Windows Explorer?

As with My Computer (see Lesson 1), you use the Windows Explorer to view and organize your drives, folders, and files.

Unlike My Computer, the Explorer doesn't open a window each time you want to see the contents of another drive or folder. Instead, everything is contained within one window. The list of drives and folders is on the left, and the contents of the selected folder or drive is on the right. This arrangement makes it easier to navigate when you need to look at different drives and folders.

Opening the Explorer

To open the Windows Explorer:

1. Click the **Start** button on the taskbar.
2. Select **Programs** from the Start menu.
3. Click **Windows Explorer** (see Figure 13.1).

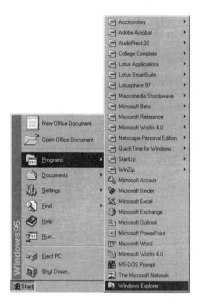

Figure 13.1 Starting up Windows Explorer.

Understanding the Explorer Window

The Explorer window (see Figure 13.2) is divided into two parts. On the left is the list of drives and folders. The right side displays the contents of the selected drive or folder.

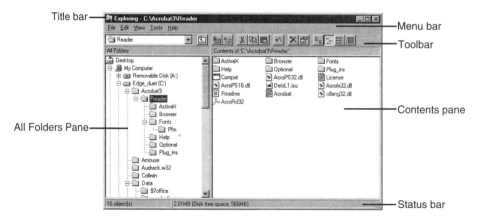

Figure 13.2 The Windows Explorer window.

With IE4 and Active Desktop Running... The Windows Explorer looks entirely different than it does here. Refer to Part V of this book for information on using the Windows Explorer with Internet Explorer 4.0.

At the top of the window is the title bar, which tells you the name of the window you have open. You can move the window by dragging the title bar.

Beneath the title bar is the menu bar, which contains commands that you may give to the program.

Below the menu bar is the toolbar. If your toolbar is not showing, choose **View**, **Toolbar** from the menu. The toolbar has buttons that perform menu commands without having to open the menu.

At the bottom of the screen is the status bar. In My Computer, the status bar displays the number of objects (files and folders) in the window and the number of bytes they take up in memory space. If you select one or more files, the status bar changes to display the number of selected files and how many bytes of memory they total. If you don't see the status bar on your window, choose **View**, **Status Bar** from the menu.

The left side of the window is the All Folders pane. Some of the icons in the All Folders pane represent drives, such as a floppy drive (A:), your hard drive (C:), or your CD-ROM drive (D:). If you have a tape drive or an additional floppy drive, icons for those items will also appear in this window. You'll also see icons for the Recycle Bin, My Briefcase, and Network Neighborhood (if you have a network).

The remaining icons in the All Folders pane look like manila folders because they're *folder* icons. When you create documents with an application such as a word processor, you save those documents as files. In order not to have the files haphazardly scattered across your hard drive, you store them in folders. Your program files are also stored in folders. Some folders contain other folders.

The All Folders pane shows you the hierarchy of drives and folders (sometimes referred to as the "tree"). It's like an organization chart turned sideways or like a computer's family tree. Here you can see clearly which folders reside inside other folders because the inside folders are indented under the main folder and are tied to the main folder by a line.

In front of some of the folder and drive icons in the All Folders pane you'll see plus (+) and minus (-) marks. A plus means the folder or drive has folders inside it but you can't see the list at the moment because it is collapsed. Click the plus to expand that folder or drive, and then you'll see the folders listed below it. A minus sign will appear in front of the drive or folder icon. To collapse the folder or drive so you no longer see the folders under it, click the minus sign.

To see the full contents of a drive or folder, click it. The folder opens up. Look to the right side of the window, to the Contents pane, to see the folders and files that the selected folder or drive contains. The files have different icons depending on what type of file they are and what program they represent or were created by.

If you need more room in either pane, point to the dividing border between them until you see the mouse pointer become a two-headed arrow (see Figure 13.3), and then drag left or right to increase the size of the left or right pane.

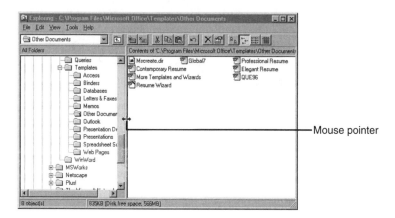

Figure 13.3   Drag the dividing border to change the pane size.

Using File Viewing Options

Not all files are displayed when you open a folder. Some system files are hidden. Also, if you are accustomed to DOS, you probably noticed that no file extensions appear in Windows 95.

To change how and what files the Explorer displays:

1. Choose **View**, **Options** from the menu. The Options dialog box opens.

2. Click the **View** tab to select it (see Figure 13.4).

Figure 13.4 The Options dialog box with the View tab selected.

3. Under **Hidden** files, select **Show All Files** to see hidden and system files when you open a folder. To selectively hide files of certain types, select **Hide Files of These Types** and then click the type of file you want to hide.

4. Check **Display the Full MS-DOS Path in the Title Bar** if you would like the Explorer title bar to show **C:\Data\Student** instead of displaying just **Student**.

5. If you don't want file extensions to appear with every file name, check **Hide MS-DOS File Extensions for File Types that are Registered**.

6. To see a description bar at the top of the All Folders and Contents panes, check **Include Description Bar for Right and Left Panes**.

7. Click **OK**.

In this lesson, you learned what the Windows Explorer is, how it differs from My Computer, what the elements of the Explorer window are, and how to set the file viewing options. In the next lesson, you learn more about the Explorer and changing views, using the toolbar and menu, and searching for files.

Navigating Explorer

In this lesson you go deeper into the Explorer window. You learn how to change the way files are viewed by using the toolbar and menus. You also learn how to search for a file and close the Explorer.

 Active Desktop? This lesson describes using My Computer without Shell Integration active. Shell Integration can be installed with Internet Explorer 4 and makes your system's desktop function like a Web browser. If you have Shell Integration active, please go to Part V to learn how to use My Computer with this feature.

Changing Displays

You can view the icons in the Contents pane a number of ways as shown in Figure 14.1. Available choices on the **View** menu are:

- **Large Icons** show the icons scattered in the window. Only the names of the files or folders appear below the icons.

- **Small Icons** show the icons in reduced size lined up alphabetically in a row.

- **List** looks like small icons except that it's organized vertically.

- With **Details**, the small icons are listed vertically, with each row providing information on the size (in kilobytes) of the file, the type of file or folder, and the date and time last modified. You can click the column headers to sort the files by the information in that column. Click once for ascending order (A–Z) and again for descending order (Z–A).

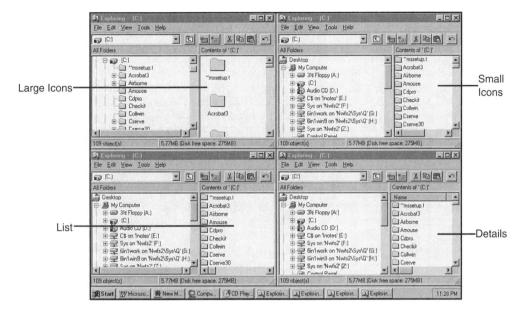

Figure 14.1 Available views of icons in the Contents pane.

The icons are generally shown in alphabetical order, but you can change the order by choosing **View**, **Arrange Icons** from the menu and then selecting the order you want—**By Drive Letter**, **By Name**, **By Type** (file type), **By Size** for files(in kilobytes**), By Date**, or **Auto Arrange** to let Windows 95 arrange them for you.

If you've accidentally moved the icons around and you want them put in straight lines again, choose **View**, **Line Up Icons**. This option is only available for the large and small icons views.

If you've made changes to the folder you're currently viewing and they haven't appeared yet, choose **View**, **Refresh** from the menu to bring the window up to date.

Using the Explorer Toolbar

To see the toolbar (see Figure 14.2), choose **View**, **Toolbar** from the menu. Table 14.1 lists the buttons and what they do.

Figure 14.2 The Windows Explorer toolbar.

Table 14.2 The Toolbar Buttons

Button	Name	Use
Reader	Go to a Different Folder	This drop-down list shows the drives and folders on your computer. Click one to open a window of that drive or folder.
	Up One Level	If the window you are in is a folder on a drive or a folder within another folder, click this button to move up one level to the drive or folder that is the "parent" of the one you have open.
	Map Network Drive	When you work on a network, you have drives and resources available to you on other computers. Mapping the drives allows you to assign a drive letter to that drive, folder, or resource.
	Disconnect Net Drive	Click to disconnect your computer from a specific drive on the network.
	Cut	Click to remove a selected file or folder from the window and store it in the Clipboard.
	Copy	Click to duplicate a selected file or folder from the window and store the copy in the Clipboard.
	Paste	Click to insert the contents of the Clipboard into the active window.
	Undo	Click to undo the last action you performed.

continues

Table 14.2 Continued

Button	Name	Use
	Delete	Click to delete a selected file or folder.
	Properties	Click to bring up the Properties window for the selected drive, folder, or file.
	Large Icons	Click to see the Large Icons view of the window.
	Small Icons	Click to see the Small Icons view of the window.
	List	Click to see the List view of the window.
	Details	Click to see the Details view of the window.

Using the Menu

The menu bar on the Explorer window offers five choices: File, Edit, View, Tools, and Help. The following list explains these menu items:

The **File** menu changes depending on what you may have selected. The File menu contains commands pertaining to file management. Creating new folders, creating shortcuts, deleting and renaming files or folders, checking file and folder properties, and closing the window are all commands found in the File menu.

The **Edit** menu includes the Undo command (to undo your last action), Cut to remove a file or folder and store it in the Clipboard, Copy to store a duplicate of a file or folder and store it in the Clipboard, Paste to put the contents of the Clipboard in the selected window, Select All to select all the files and folders in the window, and Invert Selection to select all the files and folders not selected while de-selecting the currently selected files.

Under the **View** menu are a series of options for looking at the files and folders with differently sized icons or in a different order.

Use the **Tools** menu to Find files or folders, Map Network Drives, Disconnect Network Drives, or Go To a specific folder.

The **Help** menu offers a way to open the Help Topics window, as well as open the About Windows dialog box. About Windows tells you the version of Windows you're using, its copyright date, the name of the licensee, the amount of memory available to Windows 95, and the percentage of system resources that are available.

Searching for a File

Use the Explorer to search a drive to find a file or folder or search for a computer by name if you have a network.

To find a file:

1. Open the Explorer.

2. Select the drive you want to search.

3. Choose **Tools**, **Find**, **Files or Folders** from the menu. The Find dialog box appears (see Figure 14.3).

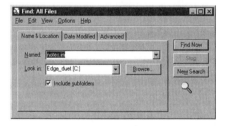

Figure 14.3 The Find dialog box.

4. In the **Named** box, enter the name of the file you want to find. If you don't know the complete name, use an asterisk (*) to substitute for the beginning or end of the name (such as "*97" to find all file names that end in "97"). Choose **Options**, **Case Sensitive** from the menu if you want to find a file that is uppercase but not find a file with the same name that is lowercase.

5. The **Look in** box should already show the name of the drive you selected.

6. To search through all the folders in the specified drive, check **Include Subfolders**.

7. If you want to look in a specific folder, click **Browse** to open the Browse for Folder dialog box (see Figure 14.4) and select the folder you want to search. Click **OK** to return to the Find dialog box.

Figure 14.4 The Browse for Folder dialog box.

8. Click **Find Now**.

9. When the search is complete, a list of files or folders matching your search criteria appears at the bottom of the dialog box (see Figure 14.5). Double-click the file you want to open.

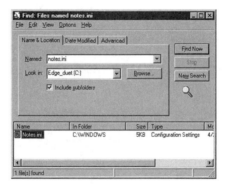

Figure 14.5 The search results appear at the bottom of the Find window.

10. Click **New Search** to clear the search criteria so you can search for another file.

You can also search for files based on the date they were created or last modified:

1. Follow steps 1 through 7 of finding a file. Don't enter a file name in the **Named** box.

2. Click the **Date Modified** tab of the Find dialog box (see Figure 14.6).

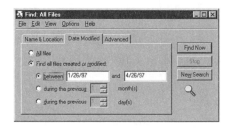

Figure 14.6   The Find dialog box with the Date Modified tab selected.

3. Select **Find All Files Created or Modified**.

4. Then choose one of the three options: **Between** (and enter the starting and ending dates) to look for all files created or modified between those dates, **During the Previous** x **Month(s)** (where x is the number of months) to return a list of files created or modified in the specified number of previous months, or **During the Previous** x **Day(s)** (where x is the number of days).

5. Click **Find Now**.

Use the advanced options of search to look for files by type, files that contain text strings, or files that are a particular size:

1. Follow steps 1 through 7 listed in Finding a File. You don't need to enter a file name in the **Named** box.

2. Click the Advanced tab of the Find dialog box (see Figure 14.7).

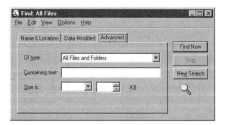

Figure 14.7   The Find dialog box with the Advanced tab selected.

3. From the **Of Type** drop-down list, select the type of file or folder you are seeking. The list depends on the types of applications or other programs you have loaded on your computer.

4. If you are searching for files containing specific text, enter all or a portion of that text in the **Containing Text** box.

5. To search for files of a particular size, choose **At Least** or **At Most** from the **Size Is** drop-down list and enter the number of kilobytes in the **KB** box.

6. Click **Find Now**.

Closing Explorer

To close the Windows Explorer, choose **File**, **Close** from the menu or click the **Close** button on the title bar.

In this lesson, you learned how to use the Explorer to look at the files and folders on your computer, how to change the views, how to use the toolbar and menu and how to search for files. In the next lesson, you explore file management as you create folders, and move, copy, delete, and rename files and folders.

Managing Files with Explorer

In this lesson, you learn to use Explorer to manage your drives, folders, and files by creating new folders to organize and store files. You also learn how to copy and move files and folders, delete files and folders, rename files and folders, and create shortcuts to put on the desktop.

 This lesson describes using My Computer without Shell Integration active. Shell Integration can be installed with Internet Explorer 4 and makes your system's desktop function like a Web browser. If you have Shell Integration active, please go to Part V to learn how to use My Computer with this feature.

Creating Folders

To organize your files, you need to sort them out into folders such as Correspondence, Memos, Accounts, and so forth. Windows 95 does provide you with a My Documents folder for your documents. You must create additional folders for yourself.

1. Open the Windows Explorer.

2. In the All Folders pane, select the drive or folder where you want to put the new folder.

3. Choose **File, New, Folder** from the menu. A new folder appears in the window with the name "New Folder" in a box and highlighted (see Figure 15.1).

CAUTION

New Isn't On My File Menu Check to make sure you don't have a folder or file selected in the Contents pane. If you do, make sure you make your selection in the All Folders pane and open the File menu again.

4. Enter a name for the folder (because "New Folder" is highlighted it will automatically disappear as you begin typing the new name, so you don't need to backspace or delete the text first). The name of the folder can be up to 255 characters long, including spaces. You cannot use any of the following characters: \, /, :, ", ", *, ?, <, >, or |.

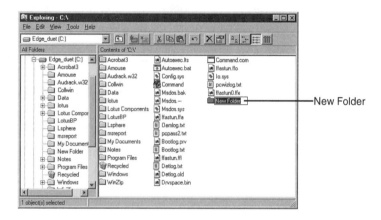

New Folder

Figure 15.1 Creating a new folder.

5. Press **Enter**.

Selecting Files and Folders

Before you can perform an operation on a file or folder, you must select (or highlight) the item so Windows knows which one you want to use.

To select files or folders:

- **Single file or folder** Click the file or folder icon, or use the arrow keys to move the highlighting to the file or folder icon you want to select.

- **Several files or folders that are together** Click the first file or folder icon, hold down the **Shift** key, and click the last file or folder icon. This method also selects all the files between. You can also hold down the **Shift** key and use an arrow key to move down to the final icon in the group you want.

- **Several files or folders that are not together**   Click the first file or folder icon, hold down the **Ctrl** key, and click each of the additional file or folder icons you want.
- **All the file or folder icons in the window**   Choose **Edit, Select All** from the menu.
- **All except the file or folder icons you have currently selected**   Choose **Edit, Invert Selection** from the menu.

Moving Files and Folders

You can move files and folders to different folders or different drives. To do this using the drag-and-drop method:

1. From the All Folders pane, open the drive or folder where the file or folder you want to move is stored by clicking on the drive or folder icon.

2. Drag the file or folder icon from the Contents to the drive or folder icon in the All Folders pane where you want to put it. Don't release the mouse button until the destination drive or folder is highlighted.

   Dragging from a file or folder on one drive to another drive copies the file, so you have to delete the original icon in the Contents pane if you do this.

To move files or folders using the cut and paste method:

1. From the All Folders pane, open the drive or folder where the file or folder you want to move is stored.

2. From the Contents pane, select the file or folder you want to move.

3. Choose **Edit, Cut** from the menu or click the **Cut** button on the toolbar. This removes the icon(s) from the current folder or drive.

4. In the All Folders pane, open the drive or folder where you want to put the file or folder.

5. Choose **Edit, Paste** from the menu or click the **Paste** button on the toolbar.

Copying Files and Folders

You can copy files and folders to different folders or different drives. To do this using the drag and drop method:

1. In the All Folders pane, open the drive or folder where the file or folder you want to copy is stored. Just click the drive or folder icon to open it.

2. Hold down the **Ctrl** key and drag the file or folder icon you want to copy from the Contents pane to the drive or folder icon in the All Folders pane, where you want to put it.

   If you are dragging the file or folder from one drive to another, you don't need to hold down the **Ctrl** key.

To copy files or folders using the cut and paste method:

1. In the All Folders pane, open the drive or folder where the file or folder you want to copy is stored.

2. In the Contents pane, select the files or folders you want to copy.

3. Choose **Edit**, **Copy** from the menu or click the **Copy** button on the toolbar. This places a duplicate of the selected files or folders in the Clipboard.

4. In the All Folders pane, open the drive or folder where you want to put the duplicate file or folder.

5. Choose **Edit**, **Paste** from the menu or click the **Paste** button on the toolbar.

 TIP **Copying to the Floppy Disk** If you want to copy selected files or folders from one of your drives to your floppy disk, click the selected icons with the right mouse button. Choose **Send To**, **3½ Floppy (A)** from the pop-up menu.

Deleting Files and Folders

When you delete files or folders from your hard disk or a network drive, they are removed from their current folder and placed in the Recycle Bin. If necessary, you can recover them from the Recycle Bin (see Lesson 12 for more information about the Recycle Bin). However, if the file is on a floppy disk it doesn't go to the Recycle Bin. Be very sure you want to delete files from your disk.

Be careful, too, when deleting folders. If you delete a folder, you're also deleting the contents of the folder. The folder doesn't have to be empty before you delete it, as in MS-DOS. Be sure you move any valuable files or folders to other locations before deleting a folder.

To delete a file or folder:

1. Select the files or folders to be deleted.

2. Press the **Delete** key, click the **Delete** button on the toolbar, or choose **File**, **Delete** from the menu.

3. A Windows 95 alert box appears asking if you are sure you want to send the selected files or folders to the Recycle Bin. If you are, select **Yes**. If not, select **No** and the operation will cease.

Renaming Files and Folders

To give a different name to a file or folder:

1. Select the file or folder you want to rename.

2. Choose **File**, **Rename** from the menu, or click the icon with the right mouse button and choose **Rename** from the pop-up menu, or click once on the name. The name gets a box around it and the text is highlighted (see Figure 15.2).

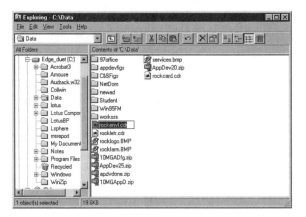

Figure 15.2 The file name when ready for renaming.

3. Enter the text for the new name.

4. Press **Enter**.

Creating Shortcuts

Shortcuts provide you with easy access to files and programs. Once you place a shortcut on the desktop, you can double-click that shortcut icon to start up a program or open a file or folder.

To create a shortcut:

1. Open the Explorer.
2. Select the drive, folder, or file for which you want to create the shortcut.
3. Choose **File**, **Create Shortcut**.
4. A copy of the icon appears in the window with the words Shortcut to in front of the name. Drag that icon onto the desktop.

In this lesson, you learned to manage your files by moving, copying, renaming, and deleting them. You saw how to create new folders and add shortcuts to your desktop. In the next lesson, you learn about backing up your files.

Using Backup

In this lesson, you learn what a back up is, how to utilize it, and how to compare and restore files.

What Is Backing Up?

Backing up is making a special copy of your files that can easily be restored should something happen to your hard drive.

You can back up your files to floppy disks, a tape drive, or another computer on your network.

You should back up your hard drive on a regular basis. At a minimum, once a week is recommended. If you're working on a network, the network drive is probably being backed up for you. If you're keeping any files on your own hard drive, it is your responsibility to back them up.

If you only have a few files that you need to back up, you can use the copying abilities of My Computer or the Windows Explorer to copy the files to a floppy disk.

Backing Up Data

Windows 95 has a built-in backup program that you can use. If you have a tape drive, backup software may have been packaged with it.

 TIP **I Don't Have Backup!** Backup is an optional component in the Windows 95 installation. If you did not select this option when Windows was installed, you need to follow the instructions in Help to install that component by running Windows setup again.

To back up your data:

1. Click the **Start** button on the taskbar.

2. Choose **Programs**, **Accessories**, **System Tools**, **Backup** from the Start menu. The Backup window opens. As you can see from Figure 16.1, the Backup window is divided into two panes, like the Windows Explorer.

TIP **My Screen Doesn't Look Like This** If this is the first time you've used the program, two screens will precede opening the program. After you read through the information, click OK to continue.

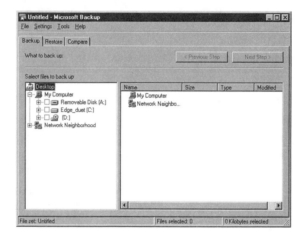

Figure 16.1 The Backup window.

3. In front of each drive or folder is a check box. Check this box to select the items you want to back up.

To do a selective backup, open the folder or drive and use the pane on the right side to select individual files or folders.

4. Click the **Next Step** button.

5. Select the drive to which you want to send the backup files (see Figure 16.2).

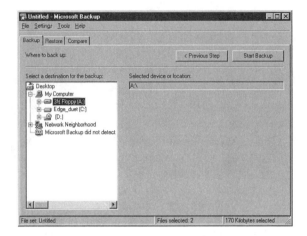

Figure 16.2 The second Backup window.

6. Click **Start Backup**.

7. The Backup Set Label dialog box appears (see Figure 16.3). Enter a label for the set and click **OK**. You can use that label later to call up the same set of files.

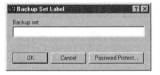

Figure 16.3 The Backup Set Label dialog box.

8. When the operation is complete, click **OK**.

Comparing Files

When you've made backups faithfully, the day may come when your diligence is rewarded—the hard disk crashes! Before you restore your files, make sure that the backup tape or disk you have is the most current. Maybe you should check one against the other, or if you still have some information on your hard disk you might want to compare that with your backup.

To compare file contents with a backup set:

1. Open the Backup program.

2. Click the **Compare** tab.

3. On the left side of the window, select the drive that holds the backup set (see Figure 16.4).

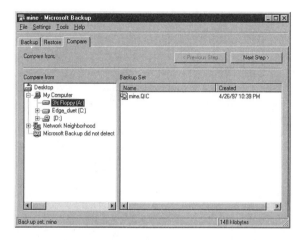

Figure 16.4 The Backup window with Compare selected.

4. On the right side of the window, select the backup set you want to compare.

5. Click **Next Step**.

6. On the left side of the window (see Figure 16.5), click the box in front of each folder you want to compare (click the plus in front of the folder to see more folders).

7. Click **Start Compare**.

8. When the operation is complete, click **OK**. The Compare dialog box appears (see Figure 16.6). The number of errors is reported in the lower-right corner.

9. Click **OK**.

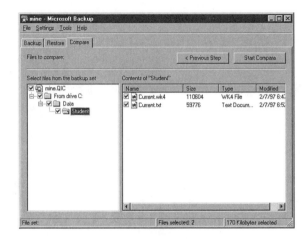

Figure 16.5   The second Compare window.

Figure 16.6   The Compare dialog box.

Restoring Files

When you need to restore your files:

1. Open the Backup program.
2. Click the **Restore** tab.
3. From the left side of the window (see Figure 16.7), select the drive where you put your backup files.

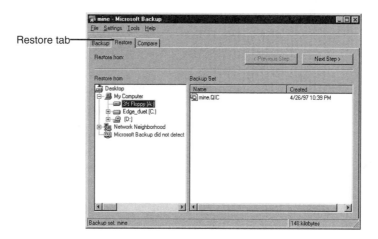

Figure 16.7 The Backup window with the Restore tab selected.

4. Select the backup set you want to restore from the right side of the window.

5. Click **Next Step**.

6. On the right side of the window (see Figure 16.8), select the files you want to restore.

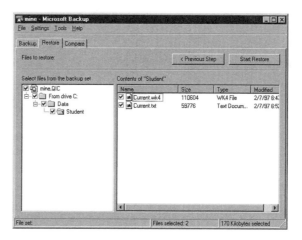

Figure 16.8 The second Restore window.

7. Click **Start Restore**.

8. If any errors occur during restoration, Backup will ask if you want to review them. If you click **OK**, an Error Log window appears (see Figure 16.9). Read the log and then close the window.

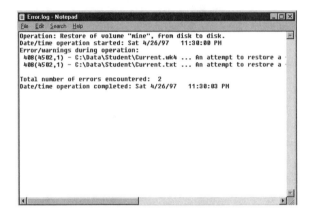

Figure 16.9 The Error Log window.

9. Click **OK**.

To exit Backup choose **File**, **Exit** from the menu.

In this lesson, you learned why it's important to back up your files, how to do it in Windows 95 Backup, how to compare backed up files, and how to restore backed up files. In the next lesson, you learn to work with some of the disk management tools of Windows 95.

Disk
Management

In this lesson, you learn about Scan Disk, DriveSpace, and Disk Defragmenter. These tools are provided by Windows 95 to help you maintain your system.

Using Disk Defragmenter

When files are stored on new disks, they are written one after another. As time goes by, one file gets deleted, leaving a "hole," and then another, and so on. The "holes" are scattered all over the disk. Then new files are stored on the disk filling up the "holes" left by the deleted files. However, one "hole" may not be enough for a file so part of it is stored there and another part is stored on another part of the disk.

Over time your files become scattered or *fragmented* across the disk. When a program retrieves a file, it takes longer to put the files' pieces together—if the file has become fragmented. You see the whole file but may not realize that it's fragmented. Slow access time to retrieve the file alerts you that the file might be fragmented.

The Disk Defragmenter puts the fragmented files together. This speeds up your file retrieval, so you get your files faster.

 TIP **Always Back Up!** Before you do anything to your hard disk, always back up your files. If any problem occurs during defragmenting, you may need to restore files. For more information on backing up, see Lesson 16.

To start Disk Defragmenter:

1. Click the **Start** button on the taskbar.
2. Choose **Programs**, **Accessories**, **System Tools**, **Disk Defragmenter**.
3. The Select Drive dialog box appears (see Figure 17.1). Select the drive you want to defragment from the drop-down list.

Figure 17.1   The Select Drive dialog box.

4. Click **OK**. If your disk does not need to be defragmented, a dialog box will appear suggesting that you cancel Defrag. You can choose to cancel, or continue.
5. When the Disk Defragmenter dialog box appears, click **Advanced** if you want to change the Defragmenter settings. The Advanced Options dialog box appears (see Figure 17.2).

Figure 17.2   The Advanced Options dialog box.

6. Under **Defragmentation Method**, you can select either **Full Defragmentation (Both Files and Free Space)**, **Defragment Files Only**, or **Consolidate Free Space Only**.
7. If you want an error report, check **Check Drive for Errors**.

8. Determine how often you want to use these settings by selecting **This Time Only, Next Time, Use the Defaults Again**, or **Save These Options and Use Them Every Time**.

9. Click **OK** to return to the Disk Defragmenter dialog box (see Figure 17.3).

Figure 17.3 The Disk Defragmenter dialog box.

10. Click **Start** to begin defragmenting your disk.

11. You can safely use your computer for other tasks while the Defragmenter is running, although your computer will run slower. You can temporarily stop the Disk Defragmenter by clicking **Pause** (see Figure 8.4). Then your other programs will run faster.

Figure 17.4 The Defragmenting Drive dialog box.

12. When the Defragmenter is finished, a dialog box will ask you if you want to work on another disk or quit. Click **Quit** unless you want to repeat the process on another disk.

Using DriveSpace

Need more space for your files? You can use DriveSpace to free up space on hard and floppy disks or to see the available space on a drive. DriveSpace compresses data on the disk, giving you 50% to 100% more free space.

TIP **Always Back Up!** Before you compress the files on your hard disk, always back up your files. If any problem occurs during compression, you may need to restore files.

To compress a drive:

1. Click **Start** on the taskbar.

2. Choose **Programs**, **Accessories**, **System Tools**, **DriveSpace**. The DriveSpace window opens (see Figure 17.5).

Figure 17.5 The DriveSpace window.

3. In the window, select the drive you want to compress.

4. Choose **Drive**, **Compress** from the menu. The Compress a Drive window appears (see Figure 17.6).

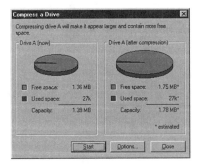

Figure 17.6 The Compress a Drive window.

5. Click **Start**.

6. If you haven't backed up your files, click **Back Up Files** and follow the instructions on the screen (or use the instructions in Lesson 16, "Using Backup").

7. Click **Compress Now**.

8. Windows may prompt you to restart your computer. Click **Yes**. Otherwise, the Compress a Drive window reappears. Then click **Close**.

In the DriveSpace window, you see two drives listed where before there was one. If you ran the compression on drive C, one is the "compressed drive C" and the other is the "host drive" for drive C.

The compressed drive isn't really a drive—it's an *artificial designation*. It appears as a drive to Windows and to your programs, but the entire contents of the compressed drive are really stored in a single file called a *compressed volume file* (CVF). The compressed volume file is located on the host drive. The default drive assignment for the host drive is H, although you can change that by clicking **Options** in the Compress a Drive window and changing the drive letter assigned to the host drive.

The host drive doesn't appear in My Computer or the Windows Explorer. It's hidden unless it has more than 2 MG of free space.

To uncompress a drive:

1. From the DriveSpace window, click on the drive you want to uncompress.
2. Choose **Drive**, **Uncompress** from the menu.
3. Click **Start**.
4. Click **Uncompress Now**.

Using ScanDisk

Check your files and folders for data errors by using ScanDisk. ScanDisk will also check the physical surface of your drive.

To start ScanDisk:

1. Click the **Start** button on the taskbar.
2. Choose **Programs**, **Accessories**, **System Tools**, **ScanDisk**. The ScanDisk window appears (see Figure 17.7).
3. Select the drive you want to scan for errors.
4. Under **Type of Test**, choose which type of test you want to run. Select **Standard** to check files and folders for data errors. Choose **Thorough** to go beyond the Standard test and scan the disk surface for errors as well.

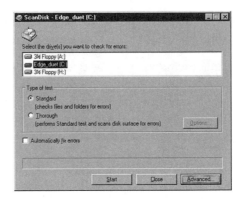

Figure 17.7 The ScanDisk window.

5. If you selected the Thorough test, you can specify how you want ScanDisk to scan the disk surface by clicking **Options** and opening the Surface Scan Options dialog box (see Figure 17.8). Select the options for the test and click **OK** to exit the dialog box.

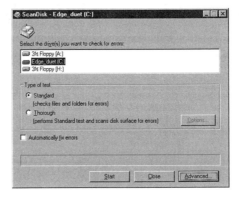

Figure 17.8 The Surface Scan Options dialog box.

You can choose to scan the **System Area Only**, the **Data Area Only**, or both the **System and Data Areas**.

When ScanDisk checks a disk it reads the contents of every sector and then writes the contents back. By doing this, it verifies that the drive can be read from and written to. Check **Do Not Perform Write-Testing** if you don't want ScanDisk to write the contents back.

ScanDisk repairs bad sectors on your disk. Data in a bad sector gets moved to a valid location. Problems may arise with system and hidden files if they are moved, as some programs require that these files be stored in a specific location. Moving the files may cause serious problems. To protect the location of these files, check **Do Not Repair Bad Sectors In Hidden and System Files**.

6. Check **Automatically Fix Errors** to have ScanDisk repair your data errors.

7. Click **Start**.

You can specify how ScanDisk works by clicking the **Advanced** button before clicking Start. The Advanced Options dialog box appears (see Figure 17.9). Table 17.3 outlines what the choices are and what they mean. Select the options you want and then click **OK**.

Figure 17.9 The Advanced Options dialog box.

Table 17.3 Advanced Options

Option	Description	Choices
Display Summary	ScanDisk displays a summary when it finishes checking a drive. When do you want to do that?	Always Never Only if errors found
Log File	A detailed record of the ScanDisk session is saved in a file named SCANDISK.LOG. Do you want to replace the previous log, add to it, or make no log?	Replace log Append to log No log

continues

121

Table 17.3   Continued

Option	Description	Choices
Cross-linked Files	Cross-linked files occur when two or more files use the same area of a disk at the same time. The data is probably correct for one of the files. Do you want to delete the cross-linked file, make copies, or ignore it?	Delete Make copies Ignore
Lost File Fragments	Do you want to delete lost file fragments and free up the space for disk storage or do you want to convert them to files that you can view and delete later. These files are stored in the root directory and are given names such as FILE0000.	Free Convert to files
Check Files For	You can't open files with invalid file names. Files with invalid dates and times may not sort properly, which could throw off date sensitive programs such as Backup.	Invalid file names Invalid dates and times
Check Host drive First	Errors on a compressed drive are often caused by errors on its host drive. If your drive is compressed, you should check this.	Enable Disable

In this lesson, you learned how to maintain your disk by compressing its files to make more room, defragmenting files to consolidate free space, and scanning the disk for data errors. In the next lesson, you learn about file properties.

File Properties

In this lesson, you learn about properties files and how to view the properties of a particular file.

File Size

All storage media (hard disks, floppy disks, CDs) measure their capacity in bytes. A *byte* is approximately the size a one character. A thousand bytes is a kilobyte (abbreviated K or KB), a million bytes is a megabyte (abbreviated MB, called "Meg"), and a billion bytes is a gigabyte (abbreviated GB, called "Gig").

The size of *files* are measured in bytes. That doesn't mean that a 1,000 character essay is going to be 1,000 bytes. All the formatting directions in a document also take up space. You can see the size of your files by looking in My Computer or the Windows Explorer and using the Details view (see Figure 18.1).

Figure 18.1 My Computer using the Details view.

If you know the size of the files you want to store and you know the storage capacity of the disk you want to store them on, you can tell if the disk is large enough to hold all the files. You have to take into account whatever files are already on the disk. It's the *free space* of the disk that must be large enough to hold your files.

File Creation Date and Time

When you first save a file, Windows automatically records the date and time that you saved it. When you open the file again and make changes, the date and time you save it is again recorded as the modified date. You can see the modified date in the details view of My Computer (as shown in Figure 18.1) or the Windows Explorer.

You need to know that date to determine which file is the most recent. The Backup programs uses that information to determine which files have been modified since the last back up.

The date and time are dependent on the system clock, so be sure to set yours for the correct time (set by selecting the **Date/Time** icon in the Control Panel).

File Attributes

There are four attributes that can be assigned to files:

Read-only   You can open a read-only file and read it or print it, but you cannot change it or delete it.

Archive   Some programs use this option to determine which files are to be backed up. In most cases, if the file is not read-only, it has an Archive attribute.

Hidden   Some files are not visible in file listings, and you can't use them unless you know the name of the file. Program files may be hidden to keep you from moving or deleting them accidentally.

System   Certain files are necessary to the operation of your system; these are system files. When you open My Computer or the Windows Explorer in the Details view, you can see which files are system files under the Type column (see Figure 18.2).

Viewing Properties

To see the properties of a file—whether you are in My Computer, Windows Explorer, or Network Neighborhood—you must first select the file and then do one of the following:

- Choose **File**, **Properties**.
- Click the right mouse button and choose **Properties** from the pop-up menu.
- Click the **Properties** button on the toolbar.

The Properties dialog box for the selected file opens (see Figure 18.2).

Figure 18.2 The Properties dialog box for a file.

The Properties dialog box provides you with information about the file:

- File name
- Type (of file)
- Location (what folder it's in)
- Size (in kilobytes and actual number of bytes)
- MS-DOS name (includes extension)
- Created (date and time the file was created)
- Modified (date and time the file was last modified)
- Accessed (date the file was last opened)

- Attributes (Read-only, Archive, Hidden, System)

Except for System files, you can change the attributes of selected files by checking the attributes you want to assign to it. For example, if you want to provide a file to several users for reference but you don't want them to change the file, change the file attribute to **Read-only**.

Click **Apply** to change an attribute without closing the Properties dialog box; click **OK** to accept the changes.

If you open the Properties dialog box for a document, you may see two additional tabs in the box: **Summary** and **Statistics** (see Figure 18.3).

Figure 18.3   Document Properties include Summary and Statistics tabs.

The **Summary** page, shown in Figure 18.4, contains information entered by the program that created it. For instance, in many word processors you can create a summary sheet. That information would appear in this Properties dialog box. You can't change it in the Properties dialog box; you must return to the original application to do that.

The **Statistics** page not only contains creation and modification dates and times but has the name of the person who last modified the file (see Figure 18.6). The Statistics page also lists the number of revisions and contains information about the number of pages and so forth. The information on this page may vary widely from application document to application document.

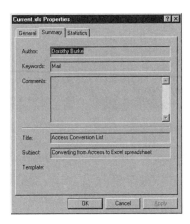

Figure 18.4 The Summary page of the Properties dialog box.

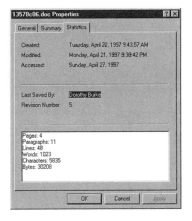

Figure 18.5 The Statistics page of the Properties dialog box.

In this lesson, you learned the various properties of a file: size, date and time, and attributes. You learned how to find the properties of a selected file and how to change the attributes. In the next lesson, you learn about registering files.

127

Registering Files

In this lesson, you look at registering files: what it means and how to do it.

What Is File Association?

In Windows version 3.1 you could associate files with particular applications. This allowed you to double-click an icon for that File Manager and have it automatically open in the associated application.

Registered files in Windows 95 work the same way. If you double-click a file icon in My Computer, the Windows Explorer, or Network Neighborhood, a file opens in it's associated application. Registering goes beyond association because you can also specify which program controls the printing of a file.

If you double-click a file icon and it isn't registered, it's probably because it wasn't created by one of the applications on your computer. Instead of opening a program, a dialog box appears asking which program to associate with the file (see Figure 19.1).

Figure 19.1 The Open With dialog box.

In the case of Figure 19.1, the Open With dialog box appeared because the file was originally created in CorelDRAW! on another computer. CorelDRAW! is not loaded on this computer, so no program can automatically opened. Select another program that can open the file (check **Always Use This Program to Open This File** if you want to make the association permanent) and click **OK**.

Registering a New File Type

You can register a new file type from either My Computer or the Windows Explorer:

1. Choose **View**, **Options**. The Options dialog box appears.

2. Select the **File Types** tab (see Figure 19.2).

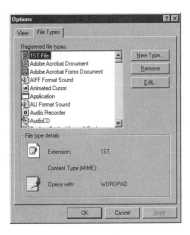

Figure 19.2 The Options dialog box with the File Types tab selected.

3. Click **New Type**. The Add New File Type dialog box appears (see Figure 19.3).

4. In the **Description** box, enter the brief description that appears under **Type** when you choose the Details view in My Computer or the Windows Explorer.

5. In the **Associated Extension** box, specify the three-letter file extension for this file type. Any files bearing this extension will automatically get the same icon and commands as in this dialog box.

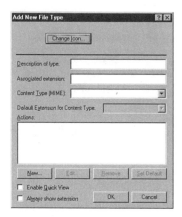

Figure 19.3   The Add New File Type dialog box.

6. From the **Content Type (MIME)** drop-down list, select the appropriate MIME type or enter the name in the box.

MIME (Multipurpose Internet Mail Extensions)   An Internet browser or Internet mail viewer associates a MIME type with a file type, which gives information about which program should run when you open the file over the Internet.

7. Once you select the MIME type, an entry may appear automatically in the **Default Extension for Content Type** box. If not, select one from the list or enter one.

8. The **Actions** box lists commands that have been defined for the selected file type. You can set up as many commands as you want and give them any name you want. To add a new command, click **New**.

9. The New Action dialog box appears (see Figure 19.4). In the Action box, enter the name of the command (such as Open or Print) that will appear on the shortcut menu for this type of file. If you want to specify a character as an accelerator key, precede it with an ampersand (&).

Figure 19.4   The New Action dialog box.

Selection Letter The one letter in each menu command is underlined. This means you can use this letter in combination with the Alt key as a keyboard shortcut.

10. In the Application Used to Perform Action box, specify the command file and path that performs the action you want. For example, if the action you entered was **Open Solitaire** then enter **SOL.EXE** here, which is the executable file for Solitaire. Click **Browse** to help locate the correct file.

11. If you know that the program or file type uses Dynamic Data Exchange (DDE) to link data, check **Use DDE** and complete the fields that appear. Click **OK**. The action appears in the **Actions** box.

12. If you know that the application supports Quick View, check **Enable Quick View**.

13. If you always want the file extension to show on this type of file, check **Always Show Extension**.

14. Click **Close** to return to the Options dialog box.

Editing an Existing File Type

To edit an existing file type:

1. Choose **View**, **Options**. The Options dialog box appears.

2. Select the **File Types** tab.

3. Under **Registered file types**, select the type you want to edit.

4. Click **Edit**. The Edit File Type dialog box appears (see Figure 19.5).

5. Make any modifications you want. Use the **New**, **Edit**, or **Remove** buttons under **Actions** to add, change, or delete actions.

6. Click **OK** to return to the Options dialog box.

7. Click **OK**.

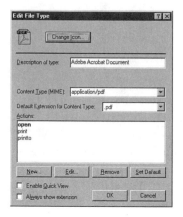

Figure 19.5 The Edit File Type dialog box.

Removing a File Type

To remove a file type:

1. Choose **View**, **Options**. The Options dialog box appears.

2. Select the **File Types** tab (see Figure 19.6).

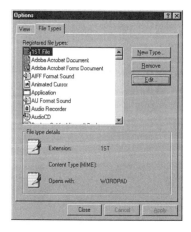

Figure 19.6 The Options dialog box with the File Types tab selected.

3. Under the **Registered File Types**, select the file type you want to remove.

4. Click **Remove**.

5. Windows requests a confirmation that you want to remove the file type. Click **Yes**.

6. Click **Close**.

Changing the Icon for a File Type

Every file type has an icon associated with it. To change the icon for an existing file type:

1. Choose **View**, **Options**. The Options dialog box appears.

2. Select the **File Types** tab.

3. Under **Registered file types**, select the type you want to edit.

4. Click **Edit**. The Edit File Type dialog box appears.

5. Click **Change Icon**. The Change Icon dialog box appears (see Figure 19.7).

Figure 19.7 The Change Icon dialog box.

6. Select one of the icons in the **Current Icon** box or click **Browse** to search for another icon.

7. Click **OK** and then **Close**.

8. Click **Close** to exit the Options dialog box.

In this lesson, you learned what registering files means, how to register a file type, how to edit it, and how to remove it. You also learned how to change an icon for a file type. In the next lesson, you learn about printing in Windows.

Printing with Windows 95

In this lesson, you learn to print from an application, control the print job, and connect to a network printer.

Installing a Printer

You can easily install a printer to work with all of your Windows applications. Windows includes many drivers for various manufacturer's computers. To install a printer, you need your Windows CD-ROM or a disk containing printer drivers that came with your printer.

Printer Drivers Software programs you install to your computer. The drivers make the printer work with Windows 95 and your Windows applications.

To install a printer, perform the following steps:

1. Choose the **Start** button, and then click **Settings**, **Printers**. The Printers window appears.

2. Double-click the **Add Printer** icon to display the **Add Printer** Wizard dialog box. Click **Next** to begin installing a new printer.

3. Choose whether to install a local printer or a network printer and then choose the **Next** button.

Local or Network Printer? A local printer is one connected directly to your computer; a network printer is one that may be connected to another computer on the network and is used by several workstations in addition to yours.

4. In the third Add Printer Wizard dialog box, choose the Manufacturer of your printer, such as Hewlett Packard, and then the model of the printer, such as DeskJet 550C as shown in Figure 20.1.

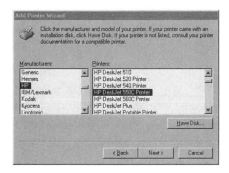

Figure 20.1 Choose the printer you want to install.

5. If you have a disk from the printer's manufacturer that contains Windows 95 drivers, insert the disk into the disk drive and click the **Have Disk** button; alternatively, insert your Windows 95 Setup CD-ROM and click the **Next** button.

6. Follow the directions on-screen. When Windows finishes setting up the printer, it returns to the Printers window.

Printing from an Application

The steps for printing from any Windows application are very similar. The biggest difference is that some dialog box options change from program to program. Most programs offer a Print icon on the toolbar that you can click to print one copy of the job; although in some programs, the print icon displays the Print dialog box. To print from a Windows application, follow these steps:

1. Choose **File**, **Print**, and the Print dialog box appears. Figure 20.2 shows the Print dialog box in the WordPad accessory program.

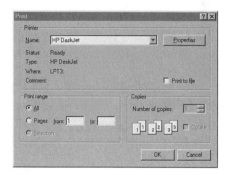

Figure 20.2   Use the Print dialog box to specify printing options.

2. Set any of the printing options described in the following list. Some applications will offer more specialized options; see a particular application's Help feature if you have questions:

> **Print Range**   Specify the pages you want to print. For example, you can print all pages, the current page, a range of pages, or a selection of text (which you select before opening the Print dialog box).
>
> **Copies**   Enter the number of copies you want to print. Often, you can choose a print order (front to back, for example) and whether to collate the copies or not.
>
> **Print to File**   Prints the document into a file, which you can use to print your document from a computer that doesn't have the program you used to create it. (You then print the file by typing print filename at the DOS prompt of any computer. All document formatting is preserved.)
>
> **Printer**   If you have several printers available, you can choose the printer to which you want to send the job.
>
> **Properties or Setup**   Usually leads to a dialog box in which you can set paper size, orientation, paper tray, graphics resolution, and other options specific to your computer.
>
> **Collate Copies**   Assembles the copies of a multiple-page document in order from 1, to 2, to 3, and so on.

3. When you're ready to print, choose **OK**. Windows sends the job to the printer.

CAUTION   **Printing Errors**   If your job doesn't print and you receive an error message from Windows, check to see that the printer is turned on and there is paper in it. If the message indicates that you may have a paper jam, check the printer and clear the jam. If you still can't print, jiggle the cable at the printer's end and again at the computer's end, to make sure the cable is not loose. Try printing again.

TIP   **Print Job**   A print job is a document you're printing. Each time you choose **OK** in the Print dialog box, you send a print job to the printer (whether that document contains one page or forty).

Working with the Print Folder

When you print a document, the printer usually begins processing the job immediately. But what if the printer is working on another job that you (or someone else, if you're working on a network printer) sent? When that happens, there is a print queue that holds the job until the printer is ready for it.

TERM   **Print Queue**   A holding area for jobs waiting to be printed. If you open the contents of the queue, the jobs appear in the order they were sent to the printer.

You can check the status of a print job you've sent by looking at the Print queue, found in the Printer's folder. Figure 20.3 shows a document in the Print Queue. The print queue window displays the information about the job.

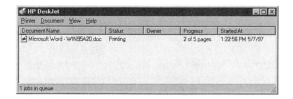

Figure 20.3   Use the Print queue to track your print jobs.

To display the Print queue, follow these steps:

1. From the Desktop, choose the **Start** button and then choose **Settings**, **Printers**.

2. In the Printers folder, double-click the icon of the printer you want to use.

Empty Print Queue? If no jobs appear in the Print queue, the job has already been sent to the printer.

CAUTION

Controlling the Print Job

It's hard to control just one or two print jobs because they usually are sent to the printer too quickly. However, if there are several jobs in the print queue, you can control them. For example, you can pause and resume print jobs, and you can delete a job before it prints.

Additionally, you can control the printer or just one particular document. You can, for example, cancel one document or all documents in the queue.

Pausing and Resuming the Queue

You may want to pause the queue and then resume printing later if, for example, the paper in the printer is misaligned or the printer is using the wrong color paper. Pausing the print queue gives you time to correct the problem. To pause the print queue, choose **Printer**, **Pause Printing**. You can also right-click the document and select Pause. To resume printing, choose **Printer**, **Pause Printing** a second time to remove the check mark beside the command.

Printer Stalled If your printer stalls while it's processing your print job, Windows displays the word `stalled` in the printer status line in the queue. Choose **Printer**, **Pause Printing** to remove the check mark from the command and start printing again. If the printer stalls again, see if there's a problem with the printer (it might be offline or out of paper, for example).

Deleting a Print Job

Sometimes you'll send a document to the printer and then change your mind. For example, you may think of additional text to add to a document or realize you forgot to check your spelling. In such a case, deleting the print job is easy, if you can catch it in time.

To delete a print job follow these steps:

1. Open the Print queue by choosing **Start**, **Settings**, **Printers**; double-click the printer icon.

2. Select the job you want to delete.

3. Choose **Document**, **Cancel**.

 Clear the Queue!   To remove all files from the print queue, choose **Purge Print Jobs**.

In this lesson, you learned to print from an application, control the print job, and connect to a network printer. In the next lesson, you learn to use Word Pad.

Using WordPad

In this lesson, you learn how to create, edit, format, and save a document in WordPad.

What Is WordPad?

WordPad is Window's word processing program. With WordPad, you can create documents such as letters, memos, reports, lists, and so on. Although WordPad is a word processor, it is a very basic word processing application. For example, you cannot check your spelling or grammar in WordPad, and there are only a limited number of toolbars and icons to help speed you work. However, you can create, edit, and format many simple documents with WordPad. Basically, it's fine to use if you don't have another word process such as Word, Word Pro, or Word Perfect.

To access WordPad:

1. From the Desktop, choose the **Start** button, select **Programs**, and then **Accessories**.

2. Click the **WordPad** option at the bottom of the Accessories menu. The program appears with a new, untitled document in the window for you to use, as shown in Figure 21.1. A blinking vertical bar, called the insertion point, appears in the upper-left corner of the document area.

 TERM   **Insertion Point**   The point at which the text you type will appear.

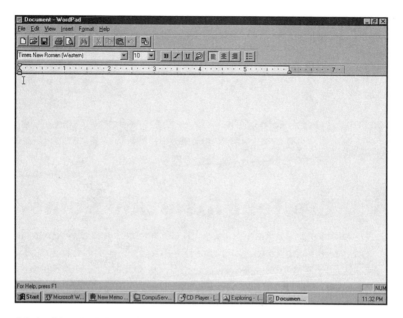

Figure 21.1   Use the WordPad program to create documents.

Like most word processing programs, WordPad has text-wrapping; you don't need to press Enter at the end of each line. Press Enter only to mark the end of a paragraph or to insert a blank line on the page.

The WordPad screen contains the following elements:

- The application name (WordPad) and the document name (the generic name is "Document" until you assign a name by saving the document) in the title bar.
- The menu bar containing WordPad menus.
- Two toolbars containing shortcuts for saving and formatting your documents.
- A ruler that enables you to set tabs and measure margins.
- The text insertion point, which marks the location of the text you enter.
- A status bar that offers helpful tips and information about the program.

Windows Elements Note that the WordPad window contains many of the same elements as other windows programs: Minimize, Maximize, and Close buttons, a Control Menu button, a window border if the window is restored, and so on.

 Need Help? The help feature in WordPad works similarly to the Help feature in Windows. If you need help, access the **Help** menu or press **F1**.

Moving the Text Insertion Point

To move the insertion point with the mouse, just click the place in the text where you want to move to. To move the insertion point using the keyboard, see the options in Table 21.1 You can use these keys to move the insertion point around without disturbing existing text. You cannot move the insertion point beyond the last character in your document.

Table 21.4 Moving the Insertion Point with the Keyboard

Press	To Move
↓	Down one line
↑	Up one line
→	Right one character
←	Left one character
Page Up	Previous screen
Page Down	Next screen
Ctrl + →	Next word
Ctrl + ←	Previous word
Ctrl + Page Up	Top of screen
Ctrl + Page Down	Bottom of screen
Home	Beginning of line
End	End of line
Ctrl + Home	Beginning of document
Ctrl + End	End of document

Inserting and Deleting Text

To insert text within existing text, simply place the insertion point in the appropriate location (using the mouse or the keyboard) and begin typing. The existing characters move to the right as you type to make room for the new text. When characters move to the right as you type, you are in *Insert* mode which is the default mode of WordPad. If you press the Insert key, insert will toggle off, putting you in overwrite mode. In *Overwrite* mode, new text that you type will replace old text.

To delete a single character to the left of the insertion point, press the **Backspace** key. To delete the character to the right of the insertion point, press the **Delete** key. To delete larger amounts of text, select the text and press the **Delete** key (see the next section to find out how to select text).

Selecting, Cutting, Copying, and Pasting Text

Before you can work with text, you must select it. To select test with the mouse, click at the beginning of the text and drag the I-beam pointer over the text so that it appears highlighted. To select text with the keyboard, place the insertion point at the beginning of the text, press and hold the **Shift** key, and use the techniques described in Table 21.1 to move to the end of the text you want to select. When you release the Shift key, the text you marked appears highlighted.

WordPad uses the Windows Clipboard to store and cut and copied text until you cut or copy again. To cut and copy text, select the text first and then use the **Edit** menu or the **Cut** and **Copy** buttons on the toolbar. To paste, move the insertion point to the location in which you want to paste the text and then choose **Edit**, **Paste**, or click the **Paste** button on the toolbar.

Formatting a Document

You can affect the appearance of your document on-screen and on-paper by changing the formatting. Formatting refers to the appearance of a document, including the font style and size, text alignment, and page layout.

You can format text before or after you type it. To format text before you type it, choose the formatting attributes and then enter the text; the formatting continues until you change the formatting again. To format text after you type it, select the text you want to change and then apply the specific formatting changes.

Formatting Text

You can change the following text attributes to improve the appearance of your text or to set it apart from other text:

Font   Choose from Arial, Times New Roman, and so on to change the look of the text.

Font Style   Apply Bold, Italic, Bold Italic, Underline, Superscript, or Subscript attributes to change the style of the text.

Font Size   Choose from 10-point, 12-point, 72-point and everything in between (or even larger) to change the size of your type for headlines, fine print, and so on. (There are about 72 points in an inch.)

To change the font, font style, or font size, follow these steps:

1. Select the text to be formatted.

2. Choose **Format**, **Font** from the WordPad menu bar. The Font dialog box appears (see Figure 21.2).

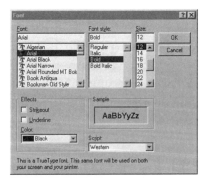

Figure 21.2   Change the look of the text on the page in Word Pad.

3. Select the font, font style, and size options you want. The Sample Area shows sample text with options you selected.

4. Choose **OK** to apply the changes.

Quick Formatting Use the Format bar above the ruler to apply a font, size, or attribute to selected text. Just click the down arrow beside the font or size drop-down list; or click the Bold, Italic, or Underline buttons on the Formatting tool bar to apply a style attribute. You will find Bold, Italic and Underline buttons in many Windows programs.

Figure 12.3 shows a document with formatting applied to selected text. Note that you can use multiple fonts and font sizes to add interest and emphasis.

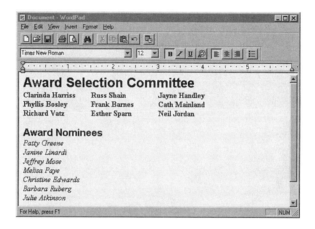

Figure 21.3 You can vary the font, size, and style of text within your document to add emphasis to important text.

Regular versus Bold A font that has no attribute applied (such as bold, italic, or underlining) is called "regular."

Aligning Text

Normally, text is aligned with the left margin. However, you can right-align text or center it between the margins.

Alignment Left-aligned text is flush along the left margin of the page and ragged along the right edge; left-aligned text is the default alignment for most word processing programs. Right-aligned text is the opposite of left-aligned. Centered text is ragged on both the left and the right sides, but each line is centered between the two side margins. Justified text makes the text flush with both the left and right edges of the page and is available in many programs; however, WordPad doesn't support justified text.

To align text:

1. Select the text.

2. Use the formatting toolbar buttons to choose the alignment:

 Left

 Center

 Right

Adjusting Page Margins

You can change the page margins using the Page Setup dialog box. You can also choose page size and orientation in this same dialog box.

 Page Settings Before you change your paper size, source, or orientation of the page, check you printer documentation to verify it can print to a special setting. Many printers, for example, cannot print to small paper or A4 envelopes and most printers have a required margin (usually at least .25 inch).

To change page margins:

1. Choose **File**, **Page Setup**. The Page Setup dialog box appears, as shown in Figure 21.4.

2. Choose **OK** to apply the margins to your document.

Figure 21.4 Change the margins in the Page Setup dialog box.

TIP **Paper Size Changes** Click the drop-down arrow beside Size in the Paper area to select another paper size, such as #10 commercial size envelope or $8\frac{1}{2}$-by-14-inch paper. You can also choose the paper tray or envelope feeder, if applicable, from the Source drop-down list.

Saving a Document and Exiting WordPad

To avoid losing the changes you've made to your WordPad document file, you need to save your work often. The first time you save a document, you assign it a name and location on the disk. From that point forward, you save the document without naming it again. If you attempt to exit WordPad or close the file without saving the file, or without saving your most recent changes, WordPad will prompt you to save the document.

To save a WordPad document:

1. Choose **File**, **Save As**. The Save As dialog box (shown in Figure 21.5) appears.
2. In the Save In drop-down list, choose a drive to save the file to.
3. In the list box, double-click the folder in which you want to save the file.
4. In the **File Name** text box, enter a name for the file; you can take advantage of Windows long file names by entering letters, numbers, and using spaces that exceed the previous DOS eight-letter limitations.

147

5. Choose **Save**. Windows saves the file, closes the dialog box, and returns to the document on-screen. The name in the title bar changes from "Untitled" to the name you assigned your document.

6. To exit WordPad, click the **Close** (X) button or choose **File, Exit**.

Figure 21.5 Give the file a name and choose a location on the disk.

Save As or Save? Choose Save As to assign a file name and location to your document the first time you save it or anytime you want to save a file under a *new* name or location. Use Save As when you need to save different version of a document. Choose Save to save any changes you make to a document that's already been named.

In this lesson, you learned how to create, edit, format, and save a document in WordPad. In the next lesson, you learn to use the Windows accessory, Paint.

Using Paint

In this lesson, you learn to open the Paint application, create a drawing with Paint, and save the drawing.

What Is Paint?

Paint is a Windows graphic program that allows you to create drawings you can use, either alone or in other Windows application such as Word, Word Pro, or Word Perfect.

To open the Paint program and begin a drawing, follow these steps:

1. From the Desktop, choose the **Start** button and then **Programs**, **Accessories**.

2. Click **Paint** from the Accessories menu. The Paint window opens as shown in Figure 22.1, ready for you to draw.

   In addition to the standard application window parts, (title bar, control button and so forth) the Paint window also has a set of drawing tools (called the toolbox) located on the left and a color palette at the bottom of the window. When drawing with Paint, you can use outline or fill colors.

 Outline and Fill Colors   The overlapping boxes to the left of the color palette show the currently selected outline color (the box on top and to the left) and the fill color (the box underneath and to the right). The outline color is the color you use when you draw lines and outlines for objects, and the fill color is the color of the inside of any objects you draw.

The box below the toolbar identifies the width of a line and the options for the currently selected tool in the toolbox. Depending on which tool is selected, you use this box to determine how wide of a line the line tool draws, how wide the eraser is, whether a shape is filled or transparent, and so on. Table 22.1 shows each of the tools in the toolbox.

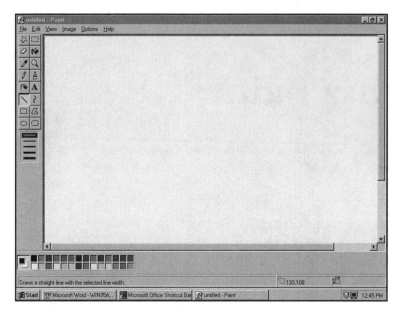

Figure 22.1 Use the Paint tools and menus to create a drawing.

Table 22.1 Tools in the Paint Toolbox

Tool	Name
	Free-Form Select
	Select
	Eraser/Color
	Pick Color
	Fill
	Magnifier
	Pencil

Tool	Name
🖌	Brush
🖍	Airbrush
A	Text
＼	Line
⟨	Curve
▭	Rectangle
◿	Polygon
○	Ellipse
▢	Rounded Rectangle

Drawing in Paint

Drawing with a mouse can be difficult at first, but practice always makes a difference. You use your mouse to draw line, curves, and shapes, as well as to enter text in Paint.

The following list describes different ways to draw:

- To select the fill color, right-click any color in the palette.
- To select the line color, click any color in the palette.
- To select the size of the drawing, choose, **Image**, **Attributes** and enter the **Width** and **Height** in the Attributes dialog box (see Figure 22.2). Click **OK**. The new size is defined by eight small black handles or boxes, outlining the specified area.

Figure 22.2   Choose the size of the drawing before you begin drawing.

- Click a drawing tool in the toolbox at the left of the screen.
- To select a line width for any line tool-line, curve, rectangle, ellipse, and so on, click the line size you want in the line box in the lower-left corner of the screen.

CAUTION

Which Tool Should I Use First?   Try starting with either the rectangle tool, the ellipse tool, or the straight line tool to experiment. Then branch out to the other tools as you learn more about the program.

- To draw an object, point at the area where you want the object to appear (within the boxed Image area), press and hold the left mouse button, and drag the mouse pointer until the object is the size you want.

CAUTION

Oops!   If you add to your graphic and then decide you don't like the addition, choose **Edit**, **Undo** (or press **Ctrl+Z**) to undo the change you made.

TIP   **A Perfect Circle Every Time**   To draw a perfect circle, select the **Ellipse** tool, hold down the **Shift** key, and click and drag the mouse pointer. You can also use this technique to draw a perfect square with Rectangle tool or a perfectly straight line with the Line tool. This method applies to many Windows graphic programs.

Adding Text to a Graphic

Using the Text tool, you can add text to a graphic such as a logo or illustration. To add text to a graphic, follow these steps:

1. Select the **Text** tool.

2. Drag the text tool to create a rectangle in which you will type the text. A rectangle that will hold the text and an insertion point appear.

3. Before you type, choose **View, Text Toolbar**. The Fonts toolbar appears, as shown in Figure 22.3. Choose the font, size and attributes from the Fonts toolbar.

4. Click the insertion point within the rectangle and type your text, pressing **Enter** at the end of each line. When you finish typing the text, choose another tool from the toolbox or click the next place you want to insert a new line of text. If you want to make a change to the formatting of the text, select the text and use the Font toolbar.

5. Click outside of the text box anywhere to accept the text you just entered.

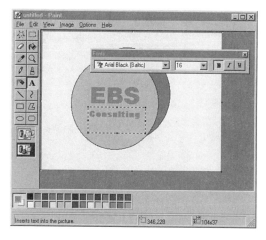

Figure 22.3 Use Paint's tools to create a company logo.

CAUTION

Once You Leave, You Can Never Go Back You can't edit or reformat text once you've accepted it; you can only erase it. To erase the text, click the **Select** tool, draw a frame around the text and choose **Edit, Cut**. (This also works for any lines or shapes you want to erase.) Be careful when cutting, however; you can cut out parts of shapes and text and leave other parts intact.

SKILLS TRANSFER

Move or Size Object To move the text (or any other part of the drawing), select it with the Select tool and then drag it to a new position, To resize an object, select it and then position the mouse pointer over one of the handles around the selection rectangle. Drag the two-headed arrow to change the size of the text or object.

153

Figure 22.4 shows a logo using graphics and text created in Paint, with the text selected and ready to move.

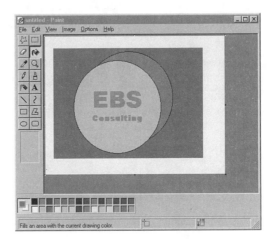

Figure 22.4 Create a company logo.

Saving a Drawing

To save a drawing, follow these steps:

1. Choose **File**, **Save As**. The Save As dialog box appears.
2. If you want to change the file type, choose a file type from the Save As Type drop-down list box.
3. In the Save In drop-down box choose a drive in which to save the file.
4. In the list box, double-click the folder to which you want to save the file.
5. In the **File Name** box, enter a name for the file. Choose **Save**, and Paint saves the file.
6. To close Paint, click the **Close** button or choose **File**, **Exit**.

In this lesson, you learned to open the Paint program, create a simple drawing with Paint, and save the drawing. In the next lesson, you are introduced to the Multimedia capabilities of Windows 95.

Using Windows 95 Multimedia

In this lesson, you learn how to use the Multimedia tools included with Windows 95.

What Is Multimedia?

Multimedia, as the name implies, is a combination of two or more mediums. Mediums can include sound, fixed pictures, moving pictures, and animation. The main components of Windows 95 Multimedia are the Sound Recorder, CD Player, Media Player, and ActiveMovie Player.

The ability to work with multimedia in Windows 95 is not automatic—you need to have the correct hardware installed before you can achieve success using multimedia tools. You need to have a sound card, CD-ROM drive, speakers, and microphone connected to use the tools here. Fortunately, most PCs come with these components as standard these days. However, even if you don't have these components today, they are pretty easy to obtain and install.

Using the Sound Recorder

If you have a sound card installed, you can use the Sound Recorder to record, play back, and manipulate sound file characteristics including adding an echo, changing playback speed, and mixing with other files. To access the Sound Recorder choose **Start**, **Programs**, **Accessories**, and **Multimedia**. From the Multimedia menu, choose **Sound Recorder**. The Sound Recorder appears (see Figure 23.1).

Figure 23.1   The Sound Recorder Program..

Recording Sounds

With the Sound Recorder open and an audio input device (microphone) connected to or built into your computer, you can record sounds by performing the following steps:

1. Select **File**, **New**.

2. To begin recording, click the **Record** button (the round circle).

3. To stop recording, click the **Stop** button (the rectangle).

4. To save your file choose **File**, **Save As**.

T I P   **Recording Your First CD?**   You can specify the default sound quality before you record a sound. On the **Edit** menu, click **Audio Properties**, and then click the quality that you want from the list

Playing Sounds

With the Sound Recorder open and an audio input device connected to your computer, you can record sounds by performing the following steps:

1. Select **File**, **Open**.

2. Open the folder containing the sound file you want to play, and then click the **Play** button (the single triangle).

3. When the file is completed, the Sound Recorder player will stop, or to stop the sound playback in progress, click the **Stop** button (the rectangle).

T I P   **Instant Replay?**   Use the Seek To Start or Seek to End buttons (the double triangles) to quickly move to the beginning or end of your recording.

Editing and Working with Effects

Using the Sound Recorder, you can cut parts of sound files and mix them with other files. You can also increase and decrease speed, play in reverse, add echo, and even change the quality by converting the file format. Descriptions of how to perform these steps follow:

- **Deleting Part of a Sound File**   Move the slider bar to the place in the file that you want to cut and using the **Edit** menu, click **Delete Before Current Position** or **Delete After Current Position**.

- **Change the Speed of a Sound File**   From the **Effects** menu, click **Increase Speed** or **Decrease Speed**.

- **Reverse Play**   From the **Effects** menu, click **Reverse** and then click **Play**.

- **Add Echo**   From the **Effects** menu, click **Add Echo** and then click **Play**.

- **Undo Changes**   From the **File** menu, click **Revert**; click **Yes** to confirm the restoration.

- **Change Sound File Quality**   From the **File** menu, click **Properties**, and from the Format Conversion area, select a format from the list. Click the **Convert Now** button, specify the format and attributes you want for the sound file, and then click **OK**.

- **Insert a Sound File into Another Sound File**   From the **File** menu, click **Open**, and then double-click the file you want to insert. Move the slider bar to where you want to insert the other sound file. On the **Edit** menu, click **Insert File**. If you insert a sound into an existing sound file, the new sound replaces the original sound after the insertion point. Type or double-click the name of the file you want to insert.

Compressed Files   You can only change the effects and edit uncompressed sound files. If you don't see the green line in Sound Recorder, the file is compressed and you cannot change it until it is uncompressed.

CAUTION

Working with the CD Player

You can use the CD-ROM drive on your computer to play music CDs. You must have a sound card installed and you may or may not use external speakers with your computer. With the CD Player, you can play CDs, switch the order in which you play tracks, and select specific tracks to play.

To use the CD Player, follow these steps:

1. Choose **Start**, **Programs**, **Accessories**, and **Multimedia**. From the Multimedia menu, choose **CD player**. The CD Player appears; if you have a data CD or no CD in the CD-ROM Drive, you see the message `Data or no disc loaded` (see Figure 23.2).

CAUTION

Still Won't Recognize the CD?   If you insert a CD and your CD player still does not recognize it, you need to make sure you have a sound card installed in your computer and that you have a Windows 95 driver for the sound card installed. Double-click the **System** icon in the Control Panel and select the Device Manager tab. Double-click the **Sound, Video, and Game Controllers** device type to see if there is an installed sound card. If you see a yellow circle with an exclamation point in it or no sound card listed, you have a problem.

2. Insert the CD. Click the **Play** button to play, the **Pause** button to temporarily stop the CD, and use the **Stop** button to stop the music.

3. To change the order of the tracks that play, as opposed to playing the tracks in the order they fall on the CD, choose **Options**, **Random Order**.

Figure 23.2   Use the CD Player to play music CDs from you computer.

TIP   **Not Loud Enough?**   To adjust the volume of the CD Player, choose **View**, **Volume Control**. The Volume Control application appears—use this to adjust the volume.

Using the Media Player

Use the Media Player to play audio, video, and animation files in Windows 95. You can play a multimedia file, rewind the file, and fast forward the file. You can also copy a multimedia file into a document that you or someone else can play back. Video for Windows files has an AVI extension.

To open and use the Media Player, perform the following steps:

1. Choose **Start**, **Programs**, **Accessories**, **Multimedia**, and then select **Media Player**. The Media Player window is now displayed (see Figure 23.3).

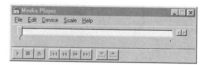

Figure 23.3 Play video and animation files with the Media Player.

2. From the Device menu, select the device type you want to play: **ActiveMovie** (animation), **Video for Windows**, or **CD Audio**.

3. If you choose the ActiveMovie or Video for Windows option, an Open dialog box appears from which you can locate and choose the file you want to play. If you choose the CD audio option, then choose **File**, **Open** to select the file you want.

4. Choose the **Play** button to play the file.

Using the ActiveMovie Player

The ActiveMovie player is similar to the Media Player; you can play animated clips or movies on both applications. Files you play using the ActiveMovie Control Box include the following types: MPEG, MPE, MPG, MPA, ENC, and DAT. These extensions represent various file types of movies or animations that have been compressed somewhat due to their very large size.

To use the ActiveMovie program, follow these steps:

1. Choose **Start**, **Programs**, **Accessories**, **Multimedia**, and then choose **ActiveMovie Control**. The Open dialog box appears.

2. Choose the file you want to play and then click the **Open** button.

3. As the file plays, you can control the movie from the ActiveMovie Control box.

Using a Multimedia File in a Document

You can place any multimedia file in a document so you or someone else can play the file at any time from within the document. You can copy the multimedia file and then paste it into the document.

To use a multimedia file in a document:

1. In the Media Player, open the **File** menu and choose **Open**.
2. Double-click the file you want to copy.
3. Choose **Edit**, **Options** and specify the options you want.
4. Open the document to which you want to paste the file and position the insertion point.
5. Choose **Edit**, **Paste**.

To play back a multimedia file from within a document, double-click the icon representing the file.

In this lesson, you learned how to use the Media player, the ActiveMovie Player, and work with multimedia files in documents. In the next section—Part II, "Customizing Windows 95"—you learn about customizing your desktop, installing software, and other Windows customization features.

Customizing
Windows 95

Understanding the Control Panel

In this lesson, you'll find out what the Control Panel is, what you can do with it, and how you can access it.

What Is the Control Panel?

When you want to set up the way your desktop looks, how your screen saver works, the fonts you're using, the time and date of your system clock, and more, you go to the Control Panel. From the Control Panel you can configure your Windows environment to work the way you want it to.

There are several ways to reach the Control Panel:

- From the taskbar, click the **Start** button and then choose **Settings, Control Panel**. The Control Panel window appears (see Figure 1.1).

- From the desktop, double-click **My Computer** and then double-click the **Control Panel** folder icon. The Control Panel window appears (refer to Figure 1.1).

- From Windows Explorer, click the **Control Panel** folder found in the left pane of the window. The contents of the Control Panel appears in the right panel (see Figure 1.2). These are the same icons that display in the Control Panel window.

Figure 1.1 The Control Panel window.

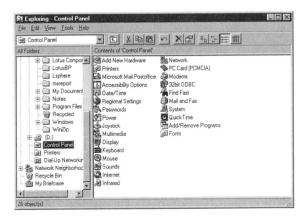

Figure 1.2 The Control Panel in Windows Explorer.

My Control Panel Isn't Like the One in The Book! Don't be alarmed if the icons in your Control Panel don't match the ones you see in these illustrations. Some of them, such as the mouse, will differ depending on the peripheral equipment you have and who manufactured it.

CAUTION

Once the Control Panel is open, you double-click the icon that represents the feature you want to change. A dialog box or properties box opens and displays options that affect that feature.

What Can You Accomplish in the Control Panel?

Using the Control Panel you can:

- **Set Accessibility Properties** If you have a disability that makes using your computer difficult, you can make adjustments to help you. You can set the keyboard to slow it down, make it ignore repeated keystrokes, or play tones when you press Caps Lock, Num Lock, or Scroll Lock. You can set up visual warnings to replace sound warnings, add more contrast to the screen for easier reading, and transfer command of the mouse pointer to the numeric pad of the keyboard.

- **Add New Hardware** Windows 95 normally detects new hardware automatically. This capability is referred to as the *plug and play* feature of Windows 95. When Windows 95 doesn't automatically detect your new hardware, use the **Add New Hardware** feature to start a wizard. The wizard searches for and identifies the new hardware so Windows 95 can work with it properly.

 Wizard A program within Windows that helps you perform a specific task. Wizards ask you questions about the task and then automatically performs operations that complete the task for you.

- **Add or Remove Software** This feature helps you install new software programs or remove old or unwanted ones.
- **Set the System Date and Time** Although the internal clock of your computer maintains the current date and time, you may occasionally have to adjust it.
- **Change Desktop Colors** You can add colors or patterns to the background of your desktop, as well as changing the look of the windows.
- **Add or Switch Screen Savers** Screen savers preserve your monitor quality, and you can select the one you want to use.
- **Add or Remove Fonts** Not only can you view your fonts from the Control Panel, but you can add new ones and remove unwanted ones.
- **Set Up a Joystick** If you have a joystick to use for games, you can set it up using the Control Panel.

- **Change Settings on Your Keyboard**   You can change the character repeat speed of your keyboard. This is the speed at which a character repeats when you hold down the key on your keyboard. You can also set the length of delay interval before a key repeats, to give you time to move your finger off a key before you get a repeat of the same character.

- **Configure Your Modem**   Use the Control Panel to adjust the settings on your modem.

- **Adjust the Settings for Your Mouse**   In the Control Panel, you can set the speed of the mouse pointer and the double-click, as well as swap buttons for left-handed users.

- **Change Settings for Multimedia Devices**   If you are using audio or video devices with your computer, you adjust the settings for those devices through the Control Panel.

- **Set or Change Passwords**   You can protect your computer so unauthorized people can't use it without first entering your password. You can set or change your password from the Control Panel.

- **Change Regional Settings**   If you're working outside the United States, you can change the standard settings for how currency, numbers, dates, and time appear.

- **Adjust System and Program Sounds**   Certain sounds signify different events, and you can choose which sounds you want to hear.

- **Find System Information and Make Advanced Settings**   You can manage the devices in your computer system and view their current settings.

The Control Panel contains a set of icons indicating the different areas that you can modify to customize your computer configuration. In this book we only discuss the most commonly used features of the Control Panel.

In this lesson you learned about the Control Panel and what it can do for you. In the next lesson you learn to customize your desktop.

Customizing the Desktop

In this lesson, you'll learn how to create shortcut icons to your favorite programs or documents, how to arrange the icons onour desktop, how to add color or background patterns to your desktop, and how to change the desktop fonts.

Creating Shortcuts

A shortcut is a quick way to access a program, printer, or document you use often. The shortcut appears as an icon on your desktop that acts as a pointer to that program, printer, or document.

To create a shortcut:

1. From My Computer or Windows Explorer, select the icon that represents the program's executable file to create a program shortcut, the printer icon from the Printers folder to create a printer shortcut, or a document icon to create a document shortcut.

Executable File An executable file is the file that starts a program. You can identify it by the icon, which should match the logo of the software product. These files have an EXE file extension (see Part I, Lesson 13, "Understanding the Windows Explorer," to learn how to display the file extensions). To test a file to see if it is the executable file, double-click its icon. The program should start.

2. From the menu, choose **File**, **Create Shortcut** or click the right mouse button and select **Create Shortcut** from the pop-up menu.

3. An icon will appear in the window labeled as **Shortcut to** the program, printer, or document you selected. The icon looks the same as the icon you originally selected, except it is smaller and has an arrow pointing up to it from its lower-left corner (see Figure 2.1).

Figure 2.1   A shortcut icon created within My Computer.

4. Drag that icon to the desktop (You will not be able to drag the printer shortcut, but Windows 95 will ask if you want to put it on the desktop. Click **Yes**.).

5. To rename the shortcut, click once on the name to place your cursor there (or right-click the icon and choose **Rename** from the pop-up menu), enter the name you want to assign to the shortcut, and press the **Enter** key.

TIP   **Using the Right Mouse Button**   A quick way to make a shortcut is to point to the icon in My Computer or Windows Explorer, hold down your right mouse button, and drag the icon to your desktop. When you release the right mouse button, a pop-up menu opens. Select **Create Shortcut**, and the shortcut icon appears on the desktop.

To use a shortcut, double-click the icon. If the shortcut is to a program, it will start the program. If the shortcut is to a document, it will start the program associated with the document and then open that document. If the shortcut is to a printer, just drag a document icon over the shortcut to print the document.

To remove a shortcut icon, drag it to the Recycle Bin or select the shortcut icon and then press the **Delete** key. If you delete the shortcut, you're not deleting the program, printer, or document—you're only removing the icon from your desktop. However, if you delete or remove the program, document, or printer, the shortcut no longer has anything to point to and double-clicking it results in an error message to that effect.

Arranging Icons

Because you can drag icons on your desktop, they have a tendency to look disordered after a while. You can control how the icons appear on the desktop by choosing their arrangement.

To arrange your desktop icons:

1. Click an open area of your desktop with the right mouse button.
2. From the pop-up menu, choose **Arrange Icons**.
3. Select **By Name** to have the desktop icons arranged in alphabetical order, **By Type** to have the icons arranged by type of file, **By Size** to order them by size of file, or **By Date** to have them appear in the order they were created. The rearrangement of icons doesn't affect My Computer, Network Neighborhood, the Recycle Bin, the Internet, the Inbox, The Microsoft Network, or My Briefcase.

To keep your icons from getting scattered all over your desktop, click the right mouse button on the desktop and select **Arrange Icons, Auto Arrange** from the pop-up menu. The icons will always return to the columns at the left side of your screen.

Choosing Colors and Backgrounds

For better viewing or just for variety, you can change the background color of your screen or choose a pattern or wallpaper for your desktop background.

To change the color of the desktop:

1. Click the **Start** button on the taskbar.
2. Choose **Settings, Control Panel**.
3. From the Control Panel window, double-click the **Display** icon. The Display Properties dialog box appears.

TIP   **Right-Click the Desktop**   To quickly access the Display Properties box, right-click an open area on your desktop and select **Properties** from the pop-up menu.

4. Click the **Appearance** tab (see Figure 2.2).

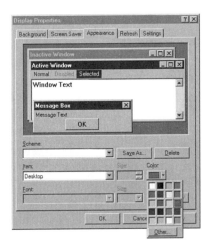

Figure 2.2   The Display Properties dialog box with the Appearance tab selected.

5. Click the down arrow on the Color list box to see a selection of background colors.

6. Click the color you want.

7. Click **Apply** to see how the desktop will look in that color.

8. Click **OK** to accept your choice and close the dialog box.

To change the desktop background:

1. Click the **Start** button on the taskbar.

2. Choose **Settings, Control Panel**.

3. From the Control Panel window, double-click the **Display** icon. The Display Properties dialog box appears with the Background tab selected (see Figure 2.3).

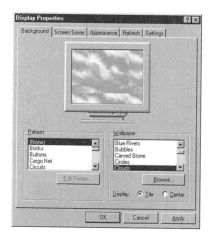

Figure 2.3   The Display Properties box with the Background tab selected.

4. From the Pattern list box, select an appropriate pattern. A sample of your selection appears in the monitor picture. The pattern uses the background color plus black. Choose **None** to remove all patterns from the background of the desktop.

5. From the Wallpaper list box, select a picture to place on your desktop. It will appear in the monitor picture so you can see how it will look on your screen. Choose **None** to remove all wallpaper from the desktop. Click the **Browse** button to select a file you created or imported (it must have a BMP extension).

6. If you want the picture to appear in the middle of your screen, select **Center** as the Display. The background color or pattern will still show around the picture.

If you want the entire screen filled with the picture, select **Tile**. The picture will be repeated across the screen until it fills the desktop background.

7. Click **Apply** to see how the desktop will look with the pattern or wallpaper you selected.

8. Click **OK** to accept your choice and close the dialog box.

Windows 95 also has a series of color schemes available from which you can choose. The color schemes not only choose a background color but also set the color for the window title bars, window borders, and text on your screen. To set a color scheme for your desktop:

1. Click the **Start** button on the taskbar.

2. Choose **Settings**, **Control Panel**.

3. From the Control Panel window, double-click the **Display** icon. The Display Properties dialog box appears.

4. Select the **Appearance** tab.

5. From the Scheme drop-down list, select a color scheme. The sample windows display the new selection (see Figure 2.4). Choose a scheme with large font if you need larger type. Select **Windows Standard** to go back to the normal color scheme.

Figure 2.4 The Display Properties box Appearance tab.

6. Click **Apply** to see how the desktop will look with the color scheme you selected.

7. Click **OK** to accept your choice and close the dialog box.

Changing Fonts

To change the size, color, and font of the screen text:

1. Click the **Start** button on the taskbar.

2. Choose **Settings**, **Control Panel**.

3. From the Control Panel window, double-click the **Display** icon. The Display Properties dialog box appears.

4. Select the **Appearance** tab (refer to Figure 2.4).

5. From the Item drop-down list, select the item for which you want to adjust the text, such as Active Title Bar, Icon, Inactive Title Bar, Menu, Message Box, Palette Title, Selected Items, or ToolTip. Unless you pick one of these items, the font choices will not be available.

6. Select the font you want to use from the Font drop-down list, the point size from the Size drop-down list, and the color of the text from the Color list. Click the **B** button for boldface and the **I** button for italic.

7. Click **Apply** to see how the desktop will look.

8. Click **OK** to accept your choice and close the dialog box.

In this lesson, you learned how to make the desktop look the way you want by arranging the icons, adding shortcuts, and changing the colors, backgrounds, and fonts. In the next lesson, you learn how to use screen savers.

Using Screen Savers

In this lesson, you'll learn what a screen saver is, why you should use one, and how to set one up.

Selecting a Screen Saver

A screen saver is a moving picture or pattern that appears on your screen when you've left the computer idle for a specified number of minutes.

Other than for looks, why do you need a screen saver? Screen savers are designed to prevent "burn in." When the same image stays on the screen for long periods of time without changing, it eventually leaves a ghost image that you can see even when the monitor is turned off. You can prevent "burn in" two ways: either turn off your monitor when you walk away from it, or use a screen saver. Because the screen saver image keeps moving, no one spot on the screen is continuously in use so that spot can't "burn in." The nice thing about using the screen saver is that it comes on automatically, so you don't have to worry about turning it on and off. Also, it automatically turns off once you move the mouse or press a key on the keyboard.

Windows 95 provides several screen savers for you to use. To select a screen saver:

1. Click the **Start** button on the taskbar (alternately, right-click the desktop, choose **Properties** from the pop-up menu, and then skip to step 4).

2. Choose **Settings, Control Panel**.

3. Double-click the **Display** icon. The Display Properties box appears.

4. Select the **Screen Saver** tab (see Figure 3.1).

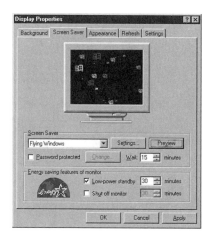

Figure 3.1 The Display Properties box with the Screen Saver tab selected.

5. From the Screen Saver drop-down list, select a screen saver. A sample appears in the monitor. Click **Preview** to see a full screen version.

6. Click **OK** to accept your choices and close the dialog box.

Screen Saver Properties

To set options or properties for your screen saver:

1. Click the **Start** button on the taskbar.

2. Choose **Settings**, **Control Panel**.

3. Double-click the **Display** icon. The Display Properties box appears.

4. Select the **Screen Saver** tab. The screen saver you selected appears in the Screen Saver box.

5. To adjust the way the screen saver works, click **Settings**. The Options dialog box appears. This dialog box differs for each screen saver, providing choices to increase or decrease the speed, the number of elements, or the colors of the elements. The options for the Scrolling Marquee screen saver allow you to enter a message you want to scroll across your screen (see Figure 3.2). Click **OK** to return to the Display Properties box.

Figure 3.2   The Options for Scrolling Marquee dialog box.

6. To assign a password to your screen saver, check **Password Protected**. If
you use a screen saver password, Windows 95 won't clear your screen
until the correct password is entered. Click **Change** to enter or change a
password (see Figure 3.3). Enter the password in the New Password box
(remember passwords are case-sensitive, so "COMPUTER" is a different
password than "computer"). You'll only see asterisks as you type, so enter
the password carefully. Repeat the password in the Confirm New Password box. Click **OK**.

Figure 3.3   The Change Password dialog box.

7. A screen saver will activate if you don't use the mouse or keyboard for a
specified period of time. To set that interval, change the value in the Wait
box by entering a number or by using the up and down arrows next to it.

 TIP **Screen Saver Timing**   Don't set your screen saver interval to such a small
interval that you keep having to clear the screen before you can continue your
project. An interval of 15 minutes is sufficient. Setting the time to 1 or 2 minutes
means you have to move your mouse or press a key before you can continue.
This is annoying if you just turn briefly to look something up or answer a short
phone call.

8. Click **OK** to accept your changes and close the dialog box.

Energy Saving Monitors

Related to the screen saver is the ability of some computers to turn the monitor off or power down the monitor if the computer mouse or keyboard is not in use. Monitors with energy saving features (they have a special logo on them that says "Energy") have this ability. Usually, this is set up before you get the computer, so you may be surprised when your computer monitor blacks out suddenly. A feature like this is especially useful for laptop computers that may be running on a battery, to keep the battery from running down too fast.

If the screen goes blank like this, try moving the mouse or pressing a key to reactivate it. It will take longer to reactivate than it takes to come back from a screen saver, but you should see it start to brighten in moments.

To control the timing of this power down feature:

1. Click the **Start** button on the taskbar.
2. Choose **Settings**, **Control Panel**.
3. Double-click the **Display** icon. The Display Properties box appears.
4. Select the **Screen Saver** tab (see Figure 3.4).

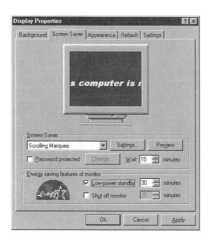

Figure 3.4 The Energy Saving settings.

5. Enable **Low-Power Standby** or **Shut Off Monitor** (you may not have both).

6. In the time interval box, enter the number of minutes the computer may stand idle before this feature is activated.

7. Click **OK**.

In this lesson, you learned how to select a screen saver and what options you could set for it. In the next lesson, you'll learn how to customize the taskbar.

Customizing the Taskbar

In this lesson, you'll learn how to move the taskbar, size it, hide it, and set its properties.

Positioning the Taskbar

By default, the taskbar appears at the bottom of your screen. It doesn't have to stay there. You can put it at the top, left, or right of the screen. In Figure 4.1, the taskbar is on the right side of the screen.

Figure 4.1 The taskbar is on the right side of the screen.

To move the taskbar:

1. Point to a spot in the middle of the taskbar where there are no buttons.

2. Hold down your mouse button.

3. Drag to the side of the screen where you want to position the taskbar. As you drag, an outline box appears representing the taskbar.

4. When the outline box is in the position where you want to put the taskbar, release the mouse button.

Sizing the Taskbar

You can make the taskbar thinner or thicker. To change the size of the taskbar:

1. Point to the border on the edge of the taskbar (your mouse pointer will become a two-headed arrow, as in Figure 4.2).

Figure 4.2   The mouse pointer becomes a two-headed arrow as you drag the Taskbar border.

2. Drag in one of the directions shown by the two-headed arrow to make the taskbar thinner or thicker. As you drag, a line appears representing the border.

3. Release the mouse button when the line is where you want the new border.

TIP   **I Lost My Taskbar!**   Did you make the taskbar so thin you can't find it? If you look closely, there is still a double line at the side of the screen where your taskbar was. Point at that line and then drag it away from the edge of the screen. Release your mouse button, and your taskbar is back.

Using Taskbar Properties

To set the taskbar properties:

1. Click the **Start** button on the taskbar.

2. Choose **Settings, Taskbar**. The Taskbar Properties box appears (see Figure 4.3).

3. There are four options in the properties box:

   Always on Top   Enable this to be able to see the taskbar even when an application is running fully maximized. Otherwise, the application window will cover the taskbar.

   Auto Hide   When enabled, the Taskbar reduces to a double-line once you activate an application. Just point to the taskbar to have it reappear. This feature allows you to see an application fully maximized and to make maximum use of your screen space, while still having the taskbar available to you.

   Show Small Icons in Start Menu   Check this to reduce the size of the Start menu icons (see the sample picture in the properties box to see the difference).

   Show Clock   Check this to have the time show on the taskbar.

4. Click **OK** to accept the choices and close the properties box.

Hiding the Taskbar

When you have applications that need the maximum screen space available for working, such as graphics and desktop publishing programs, you may want to hide your taskbar from view until you need it. It will automatically reduce to a double-line thickness when an application is open and reappear when you point to the double line.

To hide your taskbar:

1. Click the **Start** button on the taskbar.

2. Choose **Settings, Taskbar**. The Taskbar Properties box appears (see Figure 4.3).

Figure 4.3   The Taskbar Properties box.

3. Check **Auto Hide**.

4. Click **OK**.

Showing the Clock

The current time appears at the right side (if the taskbar is on the top or bottom of your screen) or bottom of the taskbar (if your taskbar is on the left or right side of your screen). If you point to the time, a pop-up appears giving you the current day of the week, month, day, and year (such as Friday, June 13, 1997).

You can show the clock or not, as you choose. To show the clock:

1. Click the **Start** button on the taskbar.

2. Choose **Settings, Taskbar**. The Taskbar Properties box appears.

3. Check **Show Clock**.

4. Click **OK**.

In this lesson, you learned to customize your taskbar. In the next lesson, you learn how to customize the menu that appears when you click the Start button.

Customizing the Start Menu

*In this lesson, you'll learn how to add and remove programs
from the menu that appear when you click the Start button on
the taskbar (referred to as the "Start menu"), how to add
programs to the StartUp window, and how to clear the document window.*

Using the Start Menu Properties

When you click the Start button on the taskbar and choose Programs, you see a list of available programs. How do these programs get added to the list? If you upgraded from a previous version of Windows, these are the old program groups you had in that version. Or, during Setup, Windows 95 adds some program groups such as Accessories to the menu. Also, as you install new software, the new programs appear on the Start menu.

You can modify the Start menu by changing its properties. To access the properties:

1. Click **Start** button on the taskbar.
2. Choose **Settings, Taskbar** from the Start menu. The Taskbar Properties box appears.
3. Select the **Start Menu Programs** tab (see Figure 5.1).
4. Set the options as outlined in this lesson.
5. Click **OK**.

Figure 5.1   The Taskbar Properties box with the Start Menu Programs tab selected.

Adding and Removing Programs

If you have a program on your hard disk or on your network that isn't listed under Programs in the Start menu, you can add it to the list:

1. Open the Taskbar Properties box as outlined in steps 1 through 3 above.

2. In the Customize Start Menu section, click **Add**. The Create Shortcut dialog box appears (see Figure 5.2).

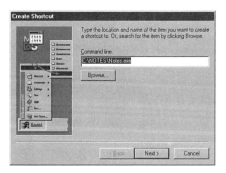

Figure 5.2   The Create Shortcut dialog box.

3. Enter the path and file name of the program file in the Command line box or click **Browse** to search for the file. If you clicked Browse, locate the file and then double-click it to have the file name and path automatically entered in the Command line box.

4. Click **Next**. The Select Program dialog box opens (see Figure 5.3).

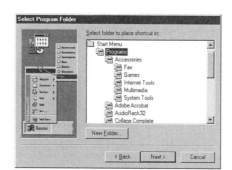

Figure 5.3 The Select Program Folder dialog box.

5. Select the folder under which you want the program to appear. Select **Programs** if you want it to be a main topic; choose another folder if you want it to appear on a submenu. Click **New Folder** if you want to create a new folder where you'll be placing more than one program.

6. Click **Next**. The Select a Title for the Program dialog box appears (see Figure 5.4).

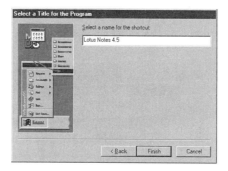

Figure 5.4 The Select a Title for the Program dialog box.

7. Enter the name of the program in the text box as you want it to appear on the menu.

8. Click **Finish**. If the program you selected doesn't have its own icon, a prompt appears asking you to choose one from a set of available Windows icons.

To remove a program from the Start menu:

1. With the Taskbar Properties box open and the Start Menu Programs tab selected, click the **Remove** button. The Remove Shortcuts/Folders dialog box appears (see Figure 5.5).

Figure 5.5   The Remove Shortcuts/Folders dialog box.

2. Select the item you want to remove.

3. Click **Remove**.

4. When Windows 95 asks you to confirm that you want to remove the folder or shortcut, click **Yes**.

5. Click **Close**.

Adding Programs to the StartUp Window

There may be some applications that you want to automatically start when Windows 95 opens, such as an anti-virus program. To make this happen you have to add the program to the StartUp Window.

1. Click the **Start** button on the taskbar.

2. Choose **Settings**, **Taskbar**. The Taskbar Properties box appears.

3. Select the **Start Menu Programs** tab.

4. Click **Add**.

5. Click **Browse**.

6. Locate the program you want to add to the StartUp window and double-click it.

7. Click **Next**. The Select Program Folder appears (see Figure 5.6).

Figure 5.6 The Select Program Folder dialog box with the StartUp folder selected.

8. Double-click the **StartUp** folder. If you are prompted to select an icon, choose one.

9. Click **Finish**. The next time you boot up your computer, the program you added will automatically start.

Clearing the Document Menu

All documents that you've opened recently appear in the Start menu under Documents. You can quickly open a document from that menu by selecting it. When you do, the associated program opens and then the document opens in that program.

However, after a time the list of documents increases beyond manageable limits. You then need to clear the list.

To clear the Document menu:

1. Click the **Start** button on the taskbar.

2. Choose **Settings**, **Taskbar**. The Taskbar Properties box appears.

3. Select the **Start Menu Programs** tab (see Figure 5.7).

Figure 5.7   The Taskbar Properties box with the Documents Menu section showing.

4. In the Documents Menu section, click **Clear**.

5. Click **OK**.

In this lesson, you learned to add and remove programs from the Start menu, to make some programs automatically start when Windows 95 did, and to clear the Documents menu. In the next lesson, you'll learn how to install new software.

Installing New Software (Programs)

In this lesson, you get an overview of how to install a new program on your computer.

When You Buy Software

There are a few things you should look for when you are purchasing software:

- Make sure the software you purchase is designed to work with Windows 95. It should say that on the package, but if you're not certain, ask the salesperson at the store before you pay. If you're buying from a catalog, and it isn't clear that the software works with Windows 95, call the catalog company and ask them before you place the order.

- All software packages have system requirements that list the hardware, operating system (that's Windows 95), memory, and disk space your system must have for the software to work on your computer. If your system does not meet these requirements, you can't use the software. Either plan to upgrade your system before you purchase the software, or find another version of the software that will work within your system's abilities.

How Do I Know What My System Has on It? Click **Start** and then choose **Settings**, **Control Panel**. Double-click the **System** icon to open the System Properties box. The General page (see Figure 6.1) will show the type of computer and the amount of RAM you have on your system.

To find how much room you have on your hard disk, open My Computer and select the icon for your hard disk. The Status Line at the bottom of the window will tell you how much free space you have (it should be more than the software requires).

Figure 6.1   The System Properties dialog box.

- Many software packages also have system recommendations. Although the system requirements list what your system *must* have for the software to run on it, the recommendations list the hardware and software specifications under which the software runs most smoothly. For example, you may have 8 MB of RAM memory, which meets the minimum requirements of the software, but the recommendation is 16 MB. This probably means that the software performance will slow if you have more than one window open or if you are performing a complicated procedure.

  If you can live with the slower performance, then you don't need to worry. However, when speed is important or when you need to have more than one application open at a time, you might want to consider upgrading your system memory to have the software perform at its best.

- Check to see if the software comes on disks or CD-ROM. You can't install software from a CD unless you have a CD-ROM drive. However, if you have both a 3½-inch disk drive and a CD-ROM drive, you should opt for the CD version of the software. Installation from a CD-ROM is much faster, you often get bonus files on a CD, and CDs are less likely to have faults or produce errors.

 RAM   The RAM (Random-Access Memory) is the working memory of your computer, as opposed to the hard disk or floppy disk which are storage memory. RAM keeps track of your current operation, each character you type or delete and each calculation you perform, until you save the file into your storage memory. RAM also keeps a copy of your current application open while you're working, plus any other applications or windows you may have open. The greater the memory (measured in megabytes) the more operations you can do or applications you can have open at the same time.

Preparing to Install

Once you remove the shrink wrap from your software package, you want to do the following:

1. Find the installation instructions for the software and read them carefully *before* you install.

2. Locate the serial number of the software. You may need it during the installation process, and you should record it for later use. The serial number may be on the outside of the package, but more often it's on the CD case or on the envelope that holds the disks. Sometimes you'll find it on the inside front cover of the software manual.

3. Read through the software license agreement before you install. It automatically becomes effective once you open the software, so it helps to know to what you're agreeing to. Software is copyrighted (unless it is *shareware*, the name for software that isn't copyrighted), and these agreements are to ensure that you don't install the software on more than one computer (unless you've purchased a software license that allows a specified number of users to be installed). Otherwise, you violate the agreement and the software company can prosecute you. Violation of this software license agreement is called "pirating."

4. Close all open programs or windows on your computer, leaving only Windows 95 running. If you don't, the installation program will request it later.

5. Any programs that start up when Windows starts may be running in RAM memory. Close down these programs before you start installation. If required by your installation instructions, you may have to temporarily remove these programs from your StartUp window. Use My Computer or Windows Explorer to find and open the StartUp folder (under Windows, Start Menu), and drag the program icon to your desktop. Then reboot your computer. After installation, drag the icon back into the StartUp folder and reboot to activate it again.

TIP   **Recording Serial Numbers**   Make sure you record your software serial number in a place where you can find it later. Should you have a problem after installation and need customer support, you'll probably have to tell the support person your serial number. Also, should your computer be permanently damaged or stolen or a fire destroy your copy of the software, you may be able to get another copy from the software company if you provide the serial number and proof of permanent loss. It may also help to record the date and place of purchase and the customer support number along with the serial number.

Installing the Software

Follow the installation instructions that come with the software package. Place the first disk in the disk drive (this is usually referred to as the *install disk*) or the CD in the CD-ROM drive. From this point, the installation differs according to how the software company set it up.

There are generally three ways installation occurs:

- An installation or setup program starts running immediately on your screen when you insert the CD. Follow the on-screen instructions.
- The instructions ask you to click the **Start** button on the taskbar and choose **Run** from the menu. The Run dialog box appears (see Figure 6.2). Enter the path and name of the file that starts the installation or setup process. This should be in your instructions, but you can find it by clicking **Browse** and looking for the file (usually called Install.exe or Setup.exe). Click **OK** to start the installation and follow any on-screen instructions.

Figure 6.2   The Run dialog box.

- The instructions ask you to click **Start** on the taskbar, select **Settings**, **Control Panel**, and then double-click the **Add/Remove Programs** icon. The Add/Remove Programs Properties box appears (see Figure 6.3). Click **Install** to start the Installation Wizard. Insert the floppy disk or CD in the drive if you haven't already. Click **Next**. Windows 95 automatically detects the installation program or asks you for the command line (enter the command or click **Browse** to find it). Click **Finish** and the installation process begins. Follow the on-screen instructions.

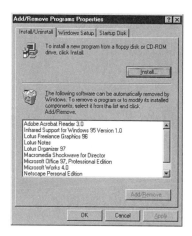

Figure 6.3   The Add/Remove Programs Properties box.

 TIP   **Quick Rebooting**   You may be asked to reboot your computer after installing the software. Hold down the **Shift** key as you click **Start**, choose **Shut Down**, select **Restart the Computer**, and click **Yes**. Instead of starting the computer from scratch, this method only restarts Windows. That's all you really need to reset certain Windows 95 parameters to work with your new program, and it saves a considerable amount of time.

In this lesson, you learned what to do when you install a program. In the next lesson, you learn how to secure your computer with a password.

Using Password Protection

In this lesson, you learn how to set a password for your computer to prevent its use by unauthorized persons.

Why Use a Password?

If you're worried that an unauthorized person might attempt to use your computer in your absence, use a password. The password is the key to your system. Unless you enter the correct password, you cannot begin working in Windows.

When Windows starts, a dialog box appears, requesting your password (see Figure 7.1). You enter your user name (if it isn't automatically entered) and then the password. When you type the password, Windows enters asterisks in the text box. Click **OK**. Windows may ask you to confirm the password by entering it again. If so, type it and click **OK**. Then your desktop appears.

Figure 7.1 The Password dialog box.

Password versus Login Don't confuse the Windows password with a network login password. If your office uses a network, the network administrator assigns a password to you that allows you to access the network. The Windows password doesn't give you access to the network. It only protects your own computer. You can use a Windows password even if you don't work with a network.

Setting Up a Password

To set up a Windows password:

1. Click **Start** from the taskbar.

2. Choose **Settings, Control Panel**.

3. Double-click the **Passwords** icon. The Passwords Properties box appears (see Figure 7.2).

Figure 7.2 The Passwords Properties box.

4. Click **Change Windows Password**. The Change Windows Password dialog box appears.

5. Enter your password (up to 25 characters) in the New Password box. Passwords are case-sensitive, so be sure to remember what words you capitalize because "LETMEIN" is a different password than "LetMeIn."

6. In the Confirm New Password box, enter the password again, exactly as you did the first time.

7. Click **OK**.

Changing Your Password

You must be careful to protect your password so other people don't learn it. It helps to change your password periodically, just in case someone has been looking over your shoulder.

To change the password:

1. Click **Start** from the taskbar.

2. Choose **Settings, Control Panel**.

3. Double-click the **Passwords** icon. The Passwords Properties box appears.

4. Click **Change Windows Password**. The Change Windows Password dialog box appears.

5. Enter your old password in the Old Password box (this proves you're authorized to make the password change).

6. In the New Password box, enter your new password.

7. In the Confirm New Password box, enter the new password again exactly as you did the first time.

8. Click **OK**.

In this lesson, you learned how to set up and change your password. In the next lesson, you learn how to change the date and time and to adjust your mouse, sound, and monitor settings.

Controlling Hardware Settings

In this lesson, you learn how to set your system clock, adjust your mouse settings for better performance, change your sound settings, and switch the mode on your monitor.

Altering the Date and Time

Your computer has an internal clock that keeps track of the date and time. The clock is attached to a battery, so it keeps time even when your system is off.

However, there are times when you want to adjust the date and time. You must do it once, when you first receive the computer, to be sure that the setting is correct. When you move to another time zone, you should adjust the time to reflect that. These may be the only instances in which you'll need to change the date and time, because Windows 95 even adjusts for daylight savings time.

To change the date and time:

1. Click the **Start** button on the taskbar.
2. Choose **Settings**, **Control Panel**.
3. Double-click the **Date/Time** icon. The Date/Time Properties box appears (see Figure 8.1).
4. In the Date section of the dialog box, click the **Month** box to select the current month from the drop-down list.
5. Use the small up and down arrows to change the year or enter the current year in the Year box.

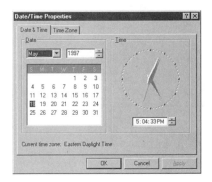

Figure 8.1 The Date/Time Properties box.

6. On the calendar picture, click the current day.

7. In the Time box, click the time component you want to change (the hours, minutes, seconds, or AM/PM). Use the small up and down arrows to adjust the setting.

8. When you have the current date and time set correctly, click OK.

To change the time zone:

1. Click the **Start** button on the taskbar.

2. Choose **Settings, Control Panel**.

3. Double-click the **Date/Time** icon. The Date/Time Properties box appears.

4. Select the Time Zone tab (see Figure 8.2).

Figure 8.2 The Date/Time Properties box with the Time Zone tab selected.

5. Select the appropriate time zone from the drop-down list or click the area on the time zone map.

6. If the time zone you selected observes daylight savings time, check **Automatically Adjust Clock for Daylight Saving Changes**.

7. Click **OK**.

Modifying Mouse Settings

When you receive your computer, the mouse is configured to work for the "average" person. You can, however, adjust it for your personal needs by switching the left and right mouse buttons (for left-handed users), speeding up or slowing down the mouse pointer, picking a look for the mouse pointer, and changing the double-click speed.

To configure your mouse:

1. Click the **Start** button on the taskbar.

2. Choose **Settings, Control Panel**.

3. Double-click the **Mouse** icon. The Mouse Properties box appears (see Figure 8.3).

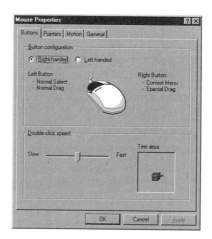

Figure 8.3 The Mouse Properties box.

4. To change the mouse for a left-handed user, click **Left-handed**. This switches the functions of the left and right mouse buttons.

5. To adjust the speed of the double-click to match the speed of your fingers, drag the triangle on the slide toward Slow or Fast. Then test the speed by double-clicking the **Test** area.

6. To change how the mouse pointer looks, select the **Pointers** tab (see Figure 8.4). Choose a Scheme from the drop-down list to see a group of pointers. To change an individual pointer, double-click it and select an alternate from the browse list; click **Open** to return to the properties box.

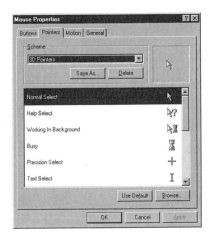

Figure 8.4   The Mouse Properties box with the Pointers tab selected.

7. To set the speed of the mouse pointer so it doesn't move across your screen too quickly for you to follow or doesn't take longer than your hand movement, select the **Motion** tab (see Figure 8.5). Drag the triangle indicator between Slow and Fast to set the speed.

8. If you have problems finding your mouse pointer on the screen, check **Show Pointer Tails** so you can see the track of the pointer. Move the triangle indicator between Short and Long to set the length of the tails.

9. To install a different mouse, select the **General** tab and then click **Change**. Select the name of the new mouse from the list that appears. You should have the installation disk that accompanies the mouse in your disk drive so Windows 95 can copy the driver file to your hard disk. Click **OK**.

10. Click **OK** to accept your changes and close the properties box.

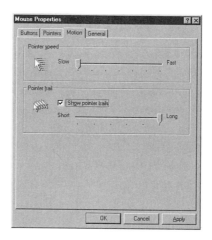

Figure 8.5 The Mouse Properties box with the Motion tab selected.

Driver A specialized file that contains the information Windows 95 needs to communicate with a peripheral device such as a mouse. The driver file translates the Windows commands to a language the device can understand and use.

These Options Are Not the Same as Mine! If your mouse is not a Microsoft mouse or if you are using a different type of pointing device (trackball, glide pad, and such), you may see different options. You may also have an additional icon for your device with settings specific to that device. Use the **What's This?** button on the dialog box or properties box to explain each option.

Changing System Sounds

Windows 95 has certain system events to which sound can be attached such as Start Windows, Exit Windows, and Program Error. If you have a sound card installed on your computer, you can play these sounds.

You can view the available events in the Sounds Properties box. You can change the sound associated with an event one-by-one or assign a sound scheme to the entire set of events.

A sound scheme is a certain combination of events and the sounds associated with them. Windows 95 includes five predefined sound schemes that you can select to help you customize your system: Musica, Windows Default, Nature, Robotz, and Utopia (there is also a No sounds setting, that disables system sounds). If you are familiar or comfortable with the sounds that are the default in Windows 3.1 you might want to use the Windows Default sound scheme.

To choose a sound scheme:

1. Click the **Start** button on the taskbar.

2. Choose **Settings**, **Control Panel**.

3. Double-click the **Sounds** icon. The Sounds Properties box appears (see Figure 8.6).

Figure 8.6 The Sounds Properties box.

4. Select one of the existing schemes from the Schemes drop-down list.

5. To test the scheme, click **Apply** and then perform a task with which a sound is associated. To test an individual sound, select the sound file and click the **Preview Play** button.

6. Click **OK** to accept your choice and close the Sound Properties box.

If you want to create your own personal sound scheme in Windows 95, all you have to do is associate the events you want with the sounds you choose. The easiest way to do this is to choose the No Sounds scheme, and save it to a new name, which gives you a blank template with which to create your own sound scheme.

1. Click the **Start** button on the taskbar.

2. Choose **Settings**, **Control Panel**.

3. Double-click the **Sounds** icon. The Sounds Properties box appears.

4. Select **No Sounds** from the Schemes list. Click **Save As**, enter a name for your new sound scheme, and click **OK**.

5. To associate an event with a sound, select an event from the Events list box and a sound from the Sound area's Name list box. When you select the sound, a speaker icon appears next to the event to which you just associated the sound. You can mix and match any of the system sounds that come with Windows 95, or you can choose your own sounds. To test an individual sound, click the right-pointing triangle button next to Preview.

   If you want to use sounds other than the ones that come with Windows 95, you must first choose the event to which you want to associate the sound. Next, click **Browse** to display the Browse dialog box (see Figure 8.7). Select a WAV file and click **OK**.

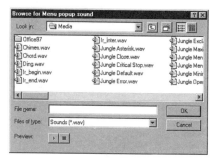

Figure 8.7 The Browse dialog box.

6. Click **OK** to close the Sounds Properties box.

It Doesn't Play My Sound! Before you can use your own WAV files, you must have them on your hard drive. Windows 95 needs to be able to find them every time you boot your system. Choosing a WAV file located on a CD can cause problems. If the CD isn't always in the player, Windows 95 can't always use it.

To change the volume of the sounds, click the **Speaker** icon on the taskbar and drag the volume indicator up or down.

203

Modifying Your Monitor Settings

If you have a VGA or SVGA color monitor, you may have the option to change the number of colors and pixels it displays depending on the video card installed on your computer. Most of the time this capability is never used, but occasionally a program will request that you switch the monitor to a 256-color palette or a 16-color palette, instead of the color palette you normally have available. Graphic artists and desktop publishers are more likely to face this problem, especially if they use image-editing software.

To change your monitor settings:

1. Click the **Start** button on the taskbar.
2. Choose **Settings**, **Control Panel** from the Start menu.
3. Double-click the **Display** icon. The Display Properties box appears.
4. Select the **Settings** tab (see Figure 8.8).

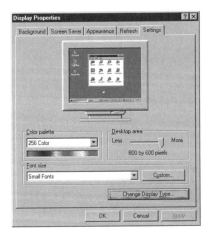

Figure 8.8 The Display Properties box with the Settings tab selected.

5. From the Color Palette drop-down list, select the color palette you need (this list shows only the palettes available for your monitor).
6. If you need to adjust the number of pixels shown on your screen, drag the triangular indicator under Desktop area to Less or More. This area will be gray if this feature is not available with your monitor.
7. Click **OK** to accept your changes (you may have to reboot your computer to see the changes).

Pixel Your computer screen is made up of rectangular dots, or pixels. Each one can be set to different colors. Together they make up the entire picture on your screen. The screen size is measured in pixels (640 x 480, 800 x 600). The higher the numbers, the better the screen resolution and the clearer your picture.

In this lesson, you learned to adjust the date and time settings, change the time zone setting, configure your mouse, change your system sounds, and modify your monitor settings. In the next lesson, you learn how to add a modem and configure it.

Installing and Configuring a Modem

In this lesson, you learn how to add a modem to your system, specify how it dials out, and change or refer to its properties.

What Is a Modem?

A modem is a piece of hardware that is either internal (inside your computer case) or external (plugged into a port on your computer). In addition to being connected to your computer, it's connected to a telephone line.

A modem is a device that allows you to send and receive data via the telephone lines. It translates your data into a form that can be carried over the phone line and then sends it; then it translates any data you receive. If you have a fax/modem, your modem can receive and send faxes also.

Adding a Modem

Installing the modem is a two-part process. The first part involves the hardware, and those instructions are included with the hardware. The second part involves setting it up for your system so Windows 95 and your communications software know it's there. The second part is covered here.

To add a modem to your system:

1. Click the **Start** button on the taskbar.
2. Choose **Settings**, **Control Panel** from the Start menu.

3. Double-click the **Modems** icon. The Modems Properties box appears (see Figure 9.1).

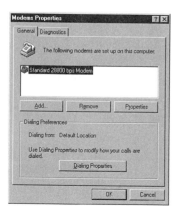

Figure 9.1 The Modem Properties box.

4. Click **Add**.

5. Windows 95 will attempt to detect your modem unless you check Don't Detect My Modem; I Will Select it From a List.

6. Click **Next**. The detection process begins.

If Windows doesn't detect the new modem it will ask you to choose it from a list. Click **Next** to view the list and make the selection. Then click **Next** to go to the next step (have the disk with the driver software available in case Windows asks for it).

7. Select the port that the modem will be using.

Port Computers have several "plugs" into which you can plug cables or peripherals. These plugs are called *ports*. Each port has a name. The ports used for modems are called COM ports and are distinguished by number (COM1, COM2, COM3, and so forth). Only one peripheral may be assigned to one COM port, so if your modem is using COM2 then no other peripheral is assigned to that COM port.

8. Click **Next**. Windows 95 sets up the modem.

9. Click **Finish**.

Modifying Dialing Properties

Before your modem can dial out using HyperTerminal, Dial-Up Networking, or a communications software package, you need to specify what area code it's calling from and how it dials outside calls.

1. Click the **Start** button on the taskbar.

2. Choose **Settings, Control Panel** from the Start menu.

3. Double-click the **Modems** icon. The Modems Properties box appears.

4. Click **Dialing Properties**. The Dialing Properties dialog box opens (see Figure 9.2).

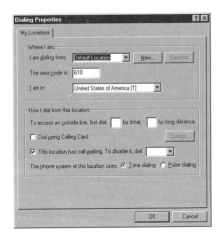

Figure 9.2   The Dialing Properties dialog box.

5. Found in the I Am Dialing From box, the Default Location setting is the location you use most often when dialing out. If your computer is a desktop located in the office, the default location is the office; if it's located at home then the default location is your home. The location only becomes an issue when you have a portable computer, and you could be dialing from anywhere. In that case you have to decide on your default location.

6. Enter the area code for the location in The Area Code Is box.

7. From the I Am In drop-down list, select the name of the country from which you're dialing.

8. You may have to enter a prefix before dialing out, such as 8 for local calls and 9 for long distance. Enter the appropriate codes in the for local and for long distance boxes.

9. If you plan to use a calling card when dialing out, check **Dial Using Calling Card**. Then click **Change**. Select the name of the card and enter the code that must be entered. Click **OK** to return to the Dialing Properties dialog box.

10. If you have call waiting on your telephone line, you must disable it in order to use the modem successfully. Otherwise, call waiting could cut off your communication. Check **This Location Has Call Waiting** and then enter or select a code from the To Disable It, Dial box.

11. Depending on the type of service you have, select **Tone Dialing** or **Pulse Dialing**.

12. You should add other locations if you're using a portable computer. You may want one for home and another for office, or even a third for hotels. To add another location, click **New**. Enter a name for the new location and click **OK**. Then follow steps 6 through 11 to set up the new location.

13. Click **OK** to accept your choices and close the dialog box.

Changing Modem Properties

You would rarely change modem properties, except for specifying a different port, unless asked to do so by customer support. However, you may need to refer to these settings while installing communications software.

To access the modem properties:

1. Click the **Start** button on the taskbar.

2. Choose **Settings, Control Panel** from the Start menu.

3. Double-click the **Modems** icon. The Modems Properties box appears.

4. Click **Properties**. The Properties dialog box appears for your modem (see Figure 9.3).

5. To change the communications port, select one from the Port list.

6. To set the Speaker Volume for the modem, drag the triangular indicator between Low and High.

7. To change the Maximum Speed, select the speed from the drop-down list.

8. Select the Connection tab to refer to the connection settings (see Figure 9.4). Do not change these without consulting the specific settings for your modem or speaking to customer support at the modem manufacturer.

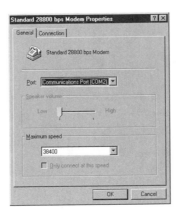

Figure 9.3   The Properties box for a specific modem.

Figure 9.4   The modem properties connection page.

9. Click **OK** to return to the Modem Properties box and then click **Close**.

In this lesson, you learned how to add a modem to your system, how to set the dialing properties for every location from which you dial out, and how to refer to the modem properties. In the next lesson, you'll look at the Device Manager.

Understanding and Using Device Manager

In this lesson, you learn what the Device Manager is and how you can use it to configure your hardware.

What Is the Device Manager?

When you install a new device on your system you should rely on Windows 95 to detect the new device and configure it. You plug the device into the computer and turn the computer on. Windows 95 reads the device ID and then loads and initializes the device drivers. It also notifies applications that the new device is available. You, the user, only have to answer a few questions that appear on the screen. This automated installation process is called Plug and Play. Most newer peripheral devices are Plug and Play compliant, so you'll have no problem installing and configuring them.

When you install older hardware devices on your system (called "legacy" devices), use the Add Hardware Wizard in the Control Panel. It will walk you through getting Windows 95 to recognize the new hardware. If Windows 95 can't find the device, you'll have to enter the name and tell it where to find the device driver, so have your device disks handy. The wizard gives you step-by-step instructions and properly configures your device for you.

So where does the Device Manager fit in? You use the Device Manager when you must manually change a device's configuration or when you need to look up information on the device's configuration.

CAUTION

Changing Device Configurations Can Cause Problems   The Device Manager is a tool for advanced users who understand configuration parameters and the consequences of changing settings, so don't treat it lightly. Don't change settings without consulting the systems person in your office or your device manufacturer's customer support.

Finding Information on Your Hardware

When you need information on the device configuration of your hardware, look in the Device Manager:

1. Click the **Start** button on the taskbar.

2. Choose **Settings**, **Control Panel** from the Start menu.

3. Double-click the **System** icon. The System Properties box appears.

4. Select the Device Manager tab (see Figure 10.1).

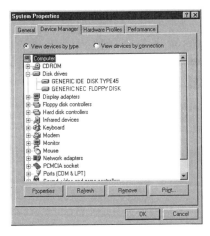

Figure 10.1   The System Properties box with the Device Manager tab selected.

5. Click the plus sign (**+**) next to the type of device about which you want more information.

6. Double-click the icon for the hardware device you're researching. The Properties box opens for that device (see Figure 10.2). The General page of the dialog box tells you the name of the device, the manufacturer, the version, and the device status. The other tabs in the dialog box change depending on the device you select:

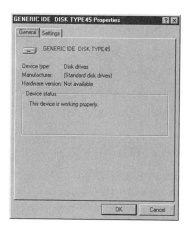

Figure 10.2   The Properties box for a hard disk drive.

Settings provides information on the current configuration settings for the device. You can't change any of the gray information. For example, on a disk drive you can't assign a new drive letter if that option is gray.

Driver tells you what device driver file is being used by your device and may offer additional driver files so you can change the driver.

Resources specifies what system resources the device is using. As long as there are no resource conflicts, you won't have to change these settings. You can double-click the resource and change the setting manually, but if you do, the resource setting becomes fixed and the system loses its flexibility to adjust resources according to changing demands. Check **Use Automatic Settings** to have Windows 95 allocate resources for you.

7. Click **OK** to accept any changes you made; click **Cancel** to close the Device Manager without making changes.

Printing Device Information

You may find it helpful to have a printout of the information concerning a hardware device as part of your disaster control plan (in case you have to set up your system after a crash).

To print hardware information:

1. Click the **Start** button on the taskbar.

2. Choose **Settings**, **Control Panel** from the Start menu.

3. Double-click the **System** icon. The System Properties box appears.

4. Select the Device Manager tab.

5. To print information about all your hardware devices, select **Computer** and then click **Print**.

   To print information about a specific device, click the icon for that device and then click **Print**.

6. When the Print dialog box appears (see Figure 10.3), choose **System Summary** to print a report organized by resource type that lists which hardware is using each resource. Choose **Selected Class or Device** to print a report of the resources and device drivers used by the hardware device you selected. Choose **All Devices and System Summary** to print a complete report about the hardware that details each piece of hardware and lists all resources used by the hardware. If you want to store this information in a file instead of having a printout, check **Print to File**. Click **OK**.

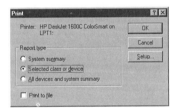

Figure 10.3 The Print dialog box.

7. Click **OK** to close the Device Manager.

In this lesson, you found out where information on your hardware devices is kept, how to look it up, and how to print it.

Using
Windows 95 on
a Network

Using Network Neighborhood

In this lesson, you learn about network basics, how to access the Network Neighborhood, and how to work with Network Neighborhood in Windows 95.

What Is a Network?

Networks connect PCs so that people can share information and resources. Some networks are small and may consist of, for example, a few PCs in an office. Other networks are global; the Internet, for example, is comprised of millions of computers spanning nearly every country (if not every country) across the world.

Most networks consist of servers and clients, although some consist solely of workstations (called "peer-to-peer" networks). Windows 95 is a client that can attach and share data with various servers—Windows NT, Novell Netware, Microsoft LAN Manager, for example—and with a peer-to-peer network, such as Windows 95, LANtastic, or Windows for Workgroups.

When you connect to a network, you gain certain advantages:

- Access to shared resources, such as modems and printers.
- Access to shared data, such as files and directories.
- The capability to send and receive electronic mail messages with others on the network using a mail program.
- The capability to back up your files to the server (see your system administrator for more information).

System Administrator The system or network administrator is the person who oversees and manages the network. The administrator can grant a user permission to access certain files and resources, troubleshoot problems with the network, and control each computer on the network. The administrator has the ability to track each user's activities on the network.

Client/Server A client/server network is one in which the workstation computer logs on to and attaches to a server that controls shared files, printers, and other resources attached to the network.

Peer-to-peer A peer-to-peer network is one in which all workstations are connected and each can share its printer, files, folders, and other resources.

Workstation Any computer that is attached to a network for the purposes of using the network resources. A workstation computer can run Windows 95, DOS, Windows 3.1, Windows NT, and other operating systems.

As a computer user, being connected to a network is usually a good thing and doesn't really impact the way you use your computer. Sometimes you might need a little help picking resources you want to use—like which printer to attach to for printing (one might be a high speed black and white laser printer for that important proposal; another might be a high resolution color printer for charts and graphics), and where to store important information that you want to ensure is backed up.

Windows 95 can connect to other computers in your office network to make it easier to share files, send electronic mail, print, and store files that require back up. The network is usually set up by people who already know how to create networks, and is managed by the network administrator. You, as a user, need only to know how to connect to the network and access the resources available to you. In Windows 95, if you are using a network, the Network Neighborhood icon appears on your desktop.

Figure 1.1 The Network Neighborhood icon indicates you are connected to a network.

What Is Network Neighborhood?

The Network Neighborhood is where Windows 95 displays your access to the PCs and printers on your network. The Network Neighborhood folder displays the resources available to you in your workgroup; the Entire Network folder, whose icon appears in the Network Neighborhood folder, displays your access to the resources shared by computers outside your workgroup.

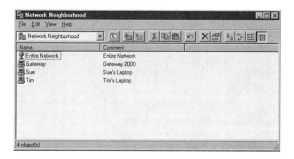

Figure 1.2   The Network Neighborhood folder provides quick access to network resources.

TIP   **Workgroup**   The group of computers your computer is in. A workgroup is generally composed of the computers you are most likely to communicate with, containing most of the network resources (such and files and printers) you will want to use. They are also likely to be within close physical location to yours (such as the same office or on the same floor in a building).

When you open Network Neighborhood, you see icons for each of the computers that are part of your workgroup, with the name of each computer under its icon. To view the resources a particular computer shares:

1. Double-click the **Network Neighborhood** icon on the desktop. This displays the networks and computers your computer is attached to.

2. Double-click any icon depicting a computer. An open folder (a folder window) appears on the desktop displaying the resources that the selected computer shares (see Figure 1.3). Shared disk resources appear as folders, with the share name of the disk serving as the name of the folder. Shared printers appear as folders with the printer's share name serving as the folder name.

TERM   **Resources**   Resources can include equipment such as disk space, printers, scanners, or modems.

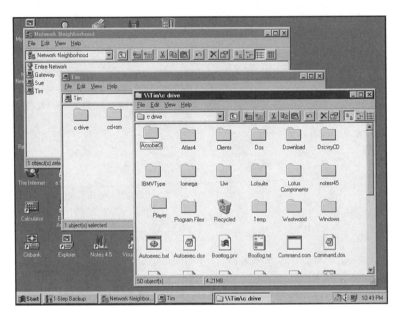

Figure 1.3   Folders display the resources shared by a computer.

This new way of sharing resources in Windows 95 is a major improvement from previous versions of Windows where you have to associate a local drive letter, M: for example, with each shared disk resource you wanted to access. Now, you simply open the remote computer's folder, open the shared folder to display its contents, then choose the file or application you want to use.

Accessing Network Neighborhood

To gain access to your network and identify your computer to other computers on your network, you are required to log on. You remain logged on until you are finished using the network and then log off. You are also logged off automatically when you shut off your computer.

Logging On

To log on, you usually need to type your user name and password. The user name that appears when you log on to Windows and the password you enter are those that you or the system administrator created. The devices provide security not only for your work, but for the entire network. Therefore, someone who does not know his or her user name and password cannot log on the network.

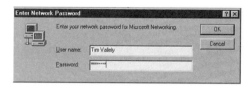

Figure 1.4 You must log on before you can access the network.

 Log On   To connect to a network, you must log on. When you log on, you're essentially telling the network that you're ready to share its resources. The network uses your log on as a key, of sorts, to identify which resources you may use.

Windows keeps a record of any applications you install, shortcuts you create, and any colors, fonts, displays, or other settings you modify on the desktop. When you log on using your user name and password, Windows displays those settings individual to you. If you logged on under a different name or just canceled the dialog box, your individual customizations would not appear when Windows opened.

Opening Network Neighborhood

When you connect to a network drive, you add a whole new set of folders, and files—not to mention other resources—to your working environment. After connecting, you can remain connected to that network while you work, and can even access other servers and resources if required.

To open Network Neighborhood and view your network connections, follow these steps:

1. From the desktop, double-click the **Network Neighborhood** icon to open that window. Figure 1.5 shows the Network Neighborhood window displaying the server to which the Windows 95 computer is attached. Depending on the network you are attached to, your Network Neighborhood may look different, but the theory and procedures are the same.

2. If you do not see your network in the Network Neighborhood window, double-click the **Entire Network** icon. The Entire Network window opens, displaying the networks and domains available to you.

3. Double-click any server or other computer listed in your Network Neighborhood window to see what resources are available to you. A list of printers, files, folders, or other peripherals, may appear.

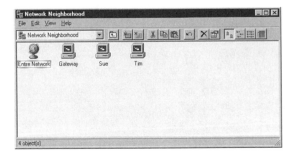

Figure 1.5   Your Network Neighborhood window displays networks and servers your Windows 95 computer is attached to.

CAUTION   **Can't Find Your Network?**   If you cannot access a network drive, don't panic. The server might be down for repair, a cable might have come loose, you may not have permission to view other computers, or some other problem might have occurred. All of these problems can easily be solved by seeing your system administrator.

To make things easier, you can use the Windows 95 shortcut feature to create shortcuts to remote computers or its shared resources on your desktop, saving even more time. To create a shortcut, open **Network Neighborhood**, locate the resource you want to create a shortcut to, and right-click it with the mouse. Next, drag (with the right mouse button) and drop the resource onto your desktop and select **Create Shortcut(s) Here** from the context menu that is displayed. Now, you can double-click the shortcut to use the resource like a local resource. Remember though, if you log off or the computer that contains the resource is disconnected from the network, the shortcut will not work.

For more information on creating shortcuts, see Part I, "Windows 95 Essentials;" Lesson 11, "Managing Files with My Computer."

Understanding the Network Neighborhood Window

You can display files or other resources on the network drive in either the Network Neighborhood or the Explorer; either way, you can treat the files and folders just as you would any files on your own hard drive. To open any server, computer, or other resource, simply double-click the icon representing the resource; as long as you see folders and files, you have permission to use those items.

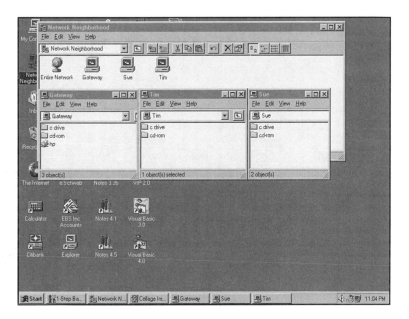

Figure 1.6 Access data and resources over the network.

The Network Neighborhood window (see Figure 1.7) contains only one Contents pane, unlike the Explorer window which is divided into two parts—drives and folders on the left, and the content of the selected drive or folder on the right.

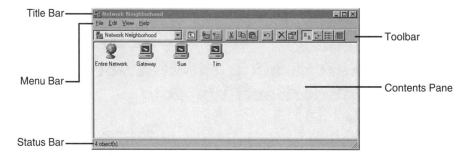

Figure 1.7   The Network Neighborhood window.

At the top of the window is the *title bar*, which tells you the name of the window you have open. You can move the window by dragging the title bar.

Beneath the title bar is the *menu bar*, which contains commands that you may give to the program.

Below the menu bar is the *toolbar*. If your Toolbar is not showing, choose **View**, **Toolbar** from the menu. The toolbar has buttons that perform menu commands without having to open the menu.

At the bottom of the screen is the status bar. In Network Neighborhood, the *status bar* displays the number of objects (files and folders) in the window and the number of bytes they take up in memory space when an object is selected. If you select one or more files, the Status Bar changes to display the number of selected files and how many bytes of memory they total. If you don't see the status bar on your window, choose **View**, **Status Bar** from the menu.

The Network Neighborhood window consists of a single Contents pane. The pane displays the Entire Network icon, and other computers which you are attached to. When you click any of the computer icons, a new window for that computer opens and displays the resources you have access to as shown in Figure 1.8.

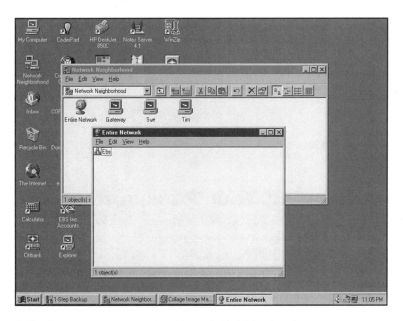

Figure 1.8 Access resources using Network Neighborhood.

Closing Network Neighborhood

You close Network Neighborhood just as you close any other window in
Windows 95, by selecting **File**, **Close** from the window menu or by clicking the
Close button (**X**) in the upper-right corner of the Network Neighborhood
window.

There may be occasions when you want to log off, then log on again as a different user. For example, you might want to log on with a different user name so
you can work with a different desktop configuration. To log off Windows 95,
choose **Start**, **Shut Down**, then **Close All Programs and Log On as a Different
User**. Windows 95 closes all programs that may be running, logs you off, resets
the Window 95 operating environment, and prompts you to log on by presenting you with a log on dialog box. Enter the user name and password that you
wish to use for logging on again.

Figure 1.9 Use the Shut Down option to log on as a different user.

Changing Your Password

For security reasons, you should change your Windows 95 password—and any other passwords you use—on a regular basis. In fact, most networks can force users to change their passwords on a periodic or predefined basis by setting a certain age limit for passwords used. Administrators can sometimes specify that passwords cannot ever be re-used, forcing users to come up with creative ways to pick, and more importantly remember, passwords.

To change your passwords in Windows 95, choose **Start**, **Settings**, and select the **Control Panel;** then choose the **Passwords** folder. Windows displays a Passwords Properties window. To change your Windows 95 log on password, choose the **Change Windows Password** button. Windows 95 displays a dialog box that you use to enter your old password and then new password.

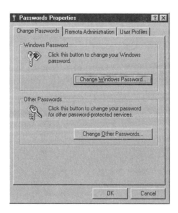

Figure 1.10 Changing your Windows passwords.

You can also change the passwords used for other network resources, like servers, using the Passwords object. To try this, choose the **Change Other Passwords** button, which opens the Select Password dialog box shown in Figure 1.11. Select the resource for which you want to change the password, and then click **Change**. Windows 95 will then prompt you for your old password, and then your new one.

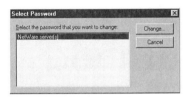

Figure 1.11 The Select Password dialog box.

In this lesson, you learned about network basics and basics of working with Network Neighborhood and network resources. In the next lesson, you learn more about navigation around Network Neighborhood.

Navigating Network Neighborhood

In this lesson, you'll go deeper into the Network Neighborhood window. You'll learn how to change the way files are viewed by using the toolbar and menus. You'll also learn how to search for a file and close the Network Neighborhood.

Changing Displays

You can view the icons in the Contents pane a number of ways (available as choices on the **View** menu):

- **Large Icons** This view shows the icons scattered in the window. Only the names of the files or folders appear below the icons (see Figure 2.1).

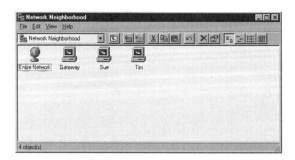

Figure 2.1 Contents pane with large icons.

- **Small Icons** Shows the icons in reduced size, lined up in a rows alphabetically (see Figure 2.2).

Figure 2.2 Contents pane with small icons.

- **List** Looks similar to small icons, except that it is organized vertically (see Figure 2.3).

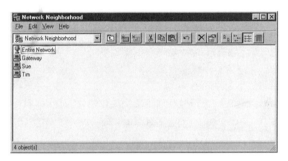

Figure 2.3 Contents pane in List view.

- **Details** With Details, the small icons are listed vertically, with each row providing comments associated with the resource (see Figure 2.4). You can click the column headers to sort the resources by the information in that column. Click once for ascending order (A–Z) and again for descending order (Z–A).

The icons are generally shown in alphabetical order, but you can change the order by choosing **View**, **Arrange Icons,** and then selecting the order you want **by Comment**, or **Auto Arrange** to let Windows 95 arrange them for you.

If you've accidentally moved the icons around and you want them put in straight lines again, choose **View**, **Line Up Icons**. This option is only available for the Large and Small Icons views.

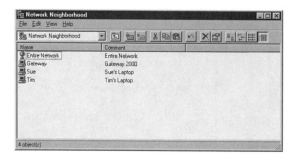

Figure 2.4   Contents pane in Details view.

If you've made changes to the folder you're currently viewing and they haven't appeared yet, choose **View**, **Refresh** from the menu to bring the window up to date.

Using the Network Neighborhood Toolbar

To see the toolbar (see Figure 2.5), choose **View**, **Toolbar** from the menu. Table 2.1 lists the buttons and what they do.

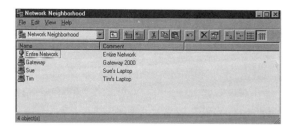

Figure 2.5   The Windows Network Neighborhood toolbar.

Table 2.1 The Toolbar Buttons

Button	Name	Use
Network Neighborhood	Go to a Different Folder	This drop-down list shows the drives and folders on your computer. Click one to open a window of that drive or folder.
	Up One Level	If the window you are in is a folder on a drive or a folder within another folder, click this button to move up one level to the drive or folder that is the "parent" of the one you have open.
	Map Network Drive	When you work on a network, you have drives and resources available to you on other computers. Mapping the drives allows you to assign a drive letter to that drive, folder, or resource.
	Disconnect Net Drive	Click to disconnect your computer from a specific drive on the network.
	Cut	Click to remove a selected file or folder from the window and store it in the Clipboard.
	Copy	Click to duplicate a selected file or folder from the window and store the copy in the Clipboard.
	Paste	Click to insert the contents of the Clipboard into the active window.
	Undo	Click to undo the last action you performed.
	Delete	Click to delete a selected file or folder.
	Properties	Click to bring up the Properties window for the selected drive, folder, or file.
	Large Icons	Click to see the Large Icons view of the window.
	Small Icons	Click to see the Small Icons view of the window.

Button	Name	Use
	List	Click to see the List view of the window.
	Details	Click to see the Details view of the window.

Using the Menu

The menu bar on the Network Neighborhood window offers four choices—File, Edit, View, and Help—detailed below:

- The **File** menu changes depending on what you may have selected. The File menu contains commands pertaining to file management. Opening new folders, mapping network drives, creating shortcuts, deleting and renaming files or folders, checking file and folder properties, and closing the window are all commands found in the File menu.

- The **Edit** menu includes the Undo command (to undo your last action), Cut to remove a file or folder and store it in the Clipboard, Copy to store a duplicate of a file or folder and store it in the Clipboard, Paste to put the contents of the Clipboard in the selected window, Select All to select all the files and folders in the window, and Invert Selection to select all the files and folders not selected while deselecting the currently selected files.

- Under the **View** menu are a series of options for looking at the files and folders with differently sized icons or in a different order.

- The **Help** menu offers a way to open the Help Topics window, as well as open the About Windows dialog box. About Windows tells you the version of Windows you're using, its copyright date, the name of the licensee, the amount of memory available to Windows 95, and the percentage of system resources that are available.

Using File Viewing Options

There are two ways to work with Contents panes in the Network Neighborhood Window:

- Browse folders by using a separate window for each folder.
- Browse folders by using a single window that changes as you open each folder.

To change how you work with the Contents pane in the Network Neighborhood window:

1. Choose **View**, **Options** from the menu. The Options dialog box opens.
2. Click the **Folders** tab to select it (see Figure 2.6).

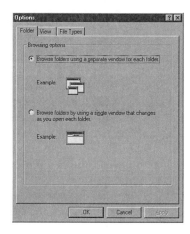

Figure 2.6 The Options dialog box with the Folder tab selected.

3. Select either **Browse Folders Using a Separate Window For Each Folder** or **Browse Folders by Using a Single Window That Changes as You Open Each Folder**.
4. Click **OK**.

Not all files are displayed when you open a folder. Some system files are hidden. Also, if you are accustomed to DOS, you probably noticed that no file extensions appear in Windows 95.

To change how and what files the Network Neighborhood displays:

1. Choose **View**, **Options** from the menu. The Options dialog box opens.
2. Click the **View** tab to select it (see Figure 2.7).
3. Under **Hidden** files, select **Show All Files** to see hidden and system files when you open a folder. To selectively hide files of certain types, select **Hide Files of These Types** and then click the type of file you want to hide.

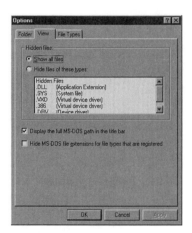

Figure 2.7   The Options dialog box with the View tab selected.

4. Check **Display the Full MS-DOS Path in the Title Bar** if you would like the Network Neighborhood title bar to show the full path instead of displaying just the file or resource.

5. If you don't want file extensions to appear with every file name, check **Hide MS-DOS File Extensions for File Types That Are Registered**.

6. To see a description bar at the top of the All Folders and Contents panes, check **Include Description Bar For Right and Left Panes**.

7. Click **OK**.

Closing Network Neighborhood

To close the Windows Network Neighborhood, choose **File**, **Close** from the menu or click the **Close** button on the title bar. Closing Network Neighborhood does not disconnect you from the network—you are only disconnected when you log off or shut down your computer.

In this lesson, you learned how to use the Network Neighborhood to look at the files and folders on your computer, how to change the views, and how to use the toolbar and menu. In the next lesson, you explore file management as you create folders, and move, copy, delete, and rename files and folders.

Managing Files and Folders with Network Neighborhood

3

In this lesson, you learn to use Network Neighborhood to manage your drives, folders, and files by creating new folders to organize and store files. You'll learn how to copy and move files and folders, delete files and folders, rename files and folders, and create shortcuts to put on the desktop.

Creating Folders

To organize your files, you need to sort them out into folders such as Correspondence, Memos, Accounts, and so forth. Windows 95 does provide you with a My Documents folder for your documents; however, you can (and usually do) create additional folders for yourself.

1. Open **Network Neighborhood**.
2. In the Content pane, select the drive or folder where you want to put the new folder.
3. Choose **File**, **New**, **Folder** from the menu.

TIP **New Isn't On My File Menu** Check to make sure you have selected a resource where you can place your new folder.

4. A new folder appears in the window with the name New Folder in a box and highlighted (see Figure 3.1). Enter a name for the folder. (Because New Folder is highlighted, it will automatically disappear as you begin typing the new name, so you don't need to backspace or delete the text first.) The name of the folder can be up to 255 characters long, including spaces. You cannot use any of the following characters: \, /, :, ", ", *, ?, <, >, or |, all of which have special meaning to the file system.

Figure 3.1   A new folder appears.

5. Press **Enter**.

Selecting Files and Folders

Before you can perform an operation on a file or folder, you must select (or highlight) the item so Windows knows which one you want to use.

To select files or folders:

- **Single file or folder**   Click the file or folder icon, or use the arrow keys to move the highlighting to the file or folder icon you want to select.

- **Several files or folders that are together**   Click the first file or folder icon, hold down the **Shift** key, and click the last file or folder icon. This method also selects all the files between. You can also hold down the **Shift** key and use an arrow key to move down to the final icon in the group you want.

- **Several files or folders that are not together**   Click the first file or folder icon, hold down the **Ctrl** key, and click each of the additional file or folder icons you want.

- **All the file or folder icons in the window**   Choose **Edit**, **Select All** from the menu.

- **All except the file or folder icons you have currently selected**   Choose **Edit**, **Invert Selection** from the menu.

Moving Files and Folders

You can move files and folders to different folders or different drives.

To do this using the drag-and-drop method:

1. From the **Contents** pane, open the drive or folder where the file or folder you want to move is stored by clicking on the drive or folder icon.

2. Drag the file or folder icon from the Contents to the drive or folder icon in the All Folders pane where you want to put it. Don't release the mouse button until the destination drive or folder is highlighted.

   Dragging from a file or folder on one drive to another drive copies instead of moving the file, so you'll have to delete the original icon in the Contents pane if you do this.

TIP **Right Mouse Button?** If you have more than one button on your mouse, try clicking the right mouse button after selecting a file or folder or any object. When you click the right mouse button, a context sensitive menu appears listing common actions (copy, move, create shortcut) you can perform on the file or folder.

Can't Open a New Window? Check your **View**, **Options** menu and select the **Folder** tab to ensure you have selected to view folders using a separate window for each folder.

CAUTION

To move files and folders using the cut and paste method:

1. From the **Contents** pane, open the drive or folder where the file or folder you want to move is stored.

2. Click the file or folder you want to move.

3. Choose **Edit, Cut** from the menu or click the **Cut** button on the toolbar. This removes the icon(s) from the current folder or drive.

4. In the Contents pane, open the drive or folder where you want to put the file or folder.

5. Choose **Edit, Paste** from the menu or click the **Paste** button on the toolbar.

Copying Files and Folders

You can copy files and folders to different folders or different drives by using methods similar to those in Explorer.

To do this using the drag-and-drop method:

1. In the **Contents** pane, open the drive or folder where the file or folder you want to copy is stored. Just click the drive or folder icon to open it.

2. Hold down the **Ctrl** key and drag the file or folder icon you want to copy from the Contents pane to the drive or folder icon in the Contents pane, where you want to put it.

If you are dragging the file or folder from one drive to another, you don't need to hold down the **Ctrl** key.

To do this using the cut and paste method:

1. In the **Contents** pane, open the drive or folder where the file or folder you want to copy is stored.

2. Select the files or folders you want to copy.

3. Choose **Edit**, **Copy** from the menu or click the **Copy** button on the toolbar. This places a duplicate of the selected files or folders in the Clipboard.

4. In the Contents pane, open the drive or folder where you want to put the duplicate file or folder.

5. Choose **Edit**, **Paste** from the menu or click the **Paste** button on the toolbar.

 TIP **Copying to the Floppy Disk** If you want to copy selected files or folders from one of your drives to your floppy disk, click one of the selected icons with the right mouse button. Choose **Send To**, **3½ Floppy (A)** from the pop-up menu.

Deleting Files and Folders

When you delete files or folders from your hard disk or a network drive, they are removed from their current folder and placed in the Recycle Bin. If necessary, you can recover them from the Recycle Bin (see Part I, Lesson 12 for more information about the Recycle Bin). However, if the file is on a floppy disk it doesn't go to the Recycle Bin. Be very sure you want to delete files from your disk.

Be careful, too, when deleting folders—especially shared folders. If you delete a folder, you're also deleting the contents of the folder. The folder doesn't have to be empty before you delete it, as in MS-DOS. Be sure you move any valuable files or folders to other secure locations and that no one else has stored valuable files in a folder before you delete it!

To delete a file or folder:

1. Select the files or folders to be deleted.
2. Press the **Delete** key, click the **Delete** button on the Toolbar, or choose **File**, **Delete** from the menu.
3. A Windows 95 alert box appears asking if you are sure you want to send the selected files or folders to the Recycle Bin. If you are, select **Yes**. If not, select **No** and the operation will cease.

Renaming Files and Folders

To give a different name to a file or folder:

1. Select the file or folder you want to rename.
2. Choose **File**, **Rename** from the menu, or click the icon with the right mouse button and choose **Rename** from the pop-up menu, or click once on the name. The name gets a box around it and the text is highlighted as shown in Figure 3.2.

Figure 3.2 The file name when ready for renaming

3. Enter the text for the new name.
4. Press **Enter**.

Creating Shortcuts

Shortcuts provide you with easy access to files and programs. Once you place a shortcut on the desktop, you can double-click that shortcut icon to start up a program or open a file or folder.

To create a shortcut:

1. Open the Network Neighborhood.

2. Select the drive, folder, or file for which you want to create the shortcut.

3. Choose **File**, **Create Shortcut**.

4. A copy of the icon appears in the window with the words Shortcut to in front of the name. Drag that icon onto the desktop.

In this lesson, you learned to manage your files and folders in Network Neighborhood by moving, copying, renaming, and deleting them. You saw how to create new folders and add shortcuts to your desktop. In the next lesson, you'll learn how to attach to a network using Dial-Up Networking.

Remote Connect to Your Office Network

In this lesson, you learn to attach to your office network using Dial-Up Networking.

Dial-Up Networking Basics

Remote access with Windows 95 is easier and more powerful than in any previous version of Windows. If you are connecting to an Internet service provider, using remote mail from home, or simply connecting to a server-based LAN, Dial-Up Networking can make the connection for you and allow you to use all the resources on the network as if you were physically connected to the LAN rather than remotely connected through a modem.

Remote access is accomplished with new Windows 95 networking components and a dial-up adapter, so you can easily use remote networking. Because remote networking is built-in at the core of Windows 95, programs that require networking automatically start the Dial-Up Networking component when they run in order to establish a connection. A good example is the Internet Explorer that is part of the Plus! Pack for Windows 95. When you attempt to connect to a resource that requires a network connection, the Internet Explorer automatically opens the Dial-Up Networking dialog box to attempt a connection to the network. For more information on Dial-Up Networking see Lesson 7, "Connecting to an Internet Service Provider."

Remote access with Windows 95 requires only the addition of a modem, installation of Dial-Up Networking components, and the phone number for the remote connection. This connection can be an Internet service account, a Windows 95 or

Windows NT dial-up server, a NetWare Connect server, or other third-party servers. This section covers connecting to a Windows NT or Windows 95 dial-up server.

Preparing Your Computer

With Dial-Up networking, you can connect to a network and access shared information, even if your computer is not a part of the network. You can use a home computer, notebook, or other computer to dial up a server on the network.

To prepare your computer, follow these steps:

1. Choose **Start**, **Settings**, and select the **Control Panel** folder. Choose the **Network** icon and the Network dialog box appears.

2. Click the **Identification** tab of the **Network** dialog box, as shown in Figure 4.1.

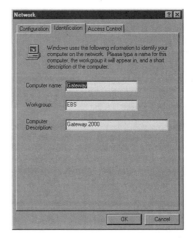

Figure 4.1   The Identification tab of the Network Dialog box.

3. Enter the name of the remote, or host, computer in the Computer name text box. Enter the Workgroup name; Workgroup refers to a Windows NT, Window 95, or Windows for Workgroups workgroup, the logical grouping of peer machines in a Windows network.

4. Click the **Access Control** tab. The Access Control tab appears as shown in Figure 4.2.

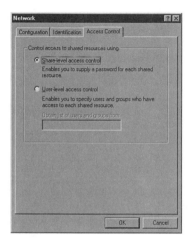

Figure 4.2 The Access Control tab.

5. For peer-to-peer networking, choose **Share-level Access Control**.

TIP **User-Level Access Control** If you normally log on to a NetWare file server or a Windows NT Server file server, you may choose **User-level Access Control**. If you choose this, you must enter the name of a NetWare file server or Windows NT Server domain controller in the **Obtain List of Users and Groups From** box. Check with your network system administrator to find out whether you can/should choose this option, and what server name to enter. If you are not sure which option to choose, then choose **Share-level Access Control**.

6. Click **OK**.

7. Windows 95 states that you must restart you computer before the new settings take effect and asks if you want to restart the computer. Choose **Yes** to restart with the new settings.

Now that you have tackled the hardest part of installation and configuration of your dial-up connection, you can proceed with configuring a dial-up connection.

Making the Connection

Windows provides a Dial-Up Connection wizard that makes it easy to create connections for Dial-Up Networking. After the wizard leads you through the process, you're ready to make your call. To run the wizard, follow these steps:

1. Open the **Start** menu and choose **Programs**, select **Accessories**, and then **Dial-Up Networking**. The Dial-Up Networking window appears.

2. Double-click **Make New Connection**. The first box of the Make New Connection wizard appears, as shown in Figure 4.3.

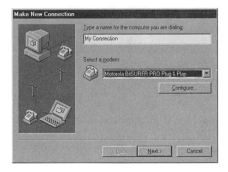

Figure 4.3   The Make New Connection Wizard.

3. Enter the name to identify the remote computer to which you will attach.

4. Select your modem.

5. Choose the **Configure** button if you need to set any specific options. The modem's Properties sheet will appear, containing such information as port, speaker volume, baud rate, data bits, parity, and so on. Choose **OK** to return to the wizard.

6. Choose **Next**. The second wizard dialog box appears, as shown in Figure 4.4.

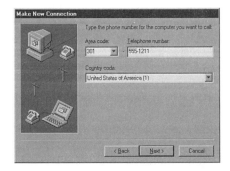

Figure 4.4   Type in the telephone number and country code for your new connection in this dialog box.

7. Enter the Telephone Number to the modem of the remote (host) computer and your Country Code.

8. Click **Next**. Another wizard box appears, telling you the connection was successfully created.

9. Click **Finish**. The new connection is added to the Dial-Up networking window.

Modifying a Connection

You can change a phone number, modem configuration, and even the server type for a Dial-Up connection. First, you must open the Dial-Up Networking window. Then follow these steps:

1. Right-click the **Dial-Up Connection** icon you want to modify.

2. Select the **Properties** command. The connection's general properties sheet appears, as shown in Figure 4.5.

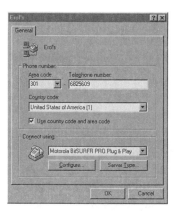

Figure 4.5   The Properties Sheet.

3. To reconfigure the modem, choose the **Configure** button. The Modem Properties sheet appears and offers options such as port, speaker volume, speed, parity, and so on.

4. To set the server, choose the **Server Type** button. The Server Types dialog box appears, as shown in Figure 4.6.

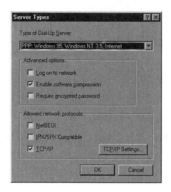

Figure 4.6   Select the Server Type you want to access.

5. In the type of **Dial-Up Server** drop-down list, choose the type of server to which you want to connect. The drop-down list may include any of the following:

- **CISPPP**   PPP connection using CompuServe networks. You will have this only if CompuServe client software has been installed on your computer.

- **CSLIP**   UNIX Connection with IP header compression. Use this to connect to the Internet, but only if your Internet Service Provider tells you to do so.

- **NRN**   NetWare Connect. Use this to connect directly to a NetWare file server that runs NetWare Connect.

- **PPP**   Windows 95, Windows NT 3.5, Internet. Use this to connect to a Windows NT computer that runs Remote Access Service (RAS), to connect to a Windows 95 computer running Dial-UP Networking Server software, or to connect to the Internet (but only if your Internet Service Provider tells you to do so).

- **SLIP**   UNIX Connection. Use this to connect to a UNIX network or to the Internet (but only if your Internet Service Provider tells you to do so).

- **Windows for Workgroups and Windows NT 3.1**   Use this to connect to a Windows NT 3.1 or Windows for Workgroups computer running Remote Access Service (RAS).

6. Other choices may appear in the list if you have installed client software for third-party remote network access products. For example, if you connect to a LAN using Shiva LANRover or Shiva NetModem products, your Shiva client software may appear in this list.

7. In the **Advanced** options area, choose from the following options:

   Log on to Network   Dial-Up Networking logs on to the network using the name and password you use to log into Windows.

   Enable Software Compression   Specifies whether data is compressed before it is sent. Speeds up the transfer, but both computers must be using compatible compression.

   Require Encrypted Password   Specifies that only encrypted passwords can be sent to or accepted by your computer.

8. In the **Allowed Network Protocols** area, choose **NetBEUI** to connect to the peer-to-peer network.

9. Choose **OK** to close the dialog box. Choose **OK** again to close the connection's properties dialog box.

Connecting to the Dial-Up Network

You can add further connections to your Dial-Up Networking window at any time. When you're ready to connect to the network, open the Dial-Up Networking window, turn on your modem, and follow these steps:

1. Double-click the **Connection** icon in the **Dial-Up Networking** window. The Connect To dialog box appears.

2. Enter your Password. You can choose **Dial Properties** if you have any last minute changes to make to the information.

3. Choose the **Connect** button. The Connecting To dialog box shows your progress. When the connection is made, Dial-Up verifies your user name and password with the remote computer.

4. When your log on is complete, Windows 95 shows the connection status dialog box that monitors the connection. You're connected to the remote network and can access any resources to which you have been given access.

The Remote Computer Hangs Up Unexpectedly   There might be noise over the phone lines that is interrupting the connection. You could try calling again and hope for a better connection. Also, you might have gone too long without typing anything and have "timed out."

CAUTION

In this lesson, you learned how to attach to a network using Dial-Up Networking and create and modify connections. In the next lesson, you learn to share your folders, files, and printers with others on your network. You also learn how to map network drives.

247

Sharing Your Folders, Files, and Printers

In this lesson, you learn to share your folders, files, and printers with others on your network. You also learn how to map network drives.

Sharing Folders on Your Computer

You can designate any folder on your computer as shared. When you share a folder, you can assign a *share name* and *password* to that folder. You can also specify what type of access users have to the shared folder. Once you have shared a folder, other users have access to the files in that folder. The computers that have the folders you want to share must be on and logged in to the network.

To share a folder, follow these steps:

1. In the Explorer, select the folder you want to share.
2. Right-click the folder, and then click **Sharing** to display the Sharing page on the Properties sheet.
3. Select the **Shared As** option.
4. You can accept the default share name for the folder or type a new name in the **Share Name** text box.
5. Enter a comment text box, if you wish.

   The comment appears in the Details view of your computer when other users select it in the Explorer or Network Neighborhood. Comments can help users locate shared information.

6. Select one of the **Access Type** options to specify the access for the shared resource.

7. You can grant users two levels of access to a shared folder. If you want users to be able only to read files and run programs in a folder, select the **Read-Only** option. If you want to be able to read, modify, rename, move, delete, or create files and run your programs, select the **Full** option.

If you want to limit access to the files in the shared folder to certain users, assign a password to the folder and give the password to only those users. If you select the **Depends on Password** option, you need to enter two passwords—one for users who have read-only access to your files and one for users with full access. If you want all users to have access to your files, don't assign a password.

8. Click **OK**.

You can share an entire disk drive by selecting the drive and following the preceding steps.

You can quickly tell if you have designated a folder as shared by looking for a hand beneath its folder icon in the Explorer or Network Neighborhood, as shown in Figure 5.1.

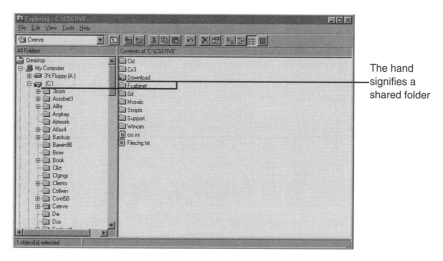

The hand signifies a shared folder

Figure 5.1   A shared disk drive and a shared folder.

To change the properties of a shared folder, click the folder with the right mouse button and change the share name, comment, access privileges, or password for the shared folder.

No Sharing Tab? If the Sharing tab is not visible when you open the Properties sheet, you must enable file and printer sharing services. To learn how to do this, see "Sharing Files on Your Computer," later in this lesson.

CAUTION

To stop sharing a folder, follow these steps:

1. Select the folder you want to stop sharing.

2. Right-click the folder and then click **Sharing**.

3. Select the **Not Shared** option and click **OK**.

Sharing Files on Your Computer

Many files on your computer are applicable only to you and your work, as are many of the files on other computers in your network. However, some of your files may be useful to your co-workers just as some of their files may be useful to you.

When working on a network, you can choose to share the file on your computer with your co-workers. Later, you can choose to stop sharing your files.

To set up file sharing on your computer, follow these steps:

1. Choose **Start**, and select **Settings**, **Control Panel**.

2. Double-click the **Network** icon in the **Control Panel**. The Network dialog box appears.

3. In the **Configuration** page, choose the **File and Print Sharing** button. The File and Print Sharing dialog box appears.

4. Select the option **I Want to be Able to Give Others Access to My Files**.

5. Choose **OK** to close the dialog box, and Windows returns to the Network dialog box.

6. Choose **OK** to close the Network dialog box.

7. Restart your computer for the change to take effect.

After choosing to share your files with others on the network, you can choose who, in particular, will have access to your files. Depending on the type of access control you have chosen you may be able to specify individual people or groups who will have access to each shared resource, or you may only be able to provide a password for each shared resource, in which case only those with the password will have access.

To set access control, open the **Network** dialog box and choose the **Access Control** tab, as shown in Figure 6.2. Select either **Share-Level Access Control** to set a password, or **User-Level Access Control** to provide a list of people. If you choose share-level access control, you can assign a password to each shared file. If you choose User-Level access control, you must specify a NetWare file server or Windows NT Server file server in the **Obtain List of Users and Groups From** box.

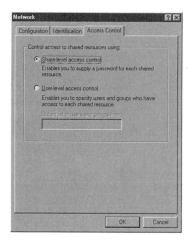

Figure 5.2 The Access Control tab.

Sharing your Printer

Peer-to-peer networks also enable printer-sharing, but if the printer is connected to your computer, you govern whether to share that printer with others on your network.

When working on a peer-to peer network, you can choose to share or stop sharing the printers on each computer.

To set printer sharing on your computer, follow these steps:

1. Choose **Start**, and select **Settings**, **Control Panel**.

2. Double-click the **Network** icon in the **Control Panel**. The Network dialog box appears.

3. In the **Configuration** page, select **Client for Microsoft Networks** from the list of installed network components.

4. Choose the **File and Print Sharing** button. The File and Print Sharing dialog box appears.

5. Select the option **I Want to be Able to Allow Others to Print to My Printer**.

6. Choose **OK** to close the dialog box and Windows returns to the Network dialog box.

7. Choose **OK** to close the Network dialog box.

After choosing to share your printer with others on the network, you can choose who, in particular, will have access to your printer. You can choose to specify people of groups who will have access to each shared resource, or you can provide a password for each shared resource and only those with the password will have access.

To set access control, open the **Network** dialog box and choose the **Access Control** tab. Select either **Share-Level Access Control** to set a password or **User-Level Access Control** to provide a list of people. If you choose share-level access control, you can assign a password to each shared printer. If you choose User-Level access control, you must specify a NetWare file server or Windows NT Server file server in the **Obtain List of Users and Groups From** box.

Mapping Drives

Windows enables you to use drive mapping when connecting to a disk or folder on another computer. Drive mapping is a method of assigning a drive letter to represent a path that included the volume, directory, and any subdirectories leading to a folder. The drive mapping you create follows the path for you, thereby saving you time; instead of opening folder after folder, you can use the drive map to quickly go to the directory or resource. Mapping is especially handy when you're constantly using a file or resource on another workstation.

To map a drive, follow these steps:

1. Open the window in which you want to place the mapped drive.

2. Choose **View, Toolbar** to display the toolbar if it is not already showing.

3. Click the **Map Network Drive** icon on the toolbar.

4. The **Map Network Drive** dialog box appears, as shown in Figure 5.1. Click the **Path** down arrow. If you have recently connected to the drive, the path appears in the list box. It the path is not in the list box, enter the path in the following format: **\\computername\sharename**.

Figure 5.3 The Map Network Drive dialog box.

5. Choose **OK** to complete the path.

To break the connection to the mapped drive, follow these steps:

1. From the Windows Explorer toolbar, select the drive you wish to disconnect and click the **Disconnect Network Drive** icon.

2. The **Disconnect Network Drive** dialog box appears; choose **OK**. The connection and the icon are now removed.

In this lesson, you learned to share your folders, files and printers with others and to disable sharing. In the next lesson, you learn to share a fax modem.

Sharing and Using a Fax Modem

In this lesson, you learn to use Microsoft Fax and share a fax modem in Windows 95.

Windows 95 Fax Modem Basics

Windows 95 users can easily share a single fax modem with other users in a workgroup using Microsoft Fax. Every user can take advantage of the service to send faxes and even editable files using the shared fax modem. Windows 95 makes faxing as easy as printing a file or sending an electronic mail message.

Microsoft Fax is compatible with Group 3 faxes worldwide, yet it also offers secure fax transmission as well as binary file transfer to another Microsoft Fax recipient. Microsoft Fax uses MAPI (Mail Application Programming Interface) so you can easily send a fax using an application's File, Send command or File, Print command, enabling fax in all users' applications. This power makes a shared fax a great addition to a workgroup. This lesson covers the basics and features of Microsoft Fax specifically when used as a shared fax server.

Understanding Fax Modem Sharing Policies

For the most part, a peer-to-peer network makes use of each computer's resources while each computer's user continues to work on the computer. When you find the shared resources are so heavily used that one computer becomes overloaded, it is time to consider changing one computer into a server.

When setting up a Windows 95 computer as a fax server, you should consider the following issues:

- How is the computer identified to be the fax server going to be used—as a fax server only, or a client workstation?
- How many users require fax service and how often?
- Are there other fax servers in your company?
- Will this computer also act as a print server?

If the fax server computer is also going to be used as a workstation, you should increase the amount of memory installed on the computer. Microsoft makes the following recommendations for fax server configurations for a stand-alone fax server:

- 80486 processor
- 8M of memory

For a dual purpose fax server and workstation, Microsoft recommends the following as a minimum configuration:

- 80486 processor
- 12M of memory

If you want to share a fax modem, you must install Microsoft Exchange on each workstation that requires use of the fax service.

All faxes are sent to the users through Microsoft Exchange. The Microsoft Exchange Inbox of the fax server receives all the incoming faxes for those using the service. The faxes are not automatically routed; this operation is done manually by the administrator of the fax server.

If the fax is the only one used by the company, the fax volume needs to be monitored to assure that the needs of the company are being met. Microsoft states that the minimum configurations above can support 25 typical users in a workgroup.

If the computer is also a print server—a common configuration since users can print their faxes from the same computer—additional monitoring may be necessary to assure that the workstation is handling the additional load.

Setting Up Fax Modem Sharing

After you have decided to install a fax server, follow these steps to set one up:

1. Install your modem.
2. Install the Microsoft Exchange client on the server computer.
3. Install Microsoft Fax on the server.
4. Establish the fax share.

Installing workstations is similar; perform the following steps to set them up:

1. Install the Microsoft Exchange client.
2. Install Microsoft Fax.
3. Connect to the shared fax.

Before configuring the fax modem for sharing, you need to install it on the sharing computer. If the fax modem is not yet set up, refer to the instructions that came with the fax modem. You also need to install Microsoft Exchange and Microsoft Fax on the server. For more information on this, read on. After that, you are ready to configure Exchange to enable fax modem sharing.

Installing Microsoft Exchange

To determine if Microsoft Exchange has been installed on your computer, look for the Inbox icon on your desktop. If it is there, Microsoft Exchange has been installed. If Microsoft Exchange has not been installed on your computer, install it as follows:

1. Choose **Start**, **Settings**, **Control Panel**. The **Control Panel** window opens.
2. In the Control Panel, double-click **Add/Remove Programs**. The Add/Remove Programs Properties dialog box opens.
3. In the Add/Remove Programs Properties dialog box, click the **Windows Setup** tab. The Windows Setup panel appears.
4. In the Windows Setup panel, click **Windows Messaging** to select it, then click **Details** to open the **Windows Messaging** dialog box.
5. In the Windows Messaging dialog box, check **Windows Messaging**. If

Internet Mail Services appears and you intend to use Microsoft Exchange to read and compose Internet mail messages, check **Internet Mail Services**. Then click **OK** twice, to close the two dialog boxes.

6. Windows may have to add files from the Windows 95 CD-ROM. If so, it may prompt you to put the CD-ROM in the drive. Do so.

Installing Microsoft Fax

To install Microsoft Fax, follow these steps:

1. Choose **Start**, **Settings**, **Control Panel**. The **Control Panel** window opens.

2. In the Control Panel, double-click **Add/Remove Programs**. The **Add/ Remove Programs Properties** dialog box opens.

3. In the Add/Remove Programs Properties dialog box, click the **Windows Setup** tab. The Windows Setup panel appears.

4. In the Windows Setup panel, look at Microsoft Fax. If a check mark appears in its check box, Microsoft Fax is already installed. If not, then click on the check box to add the check mark. Then click **OK**.

5. Windows may have to add files from the Windows 95 CD-ROM. If so, it may prompt you to put the CD-ROM in the drive.

To add the Microsoft Fax Service to a profile and set up Fax Sharing:

1. Choose **Start**, **Settings** and select the **Control Panel** folder.

2. Double-click the **Mail and Fax** icon. The *profilename* Properties sheet is displayed, where *profilename* is the name of a the default profile.

3. Microsoft Fax should appear in the window named **The Following Information Services are Set Up in this Profile**. If it does not appear, then click the **Add** button, select it in the list that appears, and click **OK**. If it does not appear in that list, then the Microsoft Fax Service is not installed on the computer; see the previous section of this lesson for the steps to \add it.

4. Select **Microsoft Fax** and click **Properties**. The Microsoft Fax Properties sheet appears, as shown in Figure 6.1.

Figure 6.1 The Microsoft Fax Properties sheet.

5. Choose the **Modem** tab and select the option **Let Other People on the Network Use My Modem To Send Faxes**, as shown in Figure 6.2.

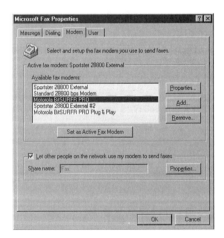

Figure 6.2 Sharing your modem.

6. Choose the **Properties** button on the **Modem** tab. The NetFax dialog box appears.

7. Enter a Share Name, a Comment (if you want to), and set the Access type for the fax modem, as shown in Figure 6.3.

Figure 6.3 Type in a share name and comments.

8. If you want to restrict access to the fax modem, enter a password. The confirmation of Password dialog box appears; enter the password again and choose **OK**.

9. Click **OK** in each dialog box to complete the configuration.

Configuring Workstations to Use a Shared Fax Modem

Once the fax server is installed, you can configure individual workstations to connect to and use the fax server. You must install Microsoft Exchange and Microsoft Fax on each workstation, but rather than looking locally for the fax modem, you configure the workstation to use the shared fax modem. To configure a workstation to use a shared fax perform the following steps:

1. Open the **Start** menu, choose **Settings**, **Control Panel**.

2. Double-click the **Mail and Fax** icon. The *profilename* Properties sheet opens, where *profilename* is the name of the default profile.

3. Select **Microsoft Fax** and click **Properties**. The Microsoft Fax Properties sheet appears.

4. Click the **Modem** tab and choose **Add**. The Add a Fax Modem dialog box appears.

5. Click **Network Fax Server**.

6. Choose **OK** and the Connect To Network Fax Server dialog box appears, as shown in Figure 6.4.

Figure 6.4   The Connect to Network Fax Server dialog box.

7. Type the UNC Share Name for the fax server (for example, *\\FAXSERVER\NETFAX*).

8. Click **OK** to close each dialog box.

Using a Shared Fax Modem

You can easily use a shared fax modem from Microsoft Exchange through Microsoft Fax, or from an application such as WordPad or Microsoft Word.

To use Microsoft Exchange to send a fax, double-click the **Inbox** to start Exchange. Compose the fax as by choosing **Compose**, **New Fax**, then filling in the screens in the Compose New Fax Wizard.

To send a fax from an application, compose the fax and then follow the application's instructions for sending a fax. In many programs you can simply choose **File**, **Print** to send a fax. In the Print dialog box choose **Microsoft Fax** as the name of the printer and choose **OK**. The Compose New Fax Wizard will then prompt you to enter the information necessary to complete the fax.

To use Microsoft Fax, open the **Start** menu and select **Programs**. Choose **Accessories**, **Fax**, and **Compose New Fax** to create a fax to send. The Compose New Fax will prompt you for the information necessary to send the fax.

 TIP   **Fax Modem Busy?**   If someone tries to access the fax modem while it is in use, the fax messages are place in a queue, similar to when jobs are places in a print queue.

 TIP   **Is Privacy Important?**   If you send or receive faxes on the network using a shared fax modem, you may want to take advantage of the security features in Microsoft Fax to ensure privacy of your fax transmissions.

In this lesson, you learned how to use and share a fax modem in Windows 95. In the next lesson, you learn to use another tool requiring a modem—Dial-Up Networking.

Connecting to an Internet Service Provider

In this lesson, you will learn to use the Dial-Up Networking capabilities in Windows 95 to communicate with an Internet Service Provider (ISP) or with other computers.

What Are Remote Access Services?

Windows 95 includes a set of communications tools named Dial-Up Networking that helps make connecting to and communicating with other computers easier. Using Dial-Up Networking, your computer can dial into a server to connect to other networks, perhaps within your company, or external networks like CompuServe, America Online, and the Internet. The software that answers the phone when you dial in to a remote computer is called a *remote access service*. For example, Windows NT Server provides a remote access service called (appropriately enough) Windows NT Remote Access Service (or "RAS" for short). When installed on a Windows NT Server computer, RAS permits remote users to connect to the entire network by dialing in to that NT server. (For more information on using Dial-Up Networking to access your office network, see Lesson 4, "Remote Connect to Your Office Network.")

Understanding Dial-Up Networking

Dial-Up Networking allows mobile users to work as if they are connected directly to the network. Establishing a network connection by using Dial-Up Networking works the same as establishing a network connection in the office—you just double-click a network resource.

The Windows 95 Dial-Up Networking feature allows remote users to designate a computer running Windows 95 as a dial-up client or server. From a remote site, you can use Dial-Up Networking to connect the dial-up client to a Windows 95 dial-up server or other remote access server. If the client and server are running the same network protocols, the dial-up client can connect to the network to access its resources.

 TIP   **Dial-Up Not Displayed?**   Dial-Up server capabilities are only available if you have Microsoft Plus! For Windows 95 installed.

Windows 95 provides the following tools to help users stay as functional as possible with the limited resources of a mobile site:

Remote Mail   With the Microsoft Exchange client and a Microsoft Mail workgroup post office, remote users can dial in to the network to send and receive electronic mail, without requiring any additional client software or a special gateway server. To send and receive mail, mobile users make a Dial-Up Networking connection to another computer running Windows 95 to another remote access server connected to their workgroup post office. After connecting, they use Microsoft Exchange to send and receive their mail.

Direct Cable Connection   This tool allows you to quickly and easily establish a connection between two computers by using a parallel cable or null-modem serial cable. After the connection is established, Direct Cable Connection facilitates the transfer of files from the host computer to the guest computer.

Windows 95 Briefcase   This file synchronization tool eases the task of keeping track of the relationships between files on a portable computer and on a desktop computer. With Briefcase, a user can simultaneously update related files.

Deferred Printing   Windows 95 supports deferred printing, which allows mobile users to generate print jobs when they are not connected to a printer. The print jobs are stored until a printer becomes available. Windows 95 detects the printer connection and automatically spools the print jobs in the background.

Dial-Up Tools From Other Vendors   This shows you how to use Dial-Up Networking with Windows NT, Shiva, and NetWare remote access servers (RAS).

To use Dial-Up Networking to connect to the network, you need the following hardware:

- An installed modem.
- About 3M of free disk space to install Dial-Up Networking.

With Dial-Up Networking, you can connect from a remote site to a computer that has been configured as a remote access server, or connect to a network through the remote access server. A Windows 95 dial-up client can connect to a wide variety of networks because support is included for a variety of connection and network protocols.

Different remote access servers provide different security systems to protect access to a network. The Windows 95 dial-up server uses pass-through user-level or share-level security.

You can use system policies and other methods to disable dial-in access so users cannot dial in to a particular desktop computer.

Dial-Up Networking uses the Windows 95 communications architecture to communicate through a modem to a network. It initializes the modem, determines its status, and dials the phone number.

The main elements of Windows 95 Dial-Up Networking are:

- Dial-Up clients and servers.
- Connection Protocols.
- Network (LAN) protocols and network servers.
- Security options.

With Dial-Up Networking, you can configure a remote computer running Windows 95 as a dial-up client to dial in to a Windows 95 dial-up server or other remote access servers. A dial-up client, running the appropriate connection protocol, can connect to many types of remote access servers, including the following:

- Windows 95 dial-up server.
- Windows NT Workstation.
- Windows NT 3.1 or later.
- Windows for Workgroups 3.11.
- NetWare Connect.

- Shiva LanRover and other dial-up routers.
- Any UNIX server that runs SLIP or PPP.

Connection protocols control the transmission of data over the wide-area network (WAN). A Windows 95 dial-up client can use the following connection protocols to connect to a remote access server:

- Point-to-Point Protocol (PPP).
- Novell NetWare Connect (IPX/SPX).
- Windows NT 3.1 or Windows for Workgroups RAS (Asynchronous NetBEUI).
- Serial Line Internet Protocol (SLIP).

The type of connection protocol you choose depends on the server you are connecting to. Some connection protocols support a subset of the common network protocols.

Following is a summary of connection protocols supported in Dial-Up Networking.

> **Point-to-Point Protocol (PPP)**   PPP has become a popular connection protocol for remote access because of its flexibility and its role as an industry standard. If a dial-up client is running PPP, it can connect to a network running IPX/SPX, TCP/IP, or NetBEUI protocols. PPP is the default protocol for the Microsoft Dial-Up adapter.
>
> **Novell NetWare Connect**   NetWare Connect is a proprietary connection protocol. It allows a computer running Windows 95 to directly connect to a NetWare Connect server and, if running a NetWare-compatible network client, connect to NetWare servers. Windows 95 can only act as a client for connecting to a NetWare Connect server. NetWare Connect clients themselves cannot connect to a Windows 95 dial-up server directly through dial-up.
>
> **RAS for Windows NT 3.1 and Windows for Workgroups 3.11 (Asynchronous NetBEUI)**   This protocol is used to connect computers running Windows 95 to remote access servers running Windows NT 3.1 or Windows for Workgroups 3.11, or to connect computers running Windows for Workgroups 3.11 or Windows NT 3.1 to a Windows 95 dial-up server.

Serial Line Internet Protocol (SLIP) SLIP is an older remote access standard that is typically used by UNIX remote access servers. Use SLIP only if your site has a UNIX system configured as a SLIP server for Internet connections. The remote access server must be running TCP/IP.

Windows 95 does not provide SLIP server capabilities; SLIP is for dial-out only. Support for SLIP can be found on the Windows 95 CD-ROM.

Installing and Configuring Dial-Up Networking

When you install Dial-Up Networking, you are installing all the components you need to connect to a network. For example, installing Dial-Up Networking also installs the Microsoft Dial-Up adapter, and connection and network protocols.

Before you dial up a remote connection using a modem and Dial-Up Networking, you need to make sure all the appropriate network protocols are bound to the Microsoft Dial-Up adapter or a network adapter. The easiest way to install Dial-Up Networking is during installation of Windows 95. If you didn't choose it during Setup, you can install it afterward.

 TIP **Upgrading from Windows 3.11 to Windows 95?** If you are currently using Windows for Workgroups 3.11 with RAS, Dial-Up Networking will automatically be installed when you upgrade to Windows 95.

Installing Dial-Up Networking

To install Dial-Up Networking after you run Setup, follow these steps:

1. Choose **Start**, **Settings** and select the **Control Panel** folder. Choose the **Add/Remove Programs** icon and click the **Windows Setup** tab.

2. In the Components list, click **Communications**, and then click the **Details** button

3. In the Communications dialog box, click **Dial-Up Networking**, as shown in Figure 7.1, and then click **OK**.

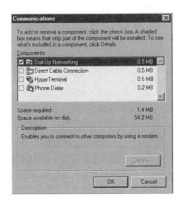

Figure 7.1 The Dial-Up Networking Component.

After Dial-Up Networking is installed, a folder for it appears in My Computer. To run Dial-Up Networking, double-click the folder.

Configuring Dial-Up Networking

Configuring computers as Dial-Up Networking clients or servers consists of the following four tasks:

- Installing the appropriate network protocols and making sure they are bound to the Microsoft Dial-Up adapter. All network protocols installed before you install Dial-Up Networking are automatically bound to the Microsoft Dial-Up adapter when you install Dial-Up Networking.

- Running the Make New Connection wizard in Dial-Up Networking to set up a connection to a remote access server for the dial-up client. If you have not yet installed a modem, the wizard guides you through installing one.

- Configuring the dial-up client in Dial-Up Networking by selecting the remote access server type it will connect to, and by choosing whether to log on to the network after connecting to the remote access server. Selecting the server type automatically enables the correct connection protocol, such as PPP or SLIP.

- Optionally, installing dial-up server capabilities and configuring a computer running Windows 95 as a dial-up server in the Dial-Up Server menu in Dial-Up Networking.

Creating a New Dial-Up Networking Connection

Windows 95 guides you through making a new remote connection when you first run Dial-Up Networking. Before creating a new Dial-Up Networking connection, you should install a modem. The Make New Connection wizard prompts you to do so, or you can install it separately by using the Install New Modem wizard in the Modems option in Control Panel.

To create a Dial-Up Networking connection using the Make New Connection wizard, follow these steps:

1. From My Computer, double-click the **Dial-Up Networking** folder.

2. In the Dial-Up Networking window, double-click the **Make New Connection** icon.

3. The Make New Connection wizard, shown in Figure 7.2, prompts you for the information needed to define a connection, including a name for the computer you are dialing, modem type, area code, telephone number, and country code (shown in Figure 7.3). After you have successfully created a connection, you will be prompted to name it (see Figure 7.4).

Figure 7.2 The Make New Connection Wizard.

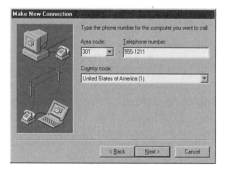

Figure 7.3 Enter the phone number for the computer you want to connect to.

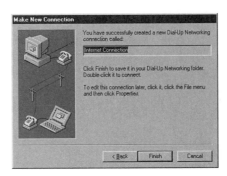

Figure 7.4 Name your connection.

The new icon for your connection appears in the Dial-Up Networking window. You need to provide this information only once for each connection you define.

 TIP **Want to Change Your Dialing String?** You can adjust the dialing string in **Dial Properties**, which is accessible from the **Connect To** dialog box that appears when you double-click a connection icon.

Displaying a Terminal Window

When a user connects to a remote server, a terminal window can be displayed to support an interactive logon session with the server. After a connection is established, remote network access becomes transparent to the user.

To make sure a network connection has been established, double-click **Network Neighborhood**, click **Map Network Drive**, and then type a path name to a network server.

To display a terminal window before or after dialing follow these steps:

1. Click a connection icon, and then click **File**, **Properties**.
2. Select the **General** properties tab, click the **Configure** button, and then click the **Options** tab.
3. In the Options dialog box, click the option named **Bring Up Terminal Window Before Dialing** or the option named **Bring Up Terminal Window After Dialing**.

Changing Location Information

With Dialing Properties, you can specify area code, special numbers needed to reach an outside line, and calling card information you may need for the connection number. Windows 95 will then automatically adjust the dial string it sends to your modem.

You can predefine Dial-Up Networking connections for users by including them as part of system policies. If you enable user profile, different users sharing the same computer can use separate dialing configurations.

You configure the Windows 95 dial-up client for each dial-in connection you define in Dial-Up Networking. Configuration consists of selecting the remote access server type to connect to and choosing whether to access the network after connecting to the remote access server. In addition, you can require an encrypted password to connect to a remote access server and check to see if the correct network protocols are installed on the dial-up client. Windows 95 automatically selects the appropriate connection protocol when you select the remote access server type for each Dial-Up Networking connection.

Using PPP, SLIP, and CSLIP Connections

While the growth of the Internet is nothing short of remarkable, many corporate networks still do not have direct connections to the Internet. This, combined with the number of home-based users or users who have non-networked standalone computers that want access to the Internet, gives good reason to describe how to work with PPP, SLIP and CSLIP connections.

Dial-Up Networking in Windows 95 supports the Microsoft TCP/IP protocol stack, which lets you dial into various types of remote access servers and Internet server providers to gain access to the Internet. Many Internet service providers (ISPs) use the Point-To-Point protocol (PPP) to provide dial-up Internet connections. PPP is the default protocol in Dial-Up Networking in Windows 95 and is used when you connect to a Windows 95 or Windows NT 3.5 or 4.0 RAS server.

Many UNIX servers, on the other hand, use Serial Line Interface Protocol (SLIP) or Compressed SLIP (CSLIP). SLIP and CSLIP drivers are available for Windows 95. The SLIP driver allows you to set up a connection to a SLIP or CSLIP server using Dial-Up Networking in Windows 95.

To install the SLIP driver, perform the following steps:

1. Insert the Windows 95 CD-ROM in the CD-ROM drive in your computer.

2. Choose **Start**, **Settings**, and then select the **Control Panel**. From the Control Panel window, select the **Add/Remove Software** icon to display the Windows setup property page.

3. Choose the **Have Disk** button to open the Install From Disk dialog box.

4. Choose the **Browse** button, then locate and select the file \Admin\ Apptools\Slip\Rnaplus.inf.

5. Choose **OK**, then **OK** again to open the Have Disk dialog box.

6. Place a check beside the **UNIX Connection For Dial-Up Networking** item in the Components list.

7. Choose **Install** to begin installing the SLIP driver.

Disabling Dial-Up Networking

You can disable the prompt that asks if you want to use Dial-Up Networking when you are attempting to connect to a network resource.

To disable the Dial-Up Networking prompt, follow these steps:

1. In **Dial-Up Networking**, click the **Connection** menu, and then click **Settings**.

2. Click the option named **Don't Prompt To Use Dial-Up Networking**, as shown in Figure 7.5.

Figure 7.5   Disabling Dial-Up Networking.

TIP   **Having Trouble with Dial-Up Networking?**   Windows 95 provides a troubleshooter for Dial-Up Networking in online Help.

In this lesson, you learned how to use, configure, and work with Dial-Up Networking. In the next lesson, you learn how to attach to printers in your network.

Attaching to Network Printers

*In this lesson, you learn to attach to printers within
your network.*

Working with Network Printers

You have already learned the basics of installing and working with local printers—those directly connected to your computer. In many workplaces, a number
of printers are shared within the network and in this lesson you learn how to
work with them.

Although Windows 95 makes network printers appear to operate as local
printers, network printing may seem more complex. Local printers usually
remain attached to the same port and are under your control. Network printers
can change location and are controlled by other users or a network administrator. If problems arise when you are using a network printer, troubleshooting is
much easier if you understand some of the differences between local and
network printing.

Printing from Applications

Printing to network printers from within an application requires the same
commands and menu items that you use to print locally. Windows handles the
network communications and creates a Printer Driver for each attached network
printer. As with local printers, you can access network printer configuration
information in the Printer Properties sheet. In this sheet, you can change the
network printer's properties for default or specific printing tasks. For example,
you can specify the default paper size, number of copies, color options, and
output quality.

When you select to print a document within an application, a print file is created by the application and sent to the printer over the network. A print file contains the spooled printer data and commands that are being temporarily stored prior to printing. The Network Redirector, which is part of the Windows 95 core network architecture, determines whether the print file destination is a local or network printer. The print file contains the data that is being sent to a printer containing—both printable and unprintable characters. Unprintable characters are used to control the printer and, ultimately, the output of your file.

Drag-and-Drop Printing

To perform drag-and drop-printing over the network, you use the same procedure as you do for local printing. However, items printed using drag-and-drop printing are sent to the computer's default printer. Windows will ask you to make it the default printer prior to printing the file. When initially connecting your PC to a network, this printer might not be available. Ensure that you are logged in to the network and verify your printer connection before setting it as the default printer.

Adding a Network Printer

Adding a network printer involves the same Add Printer Wizard, with different configuration details, as when adding a local printer described in Part 1, Lesson 20, "Printing with Windows 95."

When configuring a local printer, the location of your cable to a specific printer port determines the port's selection. The network printer, on the other hand, requires a network resource name.

If you are not sure of the correct address for the network printer, you can choose to browse the network. Browsing enables you to check which network printers are currently available. Some servers requires passwords to view what network resources they have available. If you desire access to a server, but do now know the password, contact your LAN or system administrator.

To configure a network printer, you need to know its make and model. You can get this information from your network administrator or by locating the printer and making note of these details.

To add a network printer using the Add Printer Wizard, perform the following steps:

1. Choose **Start**, **Settings**, **Printers**, and then double-click the **Add Printer** folder.

2. From the first Add Printer Wizard screen, shown in Figure 8.1, click the **Next** button. Windows 95 then displays the next Wizard screen, which asks you to decide if you are adding a Network or a Local Printer.

Figure 8.1   The first screen of the Add Printer Wizard.

3. Choose the **Network Printer** option to connect your PC to a network printer. Choose the **Next** button located at the bottom of the window.

4. Next, identify the network path to the printer. Select the **Browse** button to view Network Neighborhood.

Figure 8.2   Use the Browse option to see printers on your network.

5. Network Neighborhood displays a list of all the servers and workstations connected to your network. Find the appropriate printer and select it. Then choose the **Next** button.

   The Wizard accesses the selected printer and determines whether the computer that controls it can download an appropriate printer driver. If a driver is available, the Wizard automatically loads the driver and sets a default configuration for the printer. If a driver is not available, the Wizard asks you to specify the printer's make and model.

6. Select the manufacturer and printer model by scrolling the Wizard screen lists; then click **Next**. The screen now offers a default name for your printer. The name should adequately describe the printer for later identification.

7. The wizard asks whether you want this printer to be your default printer; select **Yes** or **No**. Follow this decision by selecting the next control, as shown in Figure 8.3.

Figure 8.3   Enter a name for your printer and set its default status.

8. The final wizard screen provides the controls to print a test page on the printer you just added. You can print the test page by selecting **Yes**; select **No** if you do not want to print the test page. As a general rule, you should always print a test page to verify the successful completion of the Add Printer Wizard.

9. Click **Finish**.

In this lesson, you learned to attach to and use a network printer.

Communications and the Internet

Understanding the Internet and the Web

In this lesson, you learn basic Internet and Web concepts and terminology, including protocols, Hypertext, and Web browsers.

What Is the Internet and World Wide Web?

The World Wide Web is part of the Internet, and is a *thing*, not a *place*. For some reason, many newcomers to the Internet and Web think that they are two different *places*. Hopefully, a little background on each will clear this up.

The Internet is a worldwide conglomeration of computer networks. The Internet is not owned and operated by any one company. This is one of the defining characteristics of the Internet. It is one network of computers that can talk to one another, and in turn, talk to other networks of computers, and so on.

The Web is a collection of documents accessible through the Internet. These documents contain a special technology called *hypertext*. When you click your mouse on hypertext, you are taken to a different document, maybe even to different computer. This works much like the green-colored text you see in Windows' Help files.

TIP **Internet or Web?** Because the Internet and the Web are not two different places, the two terms are often used interchangeably, as you may find throughout this section of the book.

Grasping Protocols

In order for computers to communicate over the Internet, they must follow sets of agreed-upon rules that are called *protocols*. The people who devised these rules were not only clever, they came up with cute names for their protocols, such as "gopher" and "World Wide Web." Other long, and often cumbersome descriptive names were shortened to acronyms, such as HyperText Markup Language (HTML) and Transmission Control Protocol/Internet Protocol (TCP/IP).

It's a good idea to understand some of these protocols as you "surf" the Web. You don't need to memorize or even fully understand all of these terms, but you'll find that as you use the Web, this list will be a good reference for you.

Surfing the Web   We're not sure who said it first, or when the phrase caught on, but it means to look around the Internet, just like the phrase "channel surfing" means to look around the channels on your TV.

- **Internet Protocol (IP)**   This is one of the most basic protocols. All computers that communicate with each other on the Internet do so using IP. This determines how data will be transferred from one computer to another, the route the data takes, and the order of the data when it arrives at the second computer.

- **Transmission Control Protocol (TCP)**   This basic protocol enhances IP and gives you a way to correct transmission errors, setting up and breaking down a communications session between computers, and many other things. Because TCP and IP generally work hand-in-hand, people refer to them together as TCP/IP.

- **File Transfer Protocol (FTP)**   Defines how to transfer for a generic file from one computer to another. The file can be a text file, a program, a picture—any type of file—and FTP will transfer it.

- **HyperText Markup Language and HyperText Transfer Protocol (HTML and HTTP)**   Together, they drive the World Wide Web. HTML defines a method of adding formatting to text files, so that when you view them with an HTML viewer (a Web browser), you see things like headlines, emphasized words, centered paragraphs, and embedded pictures. HTTP defines how computers send HTML files back and forth.

Clients and Servers

One of the things that might help clarify what's going on when your computer talks to another computer is the concept of clients and servers. On a network, computers will often assume either the role of client or server. That is, one computer—the *server*—will offer some service to the world. The other computer—the *client*—will make use of that service.

When you use the Internet, your computer is almost always acting as a client and communicating with a server of some kind. If you're transferring a file, you are using FTP server software. If you're surfing the Web, you use your Web browser as a client. A Web browser communicates with a Web server, which serves up Web pages to your browser. At work, your computer may be communicating with a file server (see Part III, "Using Windows 95 on a Network" for more on networking, clients, and servers).

Understanding Tools

From its outset, the purpose of the Internet was to help communication and research. It is to those ends that the various Internet programs are aimed, such as Internet mail programs, Internet News Groups, and Mailing Lists. Gopher, Archie, Veronica, WAIS, and Web servers are intended to help locate published material, that is, to further your research activities.

Here is a brief description of the most common Internet tools:

- **Telnet**   A protocol that defines how one computer can act like a terminal on another. Using a telnet program, you can log onto another computer and run programs on it, just as though you were sitting at its own console.

- **Mailing Lists**   Mailing lists are a way of participating in group discussions on the Internet. Mailing list server computers maintain mailing lists. Using your e-mail program, you can send a request to be added to a mailing list (or removed from it). Then, anyone can send messages addressed to the mailing list itself. The mail server will forward the message to everyone on the mailing list.

- **UseNet News**   Another way of participating in group discussions. News servers store messages and forward them to each other using a protocol called NNTP (Net News Transfer Protocol). You can read and post messages on the servers using a News Reader program.

- **Archie**   Archie servers maintain lists of the names of programs and documents and their locations on other computers on the Internet. If you need to locate a program, you can request its location from an Archie server either with an Archie client program or using Telnet or e-mail.

- **WAIS**   Wide Area Information Servers maintain searchable, full-text indexes of documents. If you need to find information about a particular subject, you can search for more than titles, as with Archie and other data-locating engines. WAIS allows you to search through the contents of the files in the database. By doing this, you may find information that the author or indexer of a document may never have realized you would want.

- **Gopher**   Gopher servers present content in the form of submenus. You pick items from menus; each menu item can be another menu, a program, or a file of some kind. The special strength of Gopher is that any menu item may actually be on a gopher server that is different from the one that presented the menu to you in the first place. So by picking items from gopher menus, you actually jump from gopher server to gopher server.

- **Veronica**   Veronica servers maintain searchable databases of gopher server contents. If you get tired of searching menus for what you want, you can compose a search request of a Veronica server, which will present the search results in the form of a Gopher menu.

- **Java**   Java is a programming language you can use to build small applications (called *applets*) that you can embed in Web pages. When a surfer downloads the Web page, his or her browser (if it is Java-aware) executes the Java applet. To the Web surfer, the executing applet may appear as a scrolling text display, an animated picture, a clock keeping real time, a stock ticker reeling of stock quotes, a graph which changes as the surfer enters numbers into a form, or any number of other whimsical or useful things, limited by the programmer's imagination and the Web surfer's browser and patience. Big Java applets may take a long time to download. Java was created by Sun Microsystems; to see examples of Java applets, go to Sun's Web site (**http://java.sun.com**).

Hypertext: The Heart of the Web

The World Wide Web, or simply the Web, is just another Internet tool. The other tools we mentioned are useful to get work done and some of them are even neat to play with, but the World Wide Web is positively exciting. There are two reasons for this: hypertext searching and the HyperText Markup Language, or HTML.

Hypertext is like computerized footnotes. If you have ever read through a footnoted book or magazine article, you have encountered an asterisk or a little number following a word in the text. If you look at the bottom of the page, or maybe at the end of the article, you'll find that little number or asterisk followed by a reference. That reference might be another book or magazine article that provides additional information about the topic being discussed. Well, not only can computers provide you with that reference, they can also take you directly to that reference, even if it is located on another computer entirely. You leap instantly through *hypertext* from one Web page located on this computer to another page located on that computer (another Web site) half-way around the world.

HTML is a set of standard notations that can be embedded in a string of text. When you view the text with an HTML reader, it interprets the HTML notations as formatting commands. Plain text becomes *formatted* text, complete with headlines, italics, centered paragraphs and, best of all, pictures. Recently, HTML has been enhanced even further so that a Web page can include audio clips, video clips, and embedded programs.

What's an Intranet?

An in*tra*net is an internal In*ter*net. Access to it is commonly restricted to company employees. In some organizations, it's cost effective to share company information in this way. The protocols and rules are the same as the Internet—the difference is that it's a closed network available only to employees connected to the network inside of the company. The information available on the intranet is company information, usually proprietary in nature.

A company can establish an intranet by installing the TCP/IP protocol, a Web server, and Web browsers. A Web server will publish documents and information in HTML format so that people with Web browsers can access this information. This Web server acts the same as the Web servers you connect with when you go out to the Internet and access information by typing in your company Web server address, or URL.

Being part of an intranet does not necessarily preclude having access to the Internet. You may have both.

Internet or Intranet?   Browser skills you learn here will apply to both a company intranet as well as the Internet.

In this lesson, you learned basic Internet and Web concepts and terminology. In the next lesson, you will learn to install Microsoft's Internet Explorer 4.0.

Installing Internet Explorer 4

In this lesson, you learn what Internet Explorer is, how to install the program, and what the program's new features are. If you know that you have Internet Explorer 4 installed on your computer, you may want to skip this lesson.

What Is Internet Explorer 4?

The Internet Explorer is Microsoft's Web browser. A browser allows you to send requests to Web servers and display pages sent by the Web server. With a browser, you can access a Web page on the Internet and follow any hypertext links contained in the page. Internet Explorer comes with Windows 95 and depending upon when Windows 95 was installed on your PC, you could have Internet Explorer version 4 or Internet Explorer version 3. In this section of the book, we discuss the Platform Preview version of Internet Explorer 4. If you have version 3, you can update to version 4 by following the installation instructions found here.

The use of the term *Explorer* by Microsoft can cause some confusion. If your computer came installed with Internet Explorer 4, you won't suffer from this confusion. If you are upgrading to Internet Explorer 4 (IE4), you need to be aware that IE4 will actually replace the Windows Explorer which you used to manage files (see Part I, Lesson 13, "Understanding the Windows Explorer"). Before IE4, both Internet Explorer version 3 and Windows Explorer came with Windows 95. Internet Explorer 3 was used to browse the Internet, and Windows Explorer was used to browse the contents of drives and file folders. When you install IE4, IE4 becomes the tool for both Internet exploration, and file and drive exploration.

Additional changes will occur when you install IE4. Desktop icons will turn into hypertext links. Even those that are not accessing the Internet become hypertext links so that they can be viewed using IE4, which is a Web browser.

Hypertext Links   The HTML code that tells the browser where the next page can be found. For more information on links, see Lesson 6, "Understanding Links."

Starting to Install Internet Explorer 4

You don't need to install or upgrade to IE4 if it came installed with your version of Windows 95. To determine which version of Internet Explorer is installed on your PC:

1. Start the Internet Explorer by clicking **The Internet** icon on your desktop.
2. Select **Help, About Internet Explorer**.
3. The version of Internet Explorer will appear in a dialog box. Click **OK** to close the dialog box. Exit Internet Explorer.

If you have IE3 or a previous version, the following installation instructions will assist you in installing and upgrading to IE4. To obtain a copy of IE4, visit the Microsoft Web site at **www.microsoft.com**. This site changes frequently, but you will find information on free downloads. Go to that section of the site and select Internet Explorer 4 for download. Follow the instructions on the screen to download the file.

TIP   **Close All Programs Before You Start the Installation**   It's a good idea to close all programs before beginning your installation. During the installation, Windows will reboot your PC. If you close programs before you start, you don't have to take a chance that you'll forget to save files later.

To install Internet Explorer 4:

1. Double-click the file you downloaded for **IE4** to start the active Setup Wizard (its name should be ie4setup.exe, or something similar). If you have IE4 supplied to you on a CD, run the Active Setup Wizard by inserting the Internet Explorer CD in your CD-ROM drive.
2. The installation program begins automatically, and the first Active Setup dialog box appears, displaying a Welcome message. Click **Next**.

3. A dialog box asks you to confirm your acceptance of the licensing agreement. To continue with the installation, you must accept the agreement.

4. Click **I Accept the Agreement**, and click **Next**.

5. The Active Setup dialog box now appears (see Figure 2.1). You must select one of the three installation options:

   - **Minimal** installs Internet Explorer 4 and multimedia enhancements.

   - **Standard** installs Internet Explorer 4, Outlook Express, Web Publishing Wizard and multimedia enhancements.

   - **Full** installs Internet Explorer 4, Microsoft Outlook Express, NetMeeting, Microsoft FrontPad, Microsoft NetShow, Microsoft Web Publishing Wizard, and multimedia enhancements.

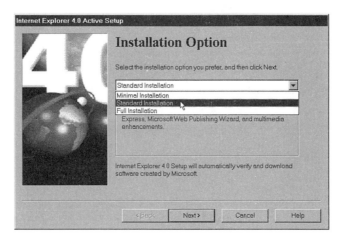

Figure 2.1 Selecting Installation options for IE4.

6. Choose your installation option. In this example, we chose **Standard Installation**. Click **Next**.

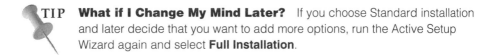

TIP **What if I Change My Mind Later?** If you choose Standard installation and later decide that you want to add more options, run the Active Setup Wizard again and select **Full Installation**.

7. The Web Integrated Desktop dialog box asks if you want to install the desktop integration features. Click **Yes**, and click **Next**.

8. The installation program will provide a default location for Internet Explorer 4. Click **Next** to confirm the default location (see Figure 2.2).

It will also tell you if it finds a previous version of Internet Explorer. You can choose to upgrade only newer items or reinstall all Internet Explorer components.

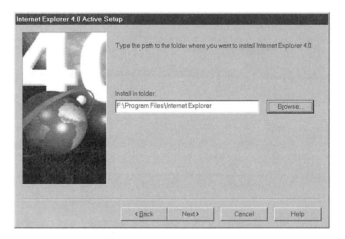

Figure 2.2   Active Setup Wizard provides a default installation directory.

9. A prompt appears, informing you that the program is preparing to set up the installation.

10. When the preparation is complete, a list of the items to be installed appears (see Figure 2.3). As each item is installed, the item is marked as complete. A progress meter at the bottom of the dialog box shows the percentage of the entire installation process that has been completed.

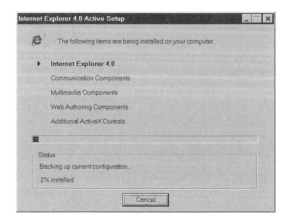

Figure 2.3   Setup installation list.

11. When the installation of the listed items is complete, you will see a message indicating that Setup has finished installing the selected components. Click **OK** to continue.

12. Windows will alert you to close open programs as shown in Figure 2.4. Windows will reboot your PC to complete the installation process. Click **OK** to close this dialog box and close any programs you have open.

Figure 2.4 Close all open programs.

13. The last installation dialog box tells you that the program is configuring your system for optimum performance, and asks you to wait. Upon completion of the performance configuration, your computer will be automatically restarted. When Windows restarts, you will be told that it is setting up some items:

- The Internet Explorer
- New tools
- Security features
- New Desktop settings

A final prompt appears, telling you that new Start menu items are being added, and the installation process is complete.

 TIP **Smart IE4 Updates** To make sure you have the latest version of Internet Explorer 4, run its update Program. Select **Start**, **Programs**, **Internet Explorer**, **Update Product**.

About the Active Desktop

Installing Internet Explorer 4 will make some significant changes to your Windows 95 Desktop, changing it to the Active Desktop shown in Figure 2.5. The Active Desktop is a shell, or outer layer, that gives you access to Internet Explorer's Web browsing capabilities.

You'll notice the following changes in your desktop, mouse, and taskbar:

- **Desktop background**   This has completely changed. Any wallpaper or pattern you were using is replaced by a solid black background containing the text Microsoft Internet Explorer 4.0.

- **Channel Guide**   The Channel Guide is a bar that allows you to quickly access premium Web sites simply by clicking buttons. It acts as a channel changer for the Web.

- **Taskbar changes**   Icons for Internet Explorer, Outlook Express Mail, View Channels, and Show Desktop now appear on your taskbar. Show Desktop returns you to the Windows desktop when you have application windows open.

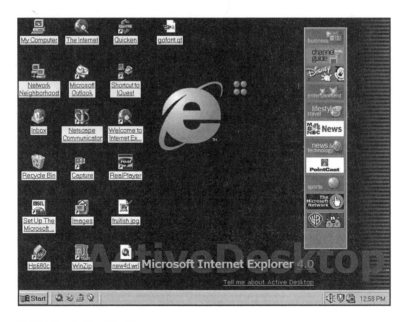

Figure 2.5   The Active Desktop.

- **Mouse changes**   As soon as you move your mouse and point to a desktop icon, you'll notice that it changes to a pointing hand (the same mouse pointer that is seen when you point to hypertext in a Web page). A single click activates the program that the icon represents. You no longer need to double-click desktop items.

TIP   **What If I Want My Old Wallpaper Back?**   You can revert to your favorite desktop background and remove the Channel Guide from your Desktop. Right-click anywhere on an empty portion of the Desktop, point to **Active Desktop**, and click **View as Web Page**. Your old wallpaper returns, but you maintain the other new features of the Active Desktop.

Uninstalling Active Desktop

If you want to completely remove the Active Desktop and all of its changes to your Windows 95 desktop, mouse, and taskbar, you have to uninstall that portion of Internet Explorer 4. Active Desktop is also referred to as the Internet Explorer Integration Shell. To uninstall the shell:

1. Close all programs.

2. From the Windows Control Panel, choose **Add/Remove Programs**.

3. From the list of programs, choose **Microsoft Internet Explorer 4.0**.

4. Click **Add/Remove**. The Add/Remove Internet Explorer 4.0 dialog box appears (see Figure 2.6).

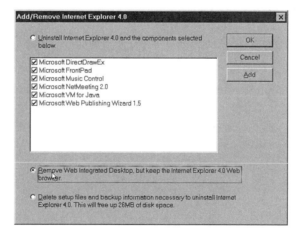

Figure 2.6   The Add/Remove Internet Explorer 4.0 dialog box.

5. Select **Remove Web Integrated Desktop, but Keep the Internet Explorer 4.0 Web Browser**. Click **OK**.

6. To refresh your Desktop, Windows automatically reboots. When Windows starts again, your standard Desktop is restored, and all traces of the Active Desktop and its features are gone.

For more information on the Control Panel, see Part II, Lesson 1, "Understanding the Control Panel."

Reinstalling the Internet Explorer 4 Integration Shell

If, after uninstalling the shell, you want to get it back, you can reverse the steps you took to remove it:

1. Establish your Internet connection.

2. From the Windows Control Panel, choose **Add/Remove Programs**.

3. Select **Microsoft Internet Explorer 4.0**.

4. Click **Add/Remove**. The Add/Remove Internet Explorer 4.0 dialog box appears.

5. Click **Add Web Integrated Desktop from Web site**, and click **OK**. Internet Explorer 4.0 starts and connects to Microsoft's Web site. The Internet Explorer 4.0 Active Setup dialog box appears.

6. Click **Yes** to allow Active Setup to determine which Internet Explorer components are installed. The Components Download page appears.

7. Place a check in the **Web Integrated Desktop** box, and click the **Next** button in the lower-right corner of the window. You are prompted to select a download site.

8. Select the desired download site and click **Install Now**. Internet Explorer downloads the required Desktop file and installs it on your computer.

9. When prompted to reboot your computer, click **Yes**. The Active Desktop and its mouse and taskbar features will return.

In this lesson, you learned about installing Internet Explorer 4, and the Active Desktop. Later in this book (Part V) you learn how to use and take full advantage of the Active Desktop. In this part of the book, you learn how to get connected to the Internet. In the next lesson, you'll learn to configure Windows 95 for Internet access.

Configuring for Internet Access

In this lesson, you'll learn to set up your Internet connection using the Connection Wizard. You also learn about Internet Service Providers.

What Is an Internet Service Provider?

The Internet is a network of computers, one talking to another, then another. In order to "jump on" the Internet, you must do so through a direct connection, or host computer. The Internet Service Provider (ISP) acts as that host computer. It is a company who provides the gateway for you to access the Internet.

ISPs come in different flavors. A commercial ISP supplies not only Internet access and mail services but the software necessary to navigate their own site. You must be a member of the commercial ISP to use their services. MSN, CompuServe, America Online, and Prodigy are examples of commercial ISPs. Commercial ISPs offer services above and beyond Internet access. For example, MSN offers services such as travel services, games, an online library, automobile research, and shopping and special interest chat groups. Each commercial ISP offers different services, and belonging to a commercial ISP is rather like belonging to an information "club."

The second kind of ISP is a local ISP who acts as your gateway to the Internet, and does not usually provide any services beyond Internet e-mail and Internet access. With a local ISP, you dial into their server, start your Web browser and surf the net. You can visit the same Web sites that you can through a commercial ISP, but the surfing, the searching and the gathering of information requires a little more effort on your part. You also don't get those extra club benefits such as travel services, games, and member chat groups.

You must pay for ISP services. A commercial service tends to be more expensive than a local ISP since they have many more services to offer. Reliability is key in selecting a service provider. Check your local newspaper and with your friends to find local ISPs and call for pricing.

If you want to see what the commercial sites have to offer, each of them gives a free trial period. Software for commercial sites undoubtedly came loaded on your computer. Try the trial memberships to see which ISP best suits your interests. If you need commercial ISP software, call 800 information to obtain a toll free number or check your local Yellow Pages for the commercial ISP and call them to request their software. The Connection Wizard, described below, also offers a listing of local ISPs.

Using the Connection Wizard

Before you can connect to the Internet, you must configure your systems' Internet connection settings. Using the Connection Wizard, you can choose from one of three options for connection settings. Those options will:

- Assist you in selecting and signing up for an Internet Service Provider and configure your setup for connection to that provider.
- Assist you in connecting to your existing Internet account or Local Area Network.

 TIP   **Check with Your System Administrator First!**   If you are at work, connected to a LAN your Internet connection has probably been configured by your system administrator. Do not set up an Internet connection without consulting your system administrator.

- Assist you if you already have a connection to the Internet and do not want to change it. For example, if you are using dial-up networking to connect to an ISP, if you don't select this option the connection Wizard will run each time you select Internet Explorer 4.

The first two choices above are covered here in this lesson. Option three is for experienced Internet users who use multiple browsers or ISPs. For more information on dial-up networking, see Part III, "Using Windows 95 on a Network;" Lesson 7 "Connecting to an Internet Service Provider."

Choosing an ISP

If you don't have an ISP, you can use the Connection Wizard to help you locate a service provider and open a new Internet account. To do this:

1. Click **Start, Programs, Internet Explorer, Connection Wizard**.

2. The Get Connected dialog box appears. This box explains the purpose of the Connection Wizard (as shown in Figure 3.1). Click **Next**.

Figure 3.1 The Connection Wizard's Get Connected dial box helps you with Internet connection.

3. The Startup Options dialog box appears (see Figure 3.2). Click **I Want To Choose An Internet Service Provider and Set Up A New Internet Account**. Click **Next**.

4. The Begin Automatic Setup dialog box appears explaining the process you have chosen. It suggests that you have your Windows setup disks available in the case you need them during the setup process. After you read this dialog box, click **Next**.

5. The Location Information dialog box appears. Fill in your area code and the first three digits of your phone number in the appropriate boxes. Click **Next**.

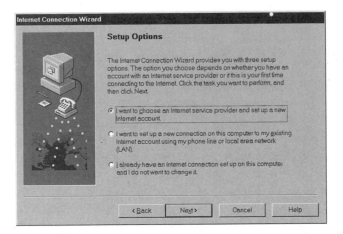

Figure 3.2   Enter Setup Options for Internet connection.

6. The Wizard now dials an 800 number which connects to the Microsoft Internet Referral server and downloads a list of Internet Service Providers for your location. This may take a few minutes. The list will appear on your screen. This list is comprised of service providers that offer Internet access in your area and for your operating systems. Information about each ISP is provided. You can select an ISP and sign up for a new Internet account from this list.

Connecting to an ISP

If you have an existing Internet account with an ISP (as you identified in step 6, above) or through a Local Area Network, you can use the Connection Wizard to set up a phone line connection to your ISP or a Internet connection through your LAN.

TIP   **Before You Begin!**   You'll need to know the following information before you connect to your ISP. Your ISP can provide you with all of the information you will need to connect to them. This may include, but is not limited to, the following:

ISP Server	Gateway
IP Address	E-Mail Pop Server
DNS Configuration	New NNTP server

If you are on a LAN, you should not use the Connection Wizard without first checking with your system administrator. If you want to create a connection to your existing ISP:

1. Click the **Start** button, **Programs**, **Internet Explorer**, **Connection Wizard**.

2. The Get Connected dialog box appears. This box explains the purpose of the Connection Wizard (refer to Figure 3.1). Click **Next**.

TIP **This Takes Time!** Configuring the Connection Wizard for the first time is a long process. You may need the name of your ISP server and the phone number for your ISP. At any time during the Wizard, you can click the **Back** button to return to previous screens, or click **Cancel** to end the configuration process. If you choose to Cancel, you can run the Wizard again at any time.

3. The Setup Options dialog box appears (refer to Figure 3.2). Choose **I Want To Set Up a New Connection On This Computer To My Existing Internet Account Using My Phone Line or Local Area Network (LAN)**.

4. Click **Next**.

5. In the Set Up Your Internet Connection dialog box, select **Connect Using My Phone Line** (see Figure 3.3). Click **Next**.

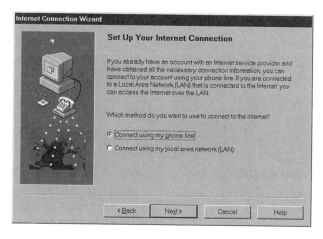

Figure 3.3 Connecting using a phone line.

6. The Dial-Up Connection dialog box appears. Choose between an existing dial-up connection or a new connection as shown in Figure 3.4. If you have used dial-up networking, you may see an existing connection available. For a new connection, click **Create A New Dial-Up Connection** and then click **Next**.

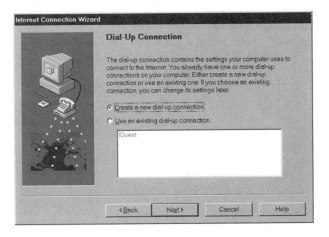

Figure 3.4   Creating a new dial-up connection.

7. The Phone Number dialog box appears. Fill in the **Area Code** and **Telephone Number** fields, providing the access number for your ISP. Confirm that the **Country Name** and **Code** are correct; if not change them. Do not select **Dial Using Area Code** and **Country Code** unless you are making a long distance call. Click **Next**.

8. The User Name and Password dialog box appears. Fill in the **User Name** field with your user name as provided by your ISP, and your Password for accessing your ISP. For security purposes (in case someone is looking over your shoulder) the password will appear in asterisks. Click **Next**.

9. The Advanced Setting dialog box appears. Select **No** so that the advanced settings are not changed. Unless you are instructed by your ISP, you need not change the default settings. Click **Next**.

10. The Dial Up Connection Name dialog box appears. Fill in a **Connection Name**, such as your Internet Service Provider's name. Click **Next**.

11. The Set Up Your Internet Mail Account dialog box appears. In order to use Internet mail, you must have an Internet Mail account with your ISP. Most ISPs provide Internet Mail and we are assuming that you want to select **Yes** on this screen. If you do not have Internet Mail, click **No** and skip to step 19. Click **Next**.

12. The Internet Mail Account Dialog box appears. Select **Use an Existing Internet Mail Account** if you already have one, otherwise, choose **Create A New Internet Mail Account**. Click **Next**.

13. In the Internet Mail Display Name dialog box, enter your name as you want it to appear in the "From" field of outgoing messages. Click **Next**.

14. In the E-mail Address dialog box, enter the addressed assigned to you by your Internet Service Provider, such as Dburke@aol.com. Click **Next**.

15. In the E-mail Server Addresses dialog box, select the type of mail server used by your ISP—the default is POP3. If you are unsure, accept the default. You can call your ISP if your Internet mail is not working and ask if they are POP3 or IMAP servers. In the Incoming Mail Server and Outgoing Mail Server boxes, enter the name of your POP3 or IMAP server and SMTP server. You can get this information from your ISP.

16. The Internet Mail Logon dialog box appears. Select **Log On Using** and enter your E-mail Account as provided by your ISP and your Password. If your ISP requires you to use Secure Password Authentication to access your e-mail account, then select **Log On Using Secure Password Authentication**. Click **Next**.

17. In the Friendly Name dialog box, enter a name for your **Internet mail account**. This can be the name of your ISP, or any descriptive name you would like it to be such as "Dorothy's Mail." Click **Next**.

18. The Set Up Your Internet News Account dialog box appears. You must have an account with an ISP to use this service. If you have a News Account, you can provide the information here. If you do not have a News account, click **No** to continue. Lesson 12 describes Internet News Accounts and teaches you how to use Outlook Express to connect to your News Account. In this example, we select **No**, then click **Next**.

19. In the Setup Your Internet Directory Service dialog box, click **No**, and then click **Next**. An Internet Directory Service provides you with an address book you can use to find people on the Internet or on a company intranet.

20. The Complete Configuration dialog box appears indicating that you have successfully completed the configuration process. Click **Finish** to continue.

TIP   **AutoDial**   To have Internet Explorer automatically establish your Internet connection when you run IE4, open Internet Explorers' **View** menu, select **Options**, and click the **Connection** tab. Select **Connect to the Internet Using a Modem**, and click the **Settings** button. Select your ISP, and enter my additional connection preferences. Click **OK**.

In this lesson, you learned to set up your Internet connection to work with Internet Explorer 4, sign up with an ISP or online service, and about commercial and local ISPs. In the next lesson, you'll learn to navigate the Internet Explorer window.

Understanding the IE4 Window

In this lesson, you'll learn about how to use the new Web browsing features of Internet Explorer 4, and how to move around within the window.

Starting Internet Explorer 4

Before running Internet Explorer, establish your Internet connection. Run My Computer, click the **Dial-Up Networking** icon, and click the icon you created for connecting to your ISP. Start Internet Explorer 4 by clicking **The Internet** icon located on your desktop if you have one or by clicking the **Launch Internet Explorer Browser** icon located on your taskbar.

When you start IE4, the program looks to see if you are connected to the Internet and if you are, opens your start page. Depending on your setup, the Internet connection process and start page displayed may vary as follows:

If you connect through a Local Area Network, you may see your company's home page, your ISP home page or a start page you designate as described in Lesson 9, "Customizing Internet Explorer 4."

If you connect to your company Intranet, you may see your company's intranet home page. It is possible that you have access to a company intranet but not the Internet. If you have any questions about your intranet or Internet access, contact your system administrator.

If you connect by dialing into an ISP, you will first see the Connect To dialog box as described later in this lesson.

If you have dialed into your ISP before you start IE4, the IE4 window will open and display your start page.

Start Page   The first page you see when you open IE4 is your Start page. The default Start page depends upon the way you set up IE4 in Lesson 3, "Configuring for Internet Access." It is either the home page of your ISP, a Microsoft site, or if you are on an Intranet, your company's intranet home page.

Home Page   The "cover page" at an Internet or intranet site is called the site's home page. This is the first page that displays when you visit a site. The home page of a site usually contains a company logo and list of information available at the site.

You can also start IE4 offline, that is, without a connection to the Internet or an intranet. Do this by clicking the **Stay Offline** button when the **Connect To** dialog box appears.

Dialing into an ISP

Assuming that you have configured a Dial-Up Network connection as described in Lesson 3, you can connect to the Internet through your ISP:

1. Click **The Internet** icon on your desktop. If you do not have Active Desktop running, double-click The Internet icon.

2. When the Connect To dialog box appears, fill in the information and click **Connect** to dial into your ISP as shown in Figure 4.1.

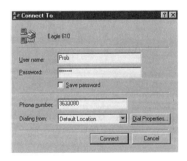

Figure 4.1   Filling in Connect information.

3. Windows will now dial into your ISP. Figure 4.2 shows the dialing dialog box.

Figure 4.2 Dialing into an ISP.

4. Depending upon your ISP, you may see a Post Dial Terminal window as shown in Figure 4.3. Type your name and ID and press the **F7** key to continue.

Figure 4.3 Post dial terminal window.

5. After your name and password have been verified by your ISP server, the Connected To dialog box will appear and minimize to the taskbar. The IE4 program window will open displaying your start page.

 TIP **Don't Forget to Hang Up!** The Connected To dialog box stays minimized on your taskbar while you are working in the IE4 window. When you are finished exploring the Internet and exit IE4, remember to maximize this dialog box and click **Disconnect** to hang up.

Figure 4.4 The Connected To dialog box.

6. You are now connected to the Internet and your start page is displayed as shown in Figure 4.5.

Navigating the IE4 Window

The Internet Explorer Window, like all Microsoft windows, contains a title bar, minimize button, maximize/restore button, close button, a menu bar, toolbar and a status bar as shown in Figure 4.5.

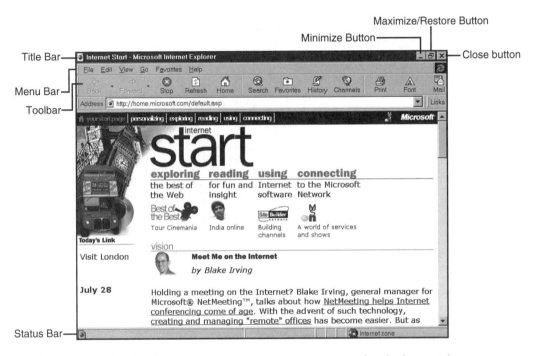

Figure 4.5   Your Start page displays when you are connected to the Internet.

The IE4 Menu Bar

The menu bar contains the features and functions of the program, and can be accessed by clicking once on the menu item or using hotkeys such as Alt+F. A drop-down menu will appear showing options within that category. All of the functions available in this program are found in the menu and the menu is context-sensitive; that is, items will be grayed out or unavailable depending upon the view and function you are performing while in IE4. If you take a moment to read the menu options by clicking each item in the menu bar, it will help you to become familiar with the features of IE4.

The IE4 Toolbar

Like all Windows products and programs, the IE4 toolbar represents shortcuts for menu commands. You can click an icon in the toolbar in lieu of selecting a menu item. Not every menu item is represented on the toolbar.

Displaying the toolbar is an option. If your toolbar is not displayed as shown in Figure 4.5, choose **View**, **Toolbar** and make sure there are check marks next to **Standard Button**, **Address Bar**, **Links**, and **Text Labels**. Use the same commands when you want to hide the toolbar.

As you point with your mouse to each icon on the toolbar, the icon displays in color and a frame appears around the icon, giving it a 3-D effect.

Table 5.1 lists each icon found on the Internet Explorer toolbar and gives a brief explanation of each icon.

Table 4.1   Internet Explorer Toolbar Icons

Tool	Name	Description	Keyboard shortcut (Hotkeys)
Back	Back	Returns you to a previously visited Web page.	Backspace
Forward	Forward	Moves forward to a Web page (only if you have gone back to a previous page).	Shift+Backspace
Stop	Stop	Stops action in progress. Stops a Web page from loading.	ESC
Refresh	Refresh	Reloads the current document.	F5
Home	Home	Returns you to your start page.	None available
Search	Search	Displays the Search Bar with tools for searching the Web.	None available

continues

Table 4.1 Continued

Tool	Name	Description	Keyboard shortcut (Hotkeys)
Favorites	Favorites	Displays a list of Web pages that you have marked as favorites.	Alt+A
History	History	Displays a list of pages you have recently visited.	None available
Channels	Channels	Displays buttons for accessing premium Web sites.	None available
Print	Print	Prints the current page.	Ctrl+P
Font	Font	Allows you to select a default font. Some Web pages will override the default font you select.	Alt+V, N
Mail	Mail	Displays the Mail menu for sending and reading messages..,	Alt+G, M
Edit	Edit	Starts Microsoft FrontPad program, where you can edit a Web page.	None available

TIP **Hidden Edit Button** If you don't see the Edit button, select **View**, **Toolbar**, **Text Labels**. This turns off the button names, providing more room for displaying buttons.

The second line of the toolbar contains an address line and a Links option as shown in Figure 4.6. To learn more about addresses, see Lesson 5, "Understanding a Web Site." To see how to customize your toolbar, see Lesson 9, "Customizing Internet Explorer 4."

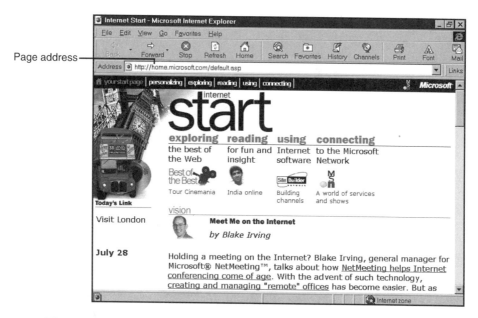

Page address

Figure 4.6   The address of the current Web page.

Double-Click **Links** on the toolbar to display the Links Bar. The Links bar opens preselected Web pages. These pages and links can be reconfigured by you to point to your frequently visited sites (see Lesson 9, "Customizing Internet Explorer 4"). Figure 4.7 shows the Links Bar. To return to the Address Bar, double-click **Links** again.

Navigating a Document

Although you may not yet know much about visiting Web sites (see Lesson 5, "Understanding a Web Site") you can still move around the document displayed in the IE4 window. Use the scrollbar to move up and down a page displayed in IE4, or use the shortcut keystrokes described in Table 4.2

Table 4.2   Keyboard Shortcuts for Moving Around a Document

Press	To
↑	Scroll up a document
↓	Scroll down a document

continues

Table 4.2   Continued

Press	To
Page Up	Move one screen up the document
Page Down	Move one screen down the document
Home	Move to beginning of document
End	Move to end of a document
Tab	Move one cell or field to the right in a form or table.

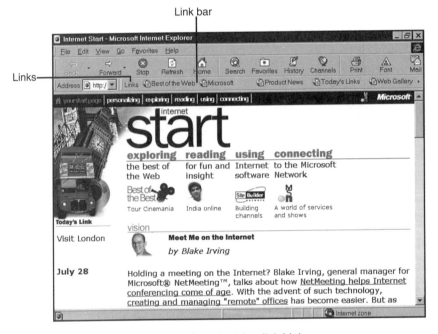

Figure 4.7   To display the Links Bar, double-click Links.

In this lesson, you learned how to start IE4, dial into an ISP, and navigate in IE4. In the next lesson, you'll visit some Web sites.

Understanding
a Web Site

*In this lesson, you'll visit some Web sites. You also learn about
reading URLs and you'll view your Web pages in the
InterNotes Web Navigator database.*

Reading URLs

Every file on every computer on the Internet has an address at which it can be
located. All Internet computers use something called Uniform Resource Loca-
tors, or URLs, to specify the locations of files. A URL looks something like this:

   http://www.mcp.com/que/filename

The first part of the URL, the part that precedes the colon (:), indicates the type
of resource being described. In the example, the resource type, http, tells you the
document is a Web page and tells the computers to use the HyperText Transfer
Protocol to transfer the file to your computer. The double slash indicating the
name of the computer follows. The computer name consists of its host name, in
this case "World Wide Web," the domain it is in, in the example "mcp," and its
zone, in this case "com," meaning that Que is a commercial enterprise. After the
computer name is the location and name of the file on the computer. It is separated from the computer name by a single slash. The file may be located in the
root directory or a subdirectory. The names of the directories precede the file
name and are separated from each other and the file name by single forward
slashes. Look at this address again:

   Protocol//name of computer and zone/directory/filename

Get it? When you want to tell your computer to locate a file, you can tell your
computer the file's URL by typing it in manually. Or the URL may be embedded

in the image on your screen, so if you click a highlighted word, your browser reads "behind" that word a URL for another file or page, and goes and retrieves that resource.

URLs seem a little backwards because you read them from right to left. The rightmost location is the filename, then the directory, then the zone, name of computer, and finally the protocol. Now, you won't always know the filename (which is the name of the page) you are looking for, so it's not unusual to visit a site by typing the protocol and the name and zone of the computer:

> http://www.mcp.com

The last (or, first if you read from right to left) piece of information, the zone, can be interpreted by you. There are three-letter zones and two-letter zones. Two-letter zones indicate a country and are used widely outside of the United States. Three-letter zones indicate a zone *type* such as "com" for commercial and are used mostly within the United States. Table 5.1 lists some three-letter zones. Table 5.2 lists some two-letter zones.

Table 5.1 Partial Listing of Three-Letter Zones

Zone	Meaning
com	Commercial establishments
edu	Educational institutions (schools, colleges)
gov	Government agencies and departments
int	International organizations
mil	Military sites
net	Networking organizations
org	Professional organizations

Table 5.2 Partial Listing of Two-Letter Zones

Zone	Meaning
au	Australia
ca	Canada
fr	France
ie	Ireland

Zone	Meaning
il	Israel
jp	Japan
nl	Netherlands
tw	Taiwan
uk	United Kingdom
us	United States

Visiting a Web Site

Okay, you're ready to take your first visit to a Web site other than your start page. For this lesson, you'll step through some basic and easy steps. In later lessons, you'll learn more about Web sites. The objective here is for you to start.

You need to have IE4 open and you need to be connected to the Internet to visit a Web site. Then:

1. Place your cursor in the **Address** field on the toolbar. Click once, and the current address (which is probably your start page) will be highlighted. Type the URL for the site you wish to visit, such as **www.mcp.com/que**. (You don't need to type the protocol—HTTP—IE4 will fill that in for you.) This is the URL for the Que Books division of the Macmillan Publishing Company. Your new text will replace the existing text.

 TIP   **Address Correctly!**   When typing addresses, it's important to use the exact space, periods, symbols and capitalization you see in the examples. Typing the address incorrectly could result in failure to locate the Web site you are seeking.

3. Press the **Enter** key. The Status bar will indicate the status of your search. It may say Finding site: www.mcp.com, then Opening page: www.mcp.com/que, then Done. When the status bar shows Done the Web page at your requested site is finished loading.

4. You should now see the Home Page for QUE Books, if you used the URL in step 2. It's a big home page, and doesn't fit within your screen, so use the scroll bars or **Page Up** or **Page Down** to examine this page.

Figure 5.1   Que's Home Page at www.mcp.com/que.

Notice the blue text on this page? This is an example of *hypertext* that was discussed in Lesson 1. If you place your mouse on hypertext, you'll see your cursor change from a pointer to a hand and the address of the linked page will display in a pop-up menu and on the status bar. Try it! Hold your mouse over hypertext.

After you've moved around a few pages, leave this Web site and go to another. You might want to go to the solar system at **nssdc.gsfc.nasa.gov/imgcat/html/ mission_page/ST_voyager_1_page1.html**. There you can see photos of Saturn as found in Figure 5.2.

You'll also notice that if you hold your mouse over the graphics on this page, your cursor will change from a pointer to a hand and the linked URL address will display. It's very likely that the page you are seeing will differ slightly than the one you see in Figure 5.2. Web pages change all the time. New information is added and designs are be updated; the links, text and information will be different. But you can continue this little surf on your own. Click underlined text and navigators to move around the site.

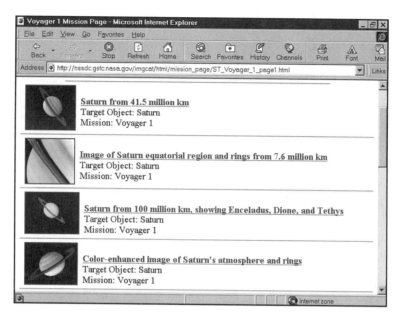

Figure 5.2   Learning about Saturn.

After you've roamed around Saturn a little, you might want to stop by NASA's Spacelink site for educators, which includes the shuttle launch schedule at **http://spacelink.nasa.gov**. Figure 5.3 shows Spacelink's Home Page and also displays how your cursor will appear when you hold the pointer over a link.

In the above examples, you visited one commercial and two government Web sites, identified as such by their three-letter zones; .com and .gov respectively.

Understanding Caching

A *cache* is a storage bin (or directory). *Caching* is to send files to the storage bin (or directory). When you use IE4, pages that you visit are cached and stored in the C:\Windows\Temporary Internet Folder. This enables you to use the back and forward buttons on the toolbar, to quickly load the graphics of pages you have visited previously, and to view pages offline when you are not connected to the Internet.

Caching helps to speed up Web page access. For example, if you visit a Web page with lots of graphics, the next time you visit the Web site you won't have to wait for all of the graphics to load again. IE4 finds the graphics files (files with

.GIF extensions) stored in your Internet Temporary Files folder and loads the Web page much faster.

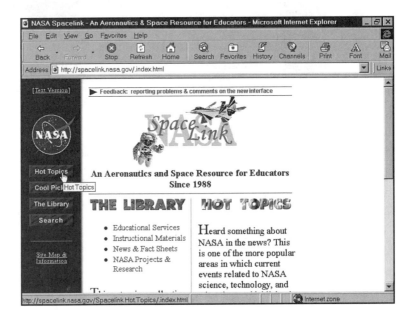

Figure 5.3   Visiting Spacelink at spacelink.nasa.gov.

IE4 has settings in which you can determine how much of your total hard drive space should be allocated for storing temporary, or cached, files. See Lesson 9, "Customizing Internet Explorer 4," for more information on controlling cache settings.

Also, be aware that caching can be somewhat of a problem when you are visiting sites that use real-time images. Real-time means that the images are changing constantly and frequently, to give you the most current image. If you have a stored image in your cache directory, you'll be viewing an out-of-date image. To see the most current information and override what is cached, click the **Refresh** button on the toolbar.

In this lesson, you learned how to read URLs and about caching. You also visited some Web sites. In the next lesson, you learn all about Internet Links.

Understanding Links

In this lesson, you will learn about the different types of Internet links and how they function.

Types of Links

Links are embedded pointers to other Web pages. They appear as colored text, pictures, or buttons. When you use your mouse to point to a link, your pointer cursor might turn into the image of a hand and a pop-up box will appear containing the URL of the Web page. When you click a link, IE4 sends a request for the page that link points to.

Several kinds of links are used on the Web, and they act as pointers to help you reach your destination. It would be impossible for you to know the URL of every Web page you want to visit. So, Web page designers create links that contain URLs. Point and click, point and click… that's all you really need to do when you're moving around a Web site. The different types of links you might see are hypertext, graphics, gopher, ftp, and image maps.

TIP **How Can I Tell if it's a Link?** It may not be as important to know what *kind* of link you're using, as long as you know it's a link. Let us give you a hand here. The secret? If you hold your pointer on something, and it changes from a pointer to a hand, it's a link!

Graphic Links

A graphics link is simply a picture with an embedded pointer (see Figure 6.1). When you double-click the picture, your computer sends out a request for the page or object named in the pointer.

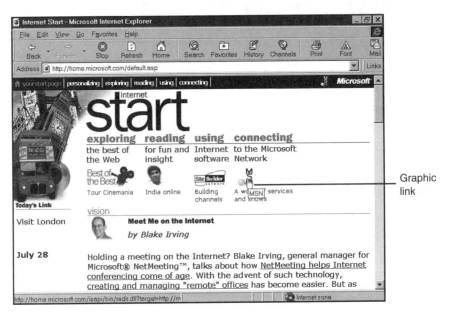

Figure 6.1   A graphics link is a picture with an embedded pointer.

Gopher Links

A Gopher link is a link to a Gopher menu. In Lesson 1, we talked about Gopher servers. Gopher servers serve up Gopher menus, and gopher links point to Gopher menus. You can recognize a gopher link because its URL begins with "gopher:". To see the URL embedded in any link, point at it and a pop-up box will appear containing the URL (see Figure 6.2).

FTP Links

A File Transfer Protocol (FTP) link is a link to an FTP server. You can recognize an FTP link because its URL begins with "ftp:" (see Figure 6.3).

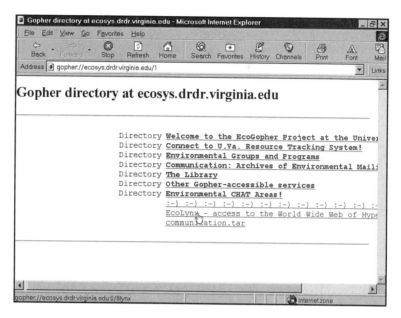

Figure 6.2 A gopher link always starts with *gopher://*

Mailto Links

A mailto link pops up a pre-addressed mail memo form when you click it (see Figure 6.4). Mailto links begin with "mailto:". When you click a mailto link, a mail memo form opens. The To: field in your mail memo form will automatically fill in the Internet address that was contained in the mailto link. Pretty handy stuff. It's very helpful and assures that you won't make any typing errors when typing the address.

Hypertext Links

If you completed Lesson 5, you've seen how hypertext looks and what it does. You've also seen that hypertext is usually underlined, and often in a different color so that it stands out and makes it clear to you that clicking on that text will take you to a different page or site. If you return or go back a page after you have visited a linked page, the hypertext will appear in a different color on your screen. This allows you to easily see where you've been.

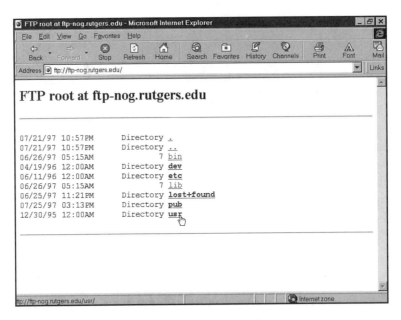

Figure 6.3 File Transfer Protocol links begin with FTP.

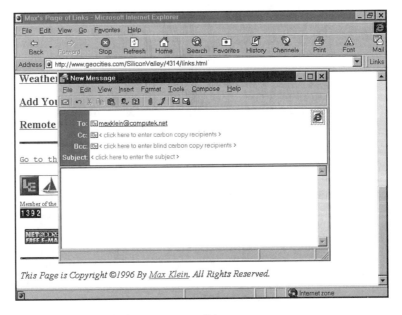

Figure 6.4 A Mailto: link brings up a e-mail form.

Hypertext originally involved just text. Now it can involve pictures, programs, and video or sound clips. To put it simply, hypertext is something that includes an embedded link to something else.

Image Maps

An image map is a single, usually large and colorful picture that has different portions of it mapped to different pointers. That is, one part of the picture will hold a pointer to Web page x, another part will hold a pointer to Web page y, and a third will hold a pointer to Web page z. You retrieve different pages depending on what part of the picture you click. It's different than graphics links, because many links are contained within one image.

Figure 6.5 shows an image map. The image map is one graphic, but it contains many embedded links.

Figure 6.5 An image map contains many embedded links.

In this lesson, you learned about some different types of Internet links including image maps and mailto: links. In the next lesson, you learn how to search the Internet.

Web, Document, and Site Searching

In this lesson, you learn the types of searches you can perform with Internet Explorer 4. You also learn about search engines and how you can search the Web, search a document, or search a Web site.

Understanding Searches

There are several kinds of searches you can perform in Internet Explorer 4. You can search the Web, you can search a Web site and you can search for text on a Web page.

Searching the Web

You search the Web when you want to find public information on, for example, "Elvis." You search the Web with the aide of a *search tool* (also referred to as a *search engine*). A search tool or engine is a program that searches the Web for a keyword or phrase you supply in your query. Many search engines are actual Web sites themselves. Internet Explorer makes it easy to use a search tool by providing a list of some of the more popular search engines, such as Yahoo, Infoseek, and Lycos. When you want to search the Web, you create a *query* (or search string), select the search engine to use, and tell IE4 to search.

The results of your search are returned to you in a Web page, as a list of list of links pointing to those sites with the most *hits* at the top of the list.

TERM **Hit** A match between your search parameters and information found on a home page on the Internet. The more specific your search parameters, the smaller number of "hits" you will find.

If you searched for "Elvis" you might see an awfully long list of links—perhaps thousands, certainly hundreds, and probably more than you need. When you search for information, create a search string that will return the links you really want. For example, if you search for "Elvis Presley," you are less likely to find Elvis Costello in your search results. And searching for "Elvis AND Sands AND Las Vegas AND October 1996" is bound to return even fewer hits! Of course, there might be an Elvis sightings Web page that covered his '96 concert, we're not sure.

Searching a Web Site

Many Web sites use search engine programs that index their own information, allowing you to search within the site itself. You can well imagine the amount of information that can be found at the Microsoft site, for example. When you visit the Microsoft site (**www.microsoft.com**) you can search the site to find information on Internet Explorer, for example. Not all Web sites are indexed, or searchable, but you will find the larger sites provide search capabilities. Search engines within a Web site work much like search engines that search the Web. You create a query, click a Search button and the results are returned to you as a list of hypertext, linking to the areas at the site that match your query. Although Web sites and search engines vary, searching a Web site is very similar to searching the Web as described later in this lesson.

Searching a Web Page

Web pages can be as long as several printed pages. Therefore, in addition to searching the Web for information, you can search the contents of a Web page for text. Searching within a Web page does not, however, return a list of links. Rather, this type of search works just like using a "Find" command in a word processing program and when you search for a word or string of words, IE4 will take you to the first occurrence it finds on that page.

Creating a Web Search

There are many search engines available on the Web. Search engines maintain indices of the contents of Web pages. Different search engines maintain different Web site information and it's possible that your search results using Yahoo may be different than your search results using Excite. As you work with search engines, you may find one that you prefer one over another.

To create a Web search:

1. Click the **Search** icon on the toolbar.
2. The IE4 screen will split into frames. The left frame displays the Search Bar.
3. Open the select provider drop-down list, and select the search tool you want to use. The Search Bar displays a search text box to enter your search string (see Figure 7.1.)
4. Enter your search criteria and click the **Search** or **Submit** button to begin your search.

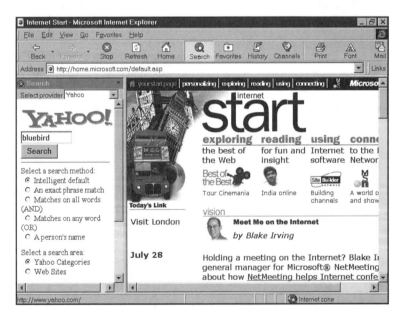

Figure 7.1   Entering search criteria.

5. Your search results appear in the left frame as shown in Figure 7.2 below your search criteria. Search results are hypertext. Scroll through the results until you find a document you would like to view and click the hypertext.

6. When you are finished with your search, click the **Search** button on the toolbar to close the search frame.

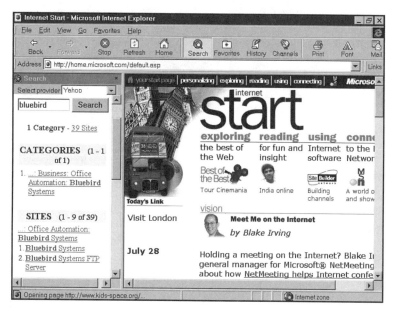

Figure 7.2 Yahoo results returned 39 hits.

 TIP **Want to Search Again?** To clear a search, or to search for something different, scroll to the bottom of the Search Bar, enter your new search text, and click **Search** or **Submit**.

Depending upon the search tool you select, search results will vary. Some search tools return categories, as Yahoo shows in Figure 7.2, as well as sites. Clicking a category reveals more sites. The search results will also tell you how many "hits" or Web sites it found that contain your search string. Remember, search results will vary from search tool to search tool. Figure 7.3 shows the results of the same search used in Figure 7.2 (bluebird). This time we searched using Lycos.

Figure 7.3   Same search, different results using a different search tool.

TIP   **Start, Find**   The **Start**, **Find** menu contain additional search options, including On the Internet and People. **On the Internet** displays the search page. **People** displays a list of tools for tracking down people on the Internet.

Working in a Search Window

The frame surrounding the search tool and its results may be a little confining for you. You can size the frame by pointing to its right border. When your pointer turns to a sizing pointer, grab the border and pull it to the right.

To close the search frame, click the **Search** button in the toolbar.

If you prefer, you can open a new window for performing your search. To open a window for your search:

1. Click the **Search** button on the toolbar.

2. In the search frame, right click the word **Search** located at the top of the search frame.

3. From the pop-up menu, select **Open in Window.**

4. You now have a second IE4 window open and the search information appears as shown in Figure 7.4.

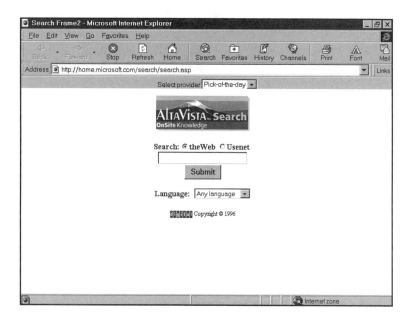

Figure 7.4 Opening Search in its own window.

CAUTION

Don't Forget to Close the Windows! Pay close attention to the number of windows you open in IE4! Unlike other programs, note the absence of the word "Window" on the menu. When you open a second window in IE4, you are actually opening a second session of the software. Two minimized program icons will appear on your task bar. Avoid opening too many sessions as this can wreak havoc on your PC, depending upon your computer's memory.

Following Search Results

Once you have completed a search and see the search results listed on your screen, simply click the hypertext links to explore Web pages that contain your search string. When you click a link in the Search Bar, the right frame displays the contents of the selected page. The contents of the Search Bar remain the same.

As stated previously, different search engines will not only return different results, their search results page can respond differently. For example, Figure 7.5 displays search results from Yahoo when searching for "bluebird". Holding the pointer over hypertext in this screen, a pop-up box appears showing the URL of the linked page.

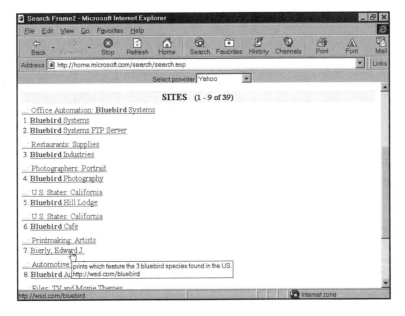

Figure 7.5 Yahoo displays URLs in search results.

Figure 7.6 displays search results from Infoseek. Holding the pointer over hypertext here, a pop-up box appears displaying actual text found on the linked page.

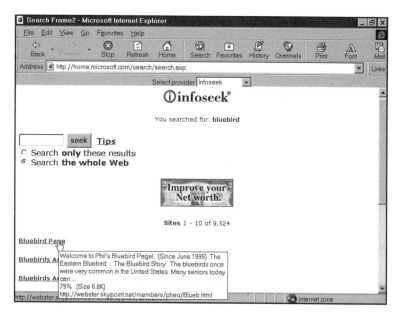

Figure 7.6 Infoseek displays text from Web pages.

Visiting a Search Engine Site

Another way to conduct a search is to visit a search engine site directly. For example, enter **www.yahoo.com** in the address on your toolbar, and you will find yourself at the Yahoo site. To obtain addresses of search engine sites, search the Web for "search engines" or search by the individual search engine name, such as "excite."

Searching for Text On a Web Page

To search the contents of a Web page, first open the page you want to search, and then:

1. Select **Edit, Find (On This Page)** or press **Ctrl+F**.

2. The Find dialog box appears (see Figure 7.7). Type the text you want to find in the **Find What** box.

3. If you want exact matches only, check the **Match Whole Word Only** box. Selecting this option, IE4 would not return occurrences of your word when found within a larger word. For example, "Nesting" will not be found if the search word is "Nest".

4. If you want IE4 to find and match the upper- and lowercase of your word, check the **Match Case** box.

5. Select **Direction Up** or **Down** to search toward the beginning or the end of the document.

6. Click **Find Next**. IE4 will move to the first occurrence of the word in your document. The Find dialog box remains open. To see the next occurrence, click **Find Next** again. If no match was found for your search, a message box appears indicating that IE4 has finished searching the document.

7. When you are finished searching, click **Cancel** to close the dialog box.

Figure 7.7   Searching for text on a Web page.

In this lesson, you learned the types of searches you can perform with Internet Explorer 4. You also learned the various methods of performing those searches.

In the next lesson, you learn more about working with Web pages.

Working with Web Pages

In this lesson, you learn how to use History to view Web pages you have visited. You also learn how to change the display of Web pages and use the Favorites folder.

Using History

IE4 keeps a history of the Web pages you visit. You can return to previously viewed Web pages by pressing the **Back** icon on the toolbar. This will display Web pages in the reverse order that you viewed them. If you need to move back several pages, click the arrow to the right of the Back button, and select the desired page.

You can also view pages you have already visited by selecting them from the File menu:

1. Select **File** from the menu.

2. In the history list of documents found at the bottom of the File menu, select the document you want to view, as shown in Figure 8.1

The File menu list is emptied when you quit Internet Explorer.

Figure 8.1 History List of Documents found on the File menu.

TIP **Don't Forget the Address list** You can also visit the pages from your current Internet session by clicking the drop-down **Address** list on the toolbar.

Although the history list is emptied from the File menu, an entire history of links to all Web pages you have viewed in all sessions is kept in a folder called History located in your C:\Windows directory.

To view the contents of your history folder:

1. Click the **History** button in the toolbar. The History Bar appears in the left frame.

2. Click the link for the day or week you visited the page. A list of folders for all the sites you visited appears. Each folder contains a list of pages you visited at that Web site.

3. Click the folder for the desired Web site. See Figure 8.2.

4. Click the page you want to view. The contents of the selected page appears in the right frame.

You can determine how many days files will stay in your history folder (the default setting is 20 days) and you can clear your history folder at any time.

To set number of days or clear the history:

1. Select **View**, **Options** from the menu. The Options Dialog Box appears with the General tab selected.

2. In the History section, click **Clear History** to empty the History folder.

3. To set the number of days that links will stay in your history folder, change the number in the **Number of Days to Keep Pages in History** field.

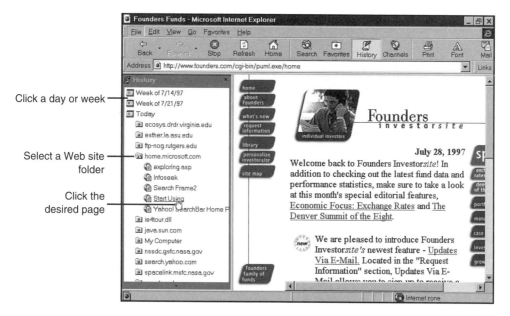

Click a day or week

Select a Web site folder

Click the desired page

Figure 8.2 The History bar lets you quickly return to pages.

4. Click **OK** to save your changes and close the dialog box.

Changing the Display of Web Pages

You can change the way Web pages display in your browser by selecting a font size and hypertext color. You can also turn off some multimedia settings, which will allow pages to load faster.

If you change the font size for your display, note that some Web pages will override your choice. The default font size is Medium.

To change the size of text do one of the following:

- Choose **View**, **Fonts** from the menu. Select the font size you want (largest, larger, medium, smaller, smallest).

- Click the **Font** icon on the toolbar. Select the font size you want.

You can also display text in a different font. Keep in mind that changes you make to the font may be overridden by Web pages.

To select a font:

1. Choose **View**, **Options**. The Options Dialog Box appears with the General tab selected.
2. Click the **Fonts** button. The Fonts dialog box appears.
3. Select the fonts you want in the **Proportional** and **Fixed-Width Font** lists.
4. Click **OK** to close the Font dialog box.
5. Click **OK** to close the Options dialog box and save your changes.

You can change the default text and background colors. The default setting tells Internet Explorer to use your Windows color settings.

To change the default text and background colors:

1. Choose **View**, **Options** from the menu. The Options Dialog Box appears with the general tab in front.
2. Click the **Colors** button. The Colors dialog box appears (see Figure 8.2).
3. In the Colors section, remove the check next to **Use Windows Colors**. Once this check is removed, you can select a text and background color by clicking the **Text** and **Background** buttons and choosing from the color palette (see Figure 8.3)

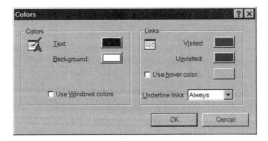

Figure 8.3   Changing the text or background colors.

4. Change link colors in the Links section by clicking the **Visited** and **Unvisited** buttons and choosing from the color palette. If you do not want hypertext links to display as underlined text, open the **Underline Links** drop-down list, and select **Never**. The **Use Hover Color** option lets you set the color of the link when the mouse pointer is resting on it.

5. When you have finished with your selections, click **OK** to close the dialog box and save your changes.

The Platform Preview version of IE4 has the ability to display Web pages in their native languages. You must add a language to your options, and adding or changing a language does not *translate* text.

To select a language for viewing Web pages:

1. Choose **View**, **Options** from the menu. The Options Dialog Box appears.
2. Click the **Languages** button.
3. Click **Add**. Select a language from the list and click **OK**.
4. Select the language you just added, and click OK.

Using the Favorites Folder

IE4 gives you the ability to save Web pages in a folder called Favorites. By saving pages in Favorites, you can give them a name (or accept the default) or organize them into folders.

To add a page to the Favorites Folder:

1. Go to the Web page you want to add.
2. Open the **Favorites** menu and select **Add to Favorites**
3. The Add To Favorites dialog box appears (see Figure 8.4). Type a name in the **Name** box or accept the default name (which is the descriptive information pulled from your Web page).

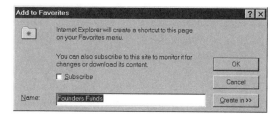

Figure 8.4 The Add To Favorites dialog box.

4. To store your favorites in a different folder, click **Create In>>**.

5. The Favorites folder structure appears as shown in Figure 8.5. To create a new folder, click **New Folder**.

6. The Create New Folder dialog box appears. Type a name for your new folder in the **Folder Name** box and click **OK**.

7. Your new folder will now appear highlighted in the Favorites folder structure. Click **OK** to save your Web page in this folder. If the folder is not highlighted, click once on the folder, and then click **OK.**

8. Click **OK**. (Ignore the Subscribe check box for now. See Lesson 10, "Subscriptions and Working Offline," for details.)

Figure 8.5   Creating a new folder.

 TIP   **Use Your Right Mouse Button**   You can add favorites by right-clicking the mouse anywhere on your Web page. From the pop-up menu, select **Add To Favorites.** To add a link, right-click the link and select **Add to Favorites.**

To open a page stored in your Favorites:

1. Click the **Favorites** button on the toolbar. The Favorites Bar appears, as shown in Figure 8.5, displaying a list of Favorites and folders.

2. If the page you want to open is in a folder, click the folder's icon in the Favorites Bar.

3. Select the page you want to view. The contents of the page appear in the right frame.

Figure 8.6   Folders appear on the Favorites menu.

You may decide that you want to delete, move, or rename pages in your Favorites folders. To reorganize your Favorites pages:

1. Click the **Favorites** icon on the toolbar. This closes the Favorites Bar.

2. Open the **Favorites** menu and select **Organize Favorites**. The Organize Favorites dialog box appears as shown in Figure 8.7.

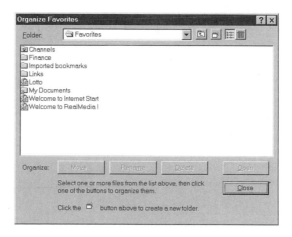

Figure 8.7   The Organize Favorites dialog box.

3. Highlight the folder or document you wish to move, rename or delete. To open a folder and view its contents, double-click the folder.

4. Once you have highlighted a document or folder, click **Move**, **Rename** or **Delete**.

   - Selecting Move opens a Browse dialog box so you can highlight the folder you want to move your document to.

   - Selecting Rename allows you to edit the folder or document name.

   - Selecting Delete will activate a Confirm Delete dialog box asking you if you are sure you want to delete this item.

5. When you are finished organizing your Favorites pages, click **Close** to close the Organize Favorites dialog box.

Downloading Files

When you need to retrieve files from a Web page, right-click the file name or link listed in the Web page, and select **Save Target As** or **Save Picture As**. Use the Save dialog box to specify the drive and folder in which you want the file saved. After you have downloaded, be certain to run a virus check on the file.

In this lesson, you learned how to change your viewing preferences and how to use and organize Favorites. In the next lesson, you learn how to customize Internet Explorer 4.

Customizing Internet Explorer 4

In this lesson, you will learn how to change the size and position of the toolbar and how to customize Quick Links. You also learn how to create a desktop shortcut to a Web page and use a Web image as wallpaper.

About Customizing the Toolbar

You can change the position of and customize the toolbar. The Address and Link buttons can be expanded or collapsed. By default, Address appears expanded and the Links button appears collapsed to the right of the Address as shown in Figure 9.1.

You can move the Address or Links sections of the toolbar by dragging them up, down, left or right.

Figure 9.1   The default toolbar shows an expanded Address and collapsed Links button.

Changing Size and Position of Buttons

To expand the toolbar so that Address and Links each display on a single line, position your pointer at the heavy gray line below Address. The pointer changes to a sizing pointer. Drag down on the toolbar. The Links and Address now each display on their own section as shown in Figure 9.2.

Figure 9.2   Expanding the toolbar displays the Address and Links section.

To reverse the order of the Address and Links bars, drag **Address** down below Links, as shown in Figure 9.3.

Figure 9.3   Rearranging the Address and Links bars.

The toolbar can have a maximum of three lines and a minimum of none. To collapse one or two lines of the toolbar into one line, drag the thick bar at the bottom edge of the toolbar upward until the buttons are hidden.

To hide the toolbar completely, choose **View**, **Toolbar** from the menu and remove the check mark next to toolbar. To reveal the toolbar again, choose **View**, **Toolbar** and select the toolbar you want to display.

Customizing the Pre-Selected Links

Five pre-selected links (called Quick Links) appear on the default Link toolbar. You can insert additional Quick Links to link to your favorite and most-visited sites.

To insert a Quick Link, simply drag a link from the current Web page up to the Links toolbar. A vertical line shows where the link will be inserted. Release the mouse button (see Figure 9.4).

Figure 9.4 Drag a link to the Links bar.

To move, delete, or rename Quick Links, open the **Favorites** menu and select **Organize Favorites**. Double-click the **Links** folder.

Creating a Desktop Shortcut

You can create a desktop shortcut to a Web page or to a hyperlink found on a Web page.

To create a shortcut to the current Web page, right-click the page and select **Create Shortcut** from the pop-up menu. To create a shortcut to a link, right-click the link and select **Create Shorcut**.

To create a shortcut to a hyperlink (hypertext), size the IE4 window so it is not maximized, and drag the hyperlink to your desktop.

When you click the shortcut on your desktop (double-click if you do not have Active Desktop running), IE4 will start and the page will be opened. If you must first dial into the Internet, IE4 will start and the **Connect To** dialog box will appear so you can dial into your ISP.

Using a Graphical Image as Wallpaper

Images that you see on Web pages can be used as desktop wallpaper. When you see an image you would like to use as your wallpaper, right-click the image and select **Set As Wallpaper** from the pop-up menu.

CAUTION

Where's My Wallpaper? With Active Desktop running, you will not be able to see wallpaper you select, as Active Desktop uses its own wallpaper (the black background and the IE4 message). To see your new wallpaper, right-click a blank area of the Windows desktop and select **Properties**. Click the **Background** tab and select **Internet Explorer Wallpaper** from the wallpaper list. Click **OK**. To restore the IE4 wallpaper, perform the same steps, but select C:\WINDOWS\Web\wallpaper from the list.

Entering Internet Explorer 4 Options

You can change most settings in Internet Explorer 4 by opening the **View** menu, selecting **Options**, and then clicking the tab for the set of options you want to change: **General**, **Security**, **Content**, **Connection**, **Programs**, and **Advanced**. The following sections provide detailed instructions on how to change the most common settings.

Going Full Screen

One of the biggest problems with any Web browser is that it occupies space that could otherwise be used to display Web pages. Internet Explorer has a simple solution: Full Screen View. To go full screen, open the **View** menu and select **Full Screen**.

Your new window contains only a scroll bar and the Standard Buttons bar—all you need to navigate the Web. To change back to Normal view, click the **Restore** button in the upper-right corner of the screen.

Loading Text-Only Pages

Although graphics liven up Web pages, they also increase the time it takes your Web browser to download pages. To speed up the process, you can tell Internet Explorer to load only text, no graphics. When you reach a page that has graphics you want to view, you can then click a placeholder to view that image. To turn off graphics, follow these steps:

1. Open the **View** menu, and select **Options**. The Options dialog box appears.
2. Click the **Advanced** tab.
3. Under Multimedia, click **Show Pictures**, **Play Animations**, **Play Sounds**, and/or **Play Videos** to turn these options off (remove the check marks).
4. Click the **OK** button to save your settings.

Using the Cache for Quick Return Trips

To increase the speed at which Internet Explorer loads the pages you've previously visited, you can change the cache settings. Take the following steps:

1. Open the **View** menu, and select **Options**. The Options dialog box appears.

2. Click the **General** tab, and click the **Settings** button under Temporary Internet Files. The Settings dialog box appears.

3. Drag the slider below **Amount of Disk Space to Use** to the right, to increase the amount of disk space reserved for the disk cache. The more space you use for the cache, the more pages Internet Explorer can store for later revisits.

4. Under Check for Newer Versions of Stored Pages, specify how often you want Internet Explorer to check a cached page against the latest page on the Web:

   Every Visit to the Page is a little excessive and will slow you down.

   Every Time You Start Internet Explorer (the default setting) checks the page the first time you revisit it in a session.

   Never is a little risky, because you might miss page updates, but it does make for speedy revisits.

5. Click the **OK** button to save your cache settings and return to the Options dialog box. Click **OK**.

In the Options dialog box, the General Settings tab also has a button called **Delete Files**, which you can click to remove all cached files from your hard drive. If you're running low on disk space, this is the button to use to free up a few megabytes.

Setting Up Security Zones

As you send data and receive active content on the Web, Internet Explorer supervises your actions and the actions of the remote server, and warns you of any risky activity. If you receive a warning dialog box, you can usually prevent similar warnings from appearing in the future by selecting the **In the Future, Do Not Show This Warning** option before giving your okay.

To access the security settings, open the **View** menu, select **Options**, and click the **Security** tab. The Zone drop-down list displays the four available security zones, as shown in Figure 9.4.

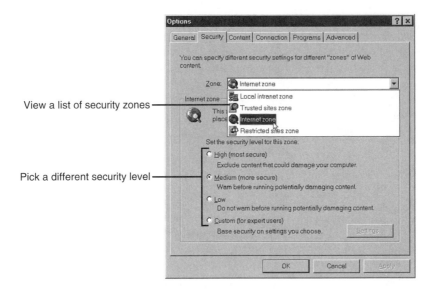

View a list of security zones

Pick a different security level

Figure 9.5   You can select a different security level for each zone.

You can add and remove sites from three of the four security zones: Corporate Intranet, Trusted Sites, and Restricted Sites. The Internet zone covers all sites not on the other three lists. When you add sites to a zone, the security settings you enter for that zone apply to all the sites in that zone. To add a site to the Restricted or Trusted sites zone, follow these steps:

1. Open the **View** menu, select **Options**, and click the **Security** tab.

2. Open the **Zone** drop-down list, and select **Restricted Sites Zone** or **Trusted Sites Zone**.

3. Click the **Add Sites** button. The resulting dialog box shows a list of sites in the selected zone, which should be empty, because you haven't specified any sites.

4. Click in the **Add this Web Site to the Zone** text box, type the site's address, and click the **Add** button. Repeat this step to add more sites to the zone.

5. To remove a site from the zone, click its address in the Web sites list, and click the **Remove** button.

6. If you want to connect to only secure Web servers (servers whose address starts with https:// rather than http://), select **Require Server Verification (https) For All Sites in This Zone**.

7. Click the **OK** button to save your list of sites.

TIP **Network Security** If you have a network connection, your network administrator is in charge of setting the security levels for trusted and untrusted sites. Because of this, the procedure for adding sites to the Corporate Intranet list is different. Check with your Network Administrator for details.

To specify a security level for a zone, open the **View** menu, select **Options**, and click the **Security** tab. Open the **Zone** drop-down list, and select the zone whose security level you want to change, and then select the desired level:

- **High** prevents you from submitting any information by way of form, even a search form. In addition, Internet Explorer won't play Java applets, download ActiveX controls, or transfer any other potentially harmful programs or scripts to your computer. The High setting is useful for sites you place on the Restricted sites list.

- **Medium** turns on prompts, so Internet Explorer displays dialog boxes whenever you attempt to send data or download scripts or other active content. The Medium setting is useful for the Internet zone, where you may want to be prompted before doing anything risky.

- **Low** turns off the prompts, allowing you to submit information using a form, and allowing sites to send you active content. The Low setting is good for Trusted sites, where you are fairly certain that nothing bad is going to happen.

- **Custom** allows you to enter specific security settings. For example, you may wish to prevent active content from being automatically downloaded to your computer, but you don't want a dialog box popping up on your screen every time you fill out a form.

TIP **Is It Safe?** You can usually tell if a site is secure by looking at its address. If the address starts with https instead of http, the site is secure. Also, Internet Explorer displays a lock icon in the status bar when you are at a secure site.

Censoring Internet Sites

If you have kids, you may want to prevent them from accessing sites that have strong language, sex, violence, or racism. To block access to these sites, follow these steps:

1. Display the Options dialog box.
2. Click the **Content** tab, and click **Enable**. A dialog box appears, prompting you to enter a password.

3 Enter the password you want to use for changing the content settings and click **OK**.

4. You can adjust the ratings system by clicking the **Settings** button and entering your desired preferences.

5. Click **OK**.

If someone tries to access a site that contains prohibited material, Internet Explorer blocks access to the site and displays a dialog box that allows you to enter a password to override the censor. If the user does not know the password, he or she cannot view the page.

The Content tab contains additional options for managing personal and site certificates. Internet Explorer uses these certificates to assure you that you are dealing with certified companies on the Web and to assure those companies that you are who you claim to be.

Selecting Default Programs

You can set up Internet Explorer to use Outlook Express as your default e-mail and newsreader and to set up NetMeeting for placing Internet phone calls. If you then click a link for mail, a newsgroup, or a NetMeeting session, Internet Explorer automatically runs the required application.

To select your default programs, display the Options dialog box, click the **Programs** tab, and select the desired program for each category. Click **OK**.

In this lesson, you learned how to size and change the toolbar and how to customize Internet Explorer. In the next lesson, you will learn how to subscribe to a Web site and how to work offline.

Subscriptions and Working Offline

In this lesson, you will learn how to update Web pages while you are away from your computer. You also learn how to work offline.

What Is a Subscription?

Internet Explorer 4 allows you to update your favorite Web pages while you are away from your computer. This can be a great time saver for you. It also allows you to see Web content while you are working *offline*, or not connected to the Internet.

IE4 uses something called Information Delivery, which allows you to update your favorite Web site pages and download them to your hard drive for viewing on- or offline.

You can schedule your Web pages to update during off hours or while you are asleep and in the morning have the most current information available to you.

To update your pages requires some set up work. You need to:

- Identify the Web pages you want to update by subscribing to them and setting a schedule for updating information.
- Have a constant Internet connection, or a dial up connection. Depending upon your ISP, you may need a dial-up networking script file. If you are using your ISPs software, there's a good chance you will *not* need a networking script file.

Dial-up Networking Script File   A file that contains instructions in Dial-Up Scripting command language. When your computer dials into another computer using this file, you need not be at the computer to login. The login information and password are contained in the script file, as well as some other commands necessary for the two computers to talk.

Subscribing to a Web Site

You can set up a site subscription for an existing Favorite, for a new Favorite, or for the currently displayed page. Follow these steps to set up a site subscription:

1. Open the page you want to subscribe to, and then choose **Favorites**, **Subscriptions**, **Subscribe**.

   Or, Right-click the shortcut that points to the page you want to subscribe to and select **Properties**. The shortcut may be on the Windows desktop, in the Quick Launch toolbar on the taskbar, or in the Organize Favorites window (Favorites, Organize Favorites). Click the **Subscription** tab and click **Subscribe Now**. The Subscribe dialog box appears, as shown in Figure 10.1.

Figure 10.1   The Subscribe dialog box.

2. Click the **Customize** button. This starts the Web Site Subscription Wizard, which informs you that Internet Explorer will monitor this page for changes (see Figure 10.2).

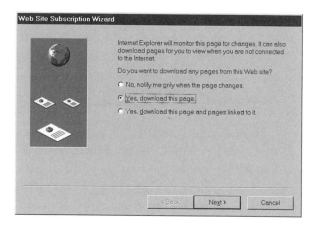

Figure 10.2 The Web Site Subscription Wizard.

3. Select one of the following options:

No, Only Notify Me When the Page Changes tells Internet Explorer to display a red asterisk on the icon when the page is updated.

Yes, Download This Page tells Internet Explorer to automatically download this page at the scheduled time. (You'll learn how to set the scheduled time later.)

Yes, Download This Page and Pages Linked to It tells Internet Explorer to automatically download not only this page but any pages that are linked to it. (If a page has lots of links, this can take a long time and quickly pack your disk with pages.)

4. Click **Next**. The Wizard asks if you want to be notified of page updates via e-mail. This is useful if you frequently travel or if you just want Internet Explorer to notify you, so you don't have to check for updates.

5. Click **No** or **Yes**. If you select Yes, you can click **Change Address** and specify the e-mail address to which you want updated notifications sent.

6. Click **Next**. The Wizard now asks how you want Internet Explorer to manage the updates.

7. Select one of the following options:

AutoSchedule is useful if you are always connected to the Internet (usually via a network connection). This allows the site itself to send updated pages on a regular basis. If you use a modem to connect, AutoSchedule is the same as selecting **Manually**.

Custom Schedule lets you specify when you want Internet Explorer to download updated pages. This is the best setting if you want to obtain updates automatically using a modem connection.

Manually tells Internet Explorer not to automatically check for updates. When you want to check for updates, you must select **Favorites, Subscriptions, Update All**.

8. Click **Next**. If you chose AutoSchedule, or Manually, skip to step 10. If you chose Custom Schedule, the next dialog box prompts you to specify an update schedule; go on to step 9.

9. Open the drop-down list, and select a general update schedule: **Daily, Weekly**, or **Monthly**. You can click the **New** or **Edit** button to select a specific day and time for Internet Explorer to download updates. Click **Allow Unattended Dial-Up for All Subscriptions**, if you want to allow Internet Explorer to establish your Internet connection while you are away from your computer.

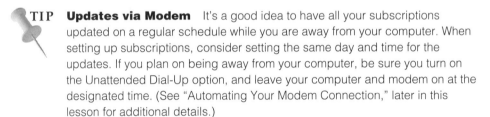

TIP **Updates via Modem**   It's a good idea to have all your subscriptions updated on a regular schedule while you are away from your computer. When setting up subscriptions, consider setting the same day and time for the updates. If you plan on being away from your computer, be sure you turn on the Unattended Dial-Up option, and leave your computer and modem on at the designated time. (See "Automating Your Modem Connection," later in this lesson for additional details.)

10. Click **Next**. The Wizard now asks if you need to enter a login name and password to access the site.

11. Click **No**, or click **Yes** and enter your login name and Password.

12. Click the **Finish** button, and the click **OK**.

Canceling Subscriptions

To cancel a subscription, you first must display the Subscriptions window. Open the **Favorites** menu, point to **Subscriptions**, and select **Manage Subscriptions**. Right-click the site whose subscription you want to terminate, click **Properties**, and click **Unsubscribe**. Click **Yes** to confirm.

Modifying Subscriptions

To change the subscription settings for a Favorite or shortcut, right-click the shortcut, and select **Properties**. The subscription properties dialog box appears, with the Subscription tab up front. Click the **Receiving** tab and take one of the following steps:

- To be notified of updates via e-mail, click **Yes, Send a Message to the Following Address**. You can click the **Change Address** button to specify the e-mail address where you want updated notices sent.

- To have Internet Explorer notify you of updates, but not download the updated page, click **No, Just Notify Me When the Site Changes**. (Internet Explorer notifies you of updates by displaying a red asterisk on the short-cut icon for the site.)

- To have Internet Explorer automatically download the page at the sched-uled time, click **Yes, Download This Site**.

If you choose Yes, Download This Site, Internet Explorer automatically down-loads the page and all related graphics at the scheduled time. To have additional related pages downloaded, and to automatically download sounds, videos, and other items on the page, click the **Advanced** button and enter select any of the following options, as shown in Figure 10.3:

Maximum Download Size (K) per Update allows you to limit the size of the download to prevent Internet Explorer from cluttering your disk with huge pages.

High Priority (Update Before Other Subscriptions) sets the update to "me first" status. Internet Explorer downloads the updates for this site before downloading updates to other sites.

Images tells Internet Explorer to download any inline images contained on the page. This is on by default.

Sound and Video tells Internet Explorer to download any background sounds and inline video clips on the page. (Audio and video files can be quite large.)

ActiveX Controls and Java Applets is another security option. It is pos-sible for programmers to develop destructive ActiveX Controls and Java Applets and place them on Web pages. If you download a page that has a destructive component, it can do a lot of damage while you're catching up on your sleep.

Download Pages that are Within ___ Levels Deep allows Internet Explorer to download any pages linked to this page. Be careful with this option. Because some pages contain many links, turning this option on can cause Internet Explorer to pack your drive with a bunch of pages you may never look at. Whatever you do, don't enter a large number in the blank.

Follow Links Outside of this Page's Web Site tells Internet Explorer to trace hyperlinks to other pages not on this site. It's a good idea to keep this option off.

You can also click the **Schedule** tab to change the frequency and time at which Internet Explorer downloads updated content. Click **OK** to save your changes.

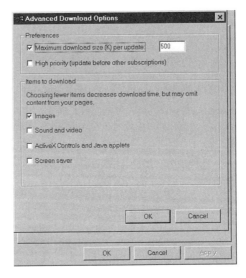

Figure 10.3 The Advanced options let you control what Internet Explorer downloads.

Automating Your Modem Connection

If you connect to the Internet via a network connection, and you stay connected to the Internet at all times, Internet Explorer automatically downloads subscribed sites at the specified times. However, if you connect using a modem, you must enter additional connection settings. These settings allow Internet Explorer to automatically "dial" your modem and establish the Internet connection required to download subscribed sites at the scheduled times. Follow these steps:

1. Open Internet Explorer's **View** menu and select **Options**.

2. Click the **Connection** tab.

3. Under Connection, click **Connect to the Internet Using a Modem**, and click the **Settings** button.

4. Open the **Use the Following Dial-up Networking Connection** drop-down list, and select the name of your Dial-Up Networking connection.

5. Check **Connect Without User Intervention**. Enter your username and password in the appropriate text boxes.

6. Enter any other desired settings to specify your dialing preferences, such as how many times Internet Explorer should dial before giving up, and how long the connection should be idle before Internet Explorer hangs up.

7. Click **OK** to return to the Options dialog box, and then click **OK** to save your settings.

Viewing Subscriptions and Working Offline

To view your subscriptions, choose **Favorites**, **Subscriptions**, **Manage Subscriptions** from the menu. The Subscriptions window opens. Click the subscription you want to view.

To work offline, choose **File**, **Work Offline**. You can then open pages as you normally do. Internet Explorer opens any subscribed pages that you automatically downloaded from the hard drive. If a page you choose has not been downloaded, Internet Explorer prompts you to go online to get the page.

Updating and Editing Subscriptions

To update subscriptions at a time other than the scheduled time, choose **Favorites**, **Subscriptions**, **Update All**. Your Internet connection will be established and your Web subscriptions will be updated. If you set up a subscription to have Internet Explorer only notify you of updates, a red asterisk appears next to the page's name to indicate that it is new. If you entered a setting to have Internet Explorer download the page, Internet Explorer saves the updated page to your disk, and you can quickly open it.

Tuning in to the Web with Channels

With Channels, you can tune in to the best sites the Web has to offer. Internet Explorer features a Channel bar that allows you to select from popular sites and then place those sites on the channel changer. To view a site, you simply click a button on the channel changer; it's just like flipping channels on your TV set.

Accessing Channels from Internet Explorer

To channel surf, you first need to display the Channel bar in Internet Explorer. Click the **Channels** button in the toolbar. Initially, the bar contains one button labeled Channel Guide, and several additional buttons for connecting to premium Web sites. Follow these steps to add a channel:

1. In the Channel bar, click **Channel Guide** to connect to Microsoft's Channel Guide. This site displays a list of popular channels.

2. Click a button for the channel you want to add. The channel appears in a preview window right on the Channel Guide page, so you can decide if you want to subscribe to the channel (see Figure 10.4).

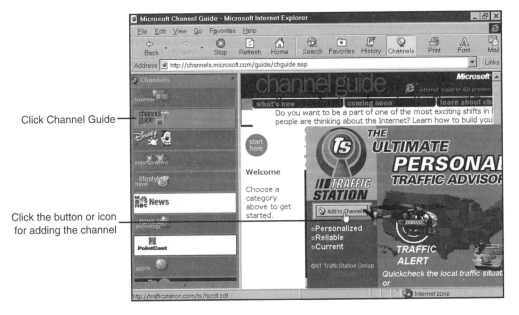

Figure 10.4   You can add channels to the Channels bar.

3. Click the link for adding the channel to the Channels list. The Subscribe dialog box appears.

4. Click the **Customize** button, and use the Channel Subscription Wizard to enter subscription settings for this site.

5. Click **OK**. A button for this site appears in the Channels bar.

 TIP **Adding Non-Channels to the Channel Changer** You can add any Web page to the Channel bar by creating a shortcut for it in the Favorites\ Channels folder. When you choose to create a Favorite, click the **Create In** button, and select the **Channels** folder.

Channel Surfing

Channels give Web developers more control over your subscriptions. Instead of allowing you to select the pages you want to subscribe to, the developer includes the list of pages related to the channel. To select a page, you click the **Channel** button, and then select the desired page, as shown in Figure 10.5.

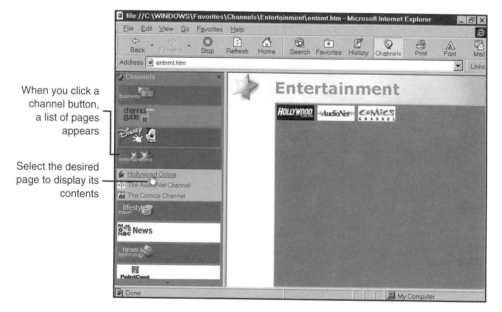

When you click a channel button, a list of pages appears

Select the desired page to display its contents

Figure 10.5 Select a channel to view pages related to the channel.

When you click a channel in the Channel bar and select a page, the Internet Explorer opens the selected page in Full Screen view, with the Internet Explorer toolbar at the top. To return to Normal view, click the **Restore** button in the upper-right corner of the window. You can return to Full Screen view at any time by selecting **View**, **Full Screen**. To close the window, click the **Close** button (X) in the upper-right corner of the window.

To give the current page more room to spread out, move the mouse pointer over the page. The pane expands, making the Channels bar thinner. You can click links on the page to skip to related pages, just as you do in the Internet Explorer window.

Tuning in on Your Windows Desktop

The Channels feature is included as a desktop component. If you turn on the Active Desktop, the Channel bar appears on the Windows desktop. If the Channel bar is not displayed, right-click the **Windows** desktop, select **Properties**, and click the **Web** tab. Make sure Disable All Web-Related Content in my Desktop is *not* checked, and make sure Internet Explorer Channel Bar is checked. Click **OK**.

To tune in to a channel, click its button, and select the desired page. This opens the page in Full Screen view, as explained in the previous section.

In this lesson, you learned about subscriptions and how to create, view and update subscriptions. In the next lesson, you learn about Outlook Express Mail.

Using Outlook Express Mail and News

In this lesson, you learn how to open and close the Outlook Express program, read and reply to mail, create mail, and use the Outlook Express News Reader.

What Is Outlook Express?

Outlook Express Mail is an Internet-standards-based e-mail and news reader program. It supports the following Internet mail standards: SMTP, POP3, and IMAP4. The news reader portion of Outlook Express Mail supports the Internet protocol NNTP. We will examine the e-mail portion of the program first, then the news reader portion.

Outlook Express Mail

With Outlook Express Mail you can send a mail message to anyone for whom you have an Internet or intranet mail address. Also, you can receive mail from other Internet and intranet users. Also, you can use Outlook Express Mail to send files—such as reports, letters, and spreadsheets—to your correspondents, as attachments to the messages you send to them.

In order to use Outlook Express Mail, you must have a connection to an Internet Service Provider or to your company's intranet. The Internet Service Provider must provide you with Internet mail services. The connection may be via modem or network.

Opening and Closing Outlook Express Mail

You can start Outlook Express Mail by clicking its icon, which appears in the taskbar, next to the Start button, or from the Start menu. To start Outlook Express Mail from its icon, take one of the following steps:

- Click **Launch Outlook Express** in the taskbar.
- Select **Start**, **Programs Internet Explorer**, **Outlook Express**.
- Open the **Go** menu in Internet Explorer and select **Mail**.

The first time you run Outlook Express, it displays the Internet Connection Wizard, which leads you through the process of setting up your mail server. To change or add servers, select **Tools**, **Accounts**.

To exit from Outlook Express Mail, choose **File, Exit** or click the **Close** button.

The Outlook Express Mail Window

Outlook Express provides a communications hub from which you can access both e-mail messages and newsgroups. Whenever you start Outlook Express, it displays the opening window, shown in Figure 11.1. The main viewing area displays icons for reading mail and newsgroup messages, composing messages, accessing the address book, updating Outlook Express, and finding people on the Internet.

From the Outlook Bar (in the left pane), you can access your Inbox, Outbox, Sent Items, Deleted Items, and Drafts, along with any news servers you set up in Outlook Express News. This provides an integrated message area where you quickly switch between Outlook Express Mail and News. It also allows you to manage your messages as easily as you manage files on your hard drive.

The Folders list appears just above the main viewing area. The name of the currently active folder is displayed (in the Figure, Outlook Express is the currently active folder). To view a list of folders where your messages are stored, click the name of the current folder. You can then select the desired folder from the list.

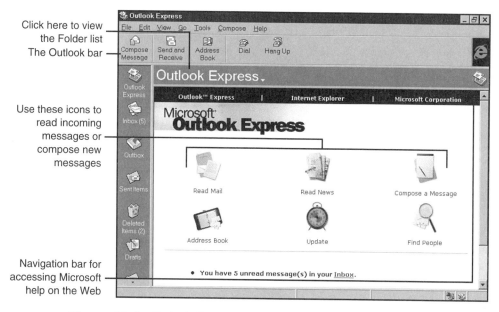

Click here to view the Folder list
The Outlook bar

Use these icons to read incoming messages or compose new messages

Navigation bar for accessing Microsoft help on the Web

Figure 11.1 Outlook Express is Windows Explorer for messages.

Sending and Retrieving Mail

When someone sends mail to you via the Internet, it arrives at your Internet mail server. To read the mail, you have to retrieve it from the server. You can do this manually or set up Outlook Express Mail to do it for you at timed intervals.

Likewise, to send mail to someone via the Internet, you have to deliver it to your mail server. If you have a network connection to the Internet, Outlook Express Mail may do this automatically for you. If you have to dial in to your Internet Service Provider by modem, you may prefer to save your outgoing messages temporarily in your Outbox, then deliver them to the server the next time you dial in.

You may send mail, retrieve mail, or do both at once. To send and retrieve mail, follow these steps:

1. Choose **Tools**, **Send and Recieve**. If you have more than one e-mail account, selecting Send and Recieve opens a submenu, which allows you to check a specific account or all accounts.

2. Outlook will then either retrieve your mail automatically from your mail server, or it will display a dialog box so you can enter your password. It will display either the Connect to *ConnectionName* dialog box if your connection is by modem, or the Logon - *Username* dialog box if your connection is by network. Whichever dialog box appears, enter your user name, if it does not appear correctly, and your password, then press **Enter**. Outlook Express Mail will then attempt to connect to your mail server to retrieve your mail.

To only deliver mail that is waiting in your Outbox to your mail server, follow these steps:

1. Choose **Tools**, **Send**.

2. If you connect to your Internet Service Provider by modem, the Connect to *ConnectionName* dialog box may appear, so you can enter your password. Do so, then press **Enter**. Outlook Express Mail will then attempt to connect to your mail server to send your mail to it.

To both send and retrieve mail, you can do one of the following:

- Choose **Tools**, **Send and Receive** in the menu.
- Press **Ctrl+M**.
- Click the **Send and Receive** button in the toolbar.

Reading Mail

Mail that you retrieve from your mail server will appear in your Inbox. To display the contents of the Inbox, click **Inbox** in the Outlook bar, or select the **Read Mail** icon in the main veiwing area. You may read it in any of the following ways:

- Select a message in the upper-right pane. Read its contents in the lower-right pane, as shown in Figure 11.2.
- Select a message in the upper-right pane. Choose **File**, **Open** in the menu to open the message in a separate window.
- Double-click a message in the upper-right pane to open the message in a separate window.

If you opened a message inside a separate window, you may close the window by pressing the **Esc** key.

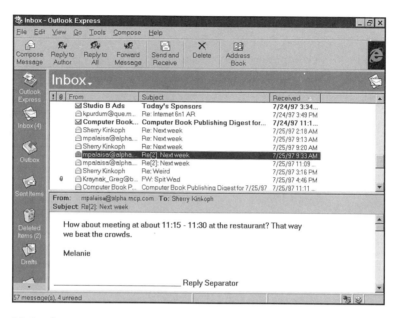

Figure 11.2 Outlook Express displays a preview pane showing the contents of the selected message.

Replying to a Message

When you reply to a message you receive, Outlook Express Mail automatically places a copy of the original message in your reply, separated from your text by a short, dashed line and identified with the > symbol preceding each line of the original message. When you reply to a message, Outlook Express Mail also addresses the reply to the author of the original message and uses the subject of the original message as the subject of the reply, but with the word RE: preceding the original subject.

To compose a reply to a message, follow these steps:

1. In either the Outlook Express Mail window or the open message window, choose **Compose**, **Reply to Author** to compose a reply addressed only to the author of the original message. Choose **Compose**, **Reply to All** to address your reply to the original author with copies addressed to all the people copied by the original author. A Reply message window opens.

2. In the Reply message window, add any additional addressees that you wish, and remove any addressees that you do not wish to include in the reply. Seperate addresses with a semicolon (;).

3. In the bottom pane of the Reply message window, above the original message, enter the text of your message.

4. When you are ready to send the message, choose **File**, **Send Message**, or press **Alt+S**, or click the **Send** icon, which is the left-most icon in the message window's toolbar.

 TIP   **Send later**   You can compose messages offline and send them later. To send a message later, compose the message, and then select File, Send Later. This places the message in the Outbox. Click Send and Receive to send all the messages.

Creating Mail

Creating a new message is similar to creating a reply, except that you will have to know the recipient's Internet address, and you will have to supply the content of the Subject line.

To create a new mail message, follow these steps:

1. In Outlook Express Mail, choose **Compose**, **New Message**, or press **Ctrl+N**, or click the **Compose Message** icon in the toolbar. A New Message window will appear.

2. In the New Message window, enter the address of the recipient in the To field. Alternately, click the **Address Book** icon next to the To field. This will display the Select Recipients dialog box, from which you can choose the recipient's name from a list, assuming you added the recipient to the Address Book.

3. If you use the Select Recipients dialog box, select a recipient's name in the left-hand window, and then click the **To**, **Cc**, or **Bcc** button to add that person's name to one of the Message Recipients fields. You can add multiple names to each of the fields. Click **OK** when you have added all the names you want. The Select Recipients dialog box will disappear and the names you selected will appear in the To, Cc, and Bcc fields in the new message.

4. Add a topic for the message in the Subject field.

5. Enter your message in the message field, which is the bottom half of the New Message window. This area of the screen is like a word processor. Your lines of text will wrap automatically when you reach the right margin. You only have to press Enter at the end of each paragraph.

6. To send the message when you are done, choose **File**, **Send Message**, or press **Alt+S**, or click the **Send** icon, which is the left-most icon in the New Message window's Toolbar.

You can also do the following things before sending a message:

- To set a high priority, or level of importance, for the message, choose **Tools**, **Set Priority**, **High**.

- To attach a file, choose **Insert File Attachment**, or click the **Insert File** icon (which looks like a paperclip) in the toolbar. In the Insert Attachment dialog box, select the file you want to attach, then click the **Attach** button. Outlook Express Mail adds the file, represented by an icon, to your message.

- If your recipient can read mail in HTML format, then you can format the text in the body of your message. To turn the formatting capability on, choose **Format, Rich Text (HTML)**. To turn formatting off, choose **Format, Plain Text**. When formatting is turned on, a formatting toolbar appears above the message area in the New Message window. You can use those tools or the choices in the Format menu to change the typeface, size, and appearance of your text, to change paragraph alignment and indentation, to create numbered and bulleted paragraphs, to insert images, and to set a background color or pattern for your message.

Outlook Express News

Outlook Express also includes an Internet News reader. Internet News is a standard method of setting up discussion forums on the Internet. Internet News-based discussion forums are called Internet newsgroups. There are over 20,000 newsgroups on the Internet. Each one specializes in a particular discussion topic. Internet Service Providers and Internet-based special interest groups maintain newsgroup discussions on computers known as News servers.

You can follow the discussions in a newsgroup or participate in them by subscribing to the newsgroup, then reading the messages (sometimes called *articles*) that others have posted in the newsgroup and, optionally, posting your replies to those messages.

Opening and Closing Outlook Express News

You can start Outlook Express News from the menu or from within Outlook Express News or Microsoft Internet Explorer.

- To start Outlook Express News from the menu, choose **Start, Programs, Internet Explorer Outlook Express News**.
- To start Outlook Express News from within Microsoft Internet Explorer, choose **Go, News**.
- To switch from Outlook Express Mail to Outlook Express News, either choose **Go, News**, or simply select your News icon (if you have set one up) in the Outlook Bar.

Connecting to a News Server

To participate in newsgroup discussions, you must first connect to a News server, from which you will retrieve messages and to which you will deliver them. To set up a connection to a News server, follow these steps:

1. Choose **Tools, Accounts** to open the Internet Accounts dialog box.
2. Click the **Add** button, then choose **News**. This starts the Internet Connection Wizard.
3. Enter a name in the Display name field. This is the name by which you will author contributions to discussions. It may be your real name or a fictitious name. Click **Next**.
4. Enter your e-mail address in the E-mail Address field. Click **Next**.
5. Enter the name of your News server in the News (NNTP) Server field.
6. If you need to provide a login name and password to your News server, check the **My News Server Requires Me To Log On** check box. Click **Next**, enter your username and password, and click **Next**.
7. Enter a name for the news server in the Internet News Account name field. This can be any name you want. Click **Next**.
8. If you have to dial in to the Internet to reach your News server, select the **Connect Using My Phone Line** option button. If you connect to your News server by network connection, or if you expect to have already dialed into the Internet when you will try to reach your News server, select the **Connect Using My Local Area Network (LAN)** option button. Click **Next**.

9. If, in the previous step, you selected the **Connect Using My Local Area Network (LAN)** option button, then click **Finish** to end this setup process. If, in the previous step, you selected the Connect Using My Phone Line radio button, then in this step either select **Create A New Dial-Up Connection** or **Use An Existing Dial-Up Connection** and choose the connection you will use from the list of available connections. Click **Next**.

10. If, in the previous step, you selected Use An Existing Dial-Up Connection, click **Finish** to end this setup process. If, in the previous step, you selected Create A New Dial-Up Connection, then in this step enter a name in the Connection name field. This may be any identifying name. Click **Next**.

11. Enter the Area Code, Phone Number, and Country Name and Code. If the phone number you will be calling is in the same area code as you, you may de-select the **Dial Using The Area Code And Country Code** check box. Click Next.

12. Enter your user name and password, as the News server you will be calling will expect to receive them. Click **Next**.

13. Choose **Yes** or **No** to the question Do you want to change the advanced settings for this connection? If you are not sure which answer to choose, then choose **No** and, if you cannot later connect to your News server, call your Internet Service Provider's support line and to solve the problem. Click **Next**.

14. If, in the previous step, you selected No, type a descriptive name for the dial-up connection, click **Next**, and click **Finish**. If, in the previous step, you selected Yes, select either the **PPP (Point to Point Protocol)** or **SLIP (Serial Line Internet Protocol)** option button. If you are not sure which one to choose, check with your Internet Service Provider. Click **Next**.

15. Choose one of the following three choices: **I Don't Need To Type Anything At Logon, I Need To Log On Manually**, or **Use This Logon Script**. If you chose the last, then enter the file name of the logon script in the text box or press the **Browse** button to choose the script from a list of available scripts. Your Internet Service Provider will tell you which one of these choices to make. Click **Next**. Then click **Finish** to end this setup process.

16. When you are finished, the news server appears in the Internet Accounts dialog box. Click **Close**. The Outlook Express dialog box apprears, asking if you want to download a list of available newsgroups.

17. Click **Yes**. Outlook Express downloads and displays a list of all newsgroups available on the news server (see the next section for details).

The result of the above process will be that a new folder appears in the folders pane of Outlook Express News. Later, when you retrieve and subscribe to newsgroups, the newsgroups and messages will appear in this folder.

Retrieving a List of Newsgroups

Next you have to dial in to your News server and retrieve from it a list of available newsgroups. The first time you do this, it may take some time, because it may be a lengthy list. However, after the first time, it should go quickly because all you will ever have to do is update the list.

To retrieve a list of newsgroups from your News server, either click the icon for your news server in the Outlook bar or choose **Tools**, **Newsgroups** in the menu. (If the icon is not displayed in the Outlook bar, click the down arrow at the bottom of the Bar.) The Newsgroups dialog box will appear. If you are already connected to your News server, Outlook Express News will automatically begin downloading newsgroup names from the News server. The Downloading Groups from the *ConnectionName* dialog box will appear and inform you of the progress of the automatic download. When it is finished, the Newsgroups dialog box will display the list of available newsgroups.

If you are not currently connected to your News server, a message box will appear asking if you would like to connect now. If you answer Yes, then the download described in the previous paragraph will proceed as soon as the connection is established.

Subscribing to and Unsubscribing from Newsgroups

To subscribe to a newsgroup, follow these steps:

1. Choose **Tools**, **Newsgroups** to view a list of available newsgroups.

2. When the download process described in the previous section of this lesson completes, scroll through the list of available newsgroups.

3. When you see a newsgroup that you would like to investigate, you can select it. Then press **Go To**. This will close the dialog box, create a subfolder for that newsgroup under the News server's folder, and fill the folder with the current set of articles in that newsgroup.

4. If you want to retrieve future articles posted in a newsgroup, select the newsgroup in the Newsgroups dialog box and click **Subscribe**, then click **OK** (see Figure 11.3.) This will close the dialog box, create a subfolder for that newsgroup under the News server's folder, fill the folder with the current set of articles, and in the future, retrieve new articles from the News server.

5. If you don't want to scroll through a long list of available newsgroups, you may enter a word in the Display Newsgroups Which Contain field at the top of the Newsgroups dialog box. As you enter words, the list of newsgroups will be automatically narrowed down to just the newsgroups that contain the words you type.

6. If you want to unsubscribe from a newsgroup, click the **Unsubscribe** button or double click the newsgroup, and then press **OK**. In the future, Outlook Express News will stop retrieving new articles from that group.

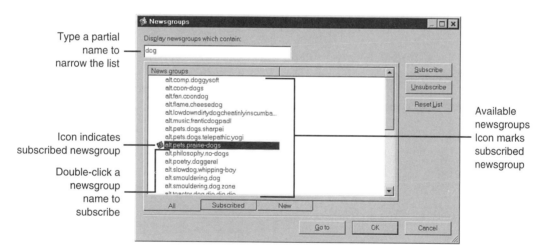

Figure 11.3 The Newsgroups dialog box.

If you want to subscribe to or unsubscribe from a newsgroup that already appears in a folder, you can select the folder and choose **Tools**, **Subscribe to This Newsgroup** or **Tools**, **Unsubscribe from This Newsgroup**.

Reading and Posting Messages

After Outlook Express News has retrieved messages from a News server, you can read the messages. Click the icon for your news server in the Outlook bar. A list of subscribed newsgroups appears in the upper right pane. Double-click the newsgroup name. A list of messages in the selected newsgroup appears. Take one of the following steps:

- Select a message in the message pane (upper left). Its contents will appear in the preview pane (lower left).
- Double-click a message in the message pane. The message will open in its own window.

After reading a message, you may post a reply to the newsgroup, or reply privately to the author of the message, or reply to both.

To post a reply to the newsgroup, either click the **Reply to Group** icon in the Toolbar or choose **Compose, Reply to Newsgroup**.

To reply privately to the author, either click the **Reply to Author** icon in the Toolbar or choose **Compose, Reply to Author** in the menu.

To reply to both, choose **Compose, Reply to Newsgroup and Author** in the menu.

Enter the text of your reply just as you would in a mail reply. When you are finished, click the **Post Message** icon in the Toolbar, or choose **File, Send Message** in the menu (or **Alt+S**).

In this lesson, you learned how to use Outlook Express Mail and Outlook Express News. You learned how to retrieve and send mail and newsgroup messages, and how to read, compose, and reply to mail and newsgroup messages. In the next, lesson you learn to create Web pages in FrontPage Express.

Understanding
FrontPage Express

*In this lesson, you'll learn how to create your own Web pages
with FrontPage Express*

What Is FrontPage Express?

 TIP **FrontPage Express?** Microsoft has announced that the name of this product will be FrontPage Express when it is released. However, at the same time the test version is still called FrontPad (the original name), which is why the scree shots in this lesson say FrontPad.

With FrontPage Express, you can create and edit your own Web pages. The FrontPage Express program is part of the Internet Explorer 4.0 package, but you must do the full installation to load it on your computer.

FrontPage Express is a trimmed-down version of Microsoft FrontPage Editor, so when you're ready for a more feature-rich Web editor, you won't have to learn a new software package from scratch. You can transfer the skills you learn in FrontPage Express to FrontPage Editor.

To start the FrontPage Express program:

1. Click the **Start** button on the taskbar.
2. Choose **Programs**.
3. Choose **Internet Explorer**, **FrontPage**. The FrontPage Express window opens. Figure 12.1 shows FrontPage displaying a Web page. Your window will be blank.

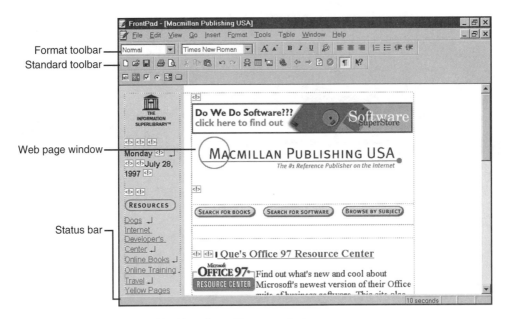

Format toolbar —
Standard toolbar —

Web page window —

Status bar —

Figure 12.1   The FrontPage Express window.

The FrontPage Express Tools

There are three toolbars in FrontPage Express—the Format toolbar, the Standard toolbar and the Forms toolbar (see Figure 12.1). If you want to know what a button does, point to the button. A small yellow box called a *ToolTip* appears beneath the button telling you what the tool is. The Status Bar at the bottom of the screen displays a short explanation of what the tool does.

The Format toolbar contains the buttons you need for changing the appearance of the text on your Web page. If you use other Microsoft products, many of the Format tools are familiar to you. Table 12.1 will help you identify the tools and how to use them.

Table 12.1   The Format Toolbar

Button	*Description*
Normal ▼	Change style

Button	Description
Times New Roman ▾	Change font
A	Increase text size
A	Decrease text size
B	Bold
I	Italic
U	Underline
	Text color
	Align left
	Center
	Align right
	Numbered list
	Bulleted list
	Decrease indent
	Increase indent

The Standard toolbar contains tools that allow you to navigate the pages, open and save, cut, copy, and paste, and more. See a description of the tools in Table 12.2.

Table 12.2   The Standard Toolbar

Button	Description
	New
	Open
	Save
	Print
	Print Preview
	Cut
	Copy
	Paste
	Undo
	Redo
	Insert WetBot Component
	Insert Table
	Insert Image
	Create or Edit Hyperlink
	Back
	Forward

Button	Description
Refresh
Stop
Show/Hide ¶
Help

Creating a Web Page

Although FrontPage Express creates and formats the Web pages in HTML (HyperText Markup Language), you don't have to worry about learning HTML. You see the Web page very much as it will appear in a Web browser, so you'll find that creat-ing a Web page in FrontPage Express is similar to making a document in a word processor.

 TERM **HyperText Markup Language (HTML)**   The standard language (or code) used to describe the contents and layout of a Web page.

To start a new Web page in FrontPage Express:

1. With the FrontPage Express application open, choose **File, New** from the menu. The New Page dialog box opens (see Figure 12.2).

Figure 12.2 The New Page dialog box.

2. Select one of the available templates or wizards to help you design the type of Web page you want. Select **Normal Page** to start with a blank page.

3. Click **OK**. If you've selected a wizard, follow the instructions on the dialog boxes to build your page; if you chose a template, put your own text and pictures in the framework. On a Normal Page, you have a blank page and can add text and pictures as you wish.

When you save the file (choose **File, Save** from the menu), FrontPage Express saves your work directly to the Web (if you installed Microsoft Web Publishing Wizard) or to a file.

Editing an Existing Web Page

You can open existing Web pages from the Web and edit them if you have the Microsoft Web Publishing Wizard installed. Otherwise, you open an HTML file from your hard disk or network.

To open an existing Web page:

1. Choose **File**, **Open** from the menu. The Open File dialog box appears (see Figure 12.3).

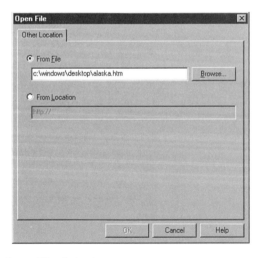

Figure 12.3 The Open File dialog box.

2. If you want to open an HTML file from your computer or network, select **From File** and enter the path and file name of the file (click **Browse** to find

the file if you don't know the path or name). If you want to open a page from the Web select **From Location** and enter the address.

3. Click **OK**.

Once the file opens, you edit it as you would a word processing document and then save it.

Formatting Text

As with a word processor, you can select text and then apply the formatting or you can turn on the format before entering the text, type the text, and then turn off the formatting.

You can apply formatting using the tools on the Format toolbar, or choose **Format, Font** to set the appearance of characters (see Figure 12.4) or **Format, Paragraph** to specify paragraph attributes in terms of HTML styles.

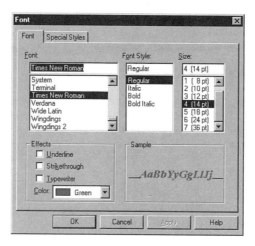

Figure 12.4 The Font dialog box.

If you're comfortable with formatting word processing pages, you won't have any difficulty applying new formatting attributes. However, you may be surprised that text size is listed as 1, 2, 3 because those are the settings you must use for HTML. To use special HTML format codes to format text on your Web page, select the **Special Styles** tab in the Font dialog box. Refer to Help for information on how to apply those codes.

CAUTION

Using HTML Codes   Because Web pages are generated based on HTML, specific codes exist to specify types of font and paragraph formatting. If you don't understand what code you're selecting from some of the dialog boxes, you are better off avoiding them. Let FrontPage Express do the work of selecting the correct code.

Changing the Page Properties

You can set margins, choose a page background or background sounds, or title your page using the Page Properties box. Although several menu commands will open different pages of this dialog box for you, the easiest way to access it is to choose **File**, **Page Properties**.

There are four tab selections on the Page Properties dialog box:

- **General**   On this page (see Figure 12.5) you can specify a title for your Web page, a default target form, base location, and a background sound (click **Browse** to find the sound file).

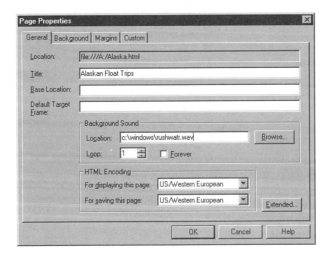

Figure 12.5   The Page Properties box with the General tab selected.

- **Background**   Select this tab (see Figure 12.6) to set a background color for your page or to choose a background image you want to appear behind your text (click **Browse** to select the file). You can choose to make the background image a watermark (faded picture). You can also pick the colors you want to use for your hyperlink text.

- **Margins**   If you want to specify a top or left margin, select the **Margins** tab.

- **Custom**   You can specify system and user variables for your page by selecting the **Custom** tab. These options are only for experienced HTML users.

Click **OK** to accept your selections.

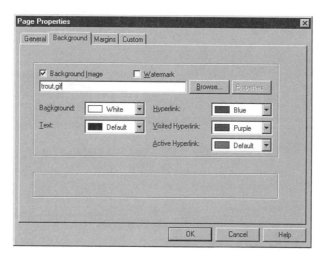

Figure 12.6   The Page Properties box with the Background tab selected.

Adding Hypertext, Images, and WebBot Components

A good Web page contains hypertext links to lead you to related Web pages and pictures to illustrate your topic.

To create a hypertext link:

1. Select the text you want to use as the hypertext link.

2. Choose **Insert**, **Hyperlink** from the menu or click the **Create or Edit Hyperlink** button on the Standard toolbar.

3. When the Create Hyperlink dialog box appears (see Figure 12.7), enter the URL to which you want to link. To link to a Web page, make sure the **Hyperlink Type** list displays **http:**.

4. Click **OK**.

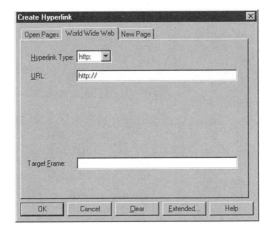

Figure 12.7 The Create Hyperlink dialog box.

To add images to your page:

1. Position your insertion point where you want to put the image (picture or drawing).

2. Choose **Insert**, **Image** from the menu or click the **Insert Image** button on the Standard toolbar.

3. When the Image dialog box appears, enter the location of the image file or click **Browse** to select the file.

4. Click **OK**. The image is inserted, and selection handles appear around it. To move the image, drag it. To resize the image, drag a handle.

WebBot Components place Include, Time Stamp, and Search features in your Web page. The Include component includes an URL in your page so another Web page opens when your page appears, Time Stamp adds the current date or the date last modified, and Search puts a search bar on your page.

To add one of these features to your page:

1. Position your insertion point where you want to put the WebBot component.

2. Choose **Insert**, **WebBot Component** or click the **WebBot Component** button on the Standard toolbar.

3. When the Insert WebBot Component dialog box opens (see Figure 12.8), select the WebBot component you want to insert and click **OK**.

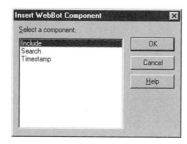

Figure 12.8 The Insert WebBot Component dialog box.

4. A dialog box opens specific to the component you selected. Enter the information requested and set the desired options. Click **OK**.

5. The WebBot Component appears on your page (see Figure 12.9 to see the Search component).

Figure 12.9 The Search Component on a page.

In this lesson, you learned the basics of creating or editing a Web page using FrontPage Express. In the next lesson, you will learn about HyperTerminal.

Using HyperTerminal

In this lesson, you learn about HyperTerminal, a communication tool that comes with Windows 95. You will also learn how to create a HyperTerminal connection and dial into another computer.

What Is HyperTerminal?

HyperTerminal allows you to remotely connect to another computer. You use HyperTerminal to connect to Bulletin Boards or to other computers (including your friends) to send and receive files. If the computer you wish to connect to is running Windows, Microsoft recommends you use Dial-Up Networking rather than HyperTerminal, but you will find HyperTerminal useful when connecting to Bulletin Boards, government agencies, and colleges.

 Bulletin Board Small online services that act as meeting places for people with common interests. Many government agencies and schools uses bulletin boards to allow people access to information regarding their services or schools. Software companies use bulletin boards as their place for users to download files, or bug fixes. Bulletin boards are fairly easy to set up and maintain, and require a computer, a modem, and bulletin board software. You'll find lots of bulletin boards run by individuals out of their home.

Creating a Connection

To connect to another computer using HyperTerminal, you need a modem and you need to establish a connection for each computer you want to communicate with.

To create a HyperTerminal connection:

1. Click the **Start** Button. Choose **Programs**, **Accessories**, **HyperTerminal**.

2. The HyperTerminal folder opens as shown in Figure 13.1.

The HyperTerminal icon ────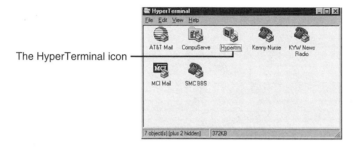

Figure 13.1 The HyperTerminal Folder contents.

3. Double-click the **HyperTerminal** icon. If you are running Active Desktop, you need only to single click.

4. The Connection Description dialog box opens (see Figure 13.2). Type a name for your connection in the **Name** box and select an icon. Click **OK**.

Figure 13.2 Choose an icon for your new connection.

5. The Phone Number dialog box appears. Type the **Phone Number** for your new connection. Check the **Country Code**, **Area Code** and modem type (in **Connect Using**) to be certain they are correct. Click **OK**.

6. The Connect dialog box appears. **Default Location** is selected in the Your Location box. If you are using a laptop and want to create a different location name, type the new name; otherwise accept Default Location as your location. Click **Dialing Properties.** The Dialing Properties dialog box appears (see Figure 13.3).

Figure 13.3   Disable call waiting in the Dialing Properties dialog box.

7. If you need to dial a prefix for an outside line, supply this information in the **How I Dial From This Location** section of the Dialing Properties box. If your phone has call waiting, disable it by placing a check mark in the **This Location Has Call Waiting** box. Select the prefix to disable call waiting from the drop-down list or type the numbers and characters yourself. Click **OK**.

CAUTION

Disable Call Waiting!   Be certain to disable call waiting before you connect to another computer, dial into the Internet or use Dial Up Networking. The signal you hear on your phone, indicating that another call is coming in, can interfere with data transfer. In many areas of the country, dialing the prefix *70 will disable call waiting. When you hang up from your call, call waiting is reactivated automatically. If you aren't sure of which prefix you should use, check the front pages of your local phone book.

8. The Connect dialog box appears. You can now dial to another computer by clicking **Dial**. If you do not want to dial out now, click **Cancel** to close the dialog box. When prompted to save your file, click **Yes**.

Your new connection icon now appears in the HyperTerminal folder. You can close this window, dial into another computer (see the following section), or if you need to change or edit this connection, right-click the icon and choose **Properties**.

Dialing Into a Computer

To dial into another computer or bulletin board:

1. If you do not have the HypterTerminal folder open, click the **Start** button and select **Programs**. Right-click your new **Connection** icon and select **Connect**.

2. The HyperTerminal window opens and the Connect dialog box appears. Click **Dial**.

3. The Connect dialog box closes and the HyperTerminal window becomes active. You are now connected to the other computer.

Connecting to a Bulletin Board

To connect to a bulletin board, establish a connection with HyperTerminal and dial into the bulletin board as described above. Different bulletin boards run different software, but once you use one bulletin board, you'll get the hang of it. All bulletin boards will require you to log in and often ask you to assign yourself a password if this is your first visit (see Figure 13.4). Some bulletin board services are free, others charge a membership fee.

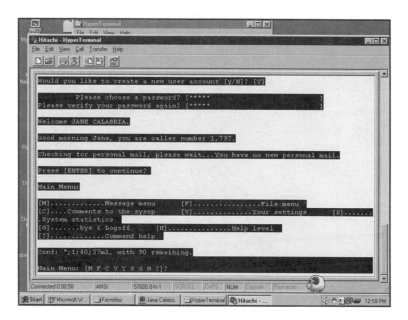

Figure 13.4 Bulletin Board log in.

Once you log on you will see a menu of services available at the site. After you have finished exploring the site, leave the bulletin board by signing out. A common method for signing out is to type G (for good-bye) at the prompt.

To download a file from a bulletin board, you select from a menu of files that can be downloaded from that server. This list is usually accessed from a menu on the first page of the bulletin board. Once you have located the file you want to download, you will need to select a File Transfer Protocol. Instructions for downloading are usually given to you by the bulletin board service.

In this lesson, you learned how to set a HyperTerminal connection and dial into another computer.

Active Desktop Essentials

Navigating the Active Desktop

In this lesson, you will learn about the components and features of the Active Desktop.

What Is the Active Desktop?

If you've installed the Platform Preview of Internet Explorer 4, you've noticed that your Desktop has changed. Your Desktop wallpaper or pattern is gone, and a solid black background (see Figure 1.1) has replaced it. You have a new Channel Bar and the Microsoft Internet Explorer 4 splash appears on the right side of the screen. Your taskbar also looks different. All of these changes have been made because Windows 95 is now completely Internet-based, and your new Active Desktop has become a Web browser. The Active Desktop is so named because you can place active content from the Web right on your Desktop.

Splash A graphic, usually a manufacturer's program logo, that appears briefly when a software application starts. In the case of the Internet Explorer 4 text on your desktop, this splash remains on the Active Desktop continuously.

Some of the changes you'll notice immediately include:

- **The mouse acts like it does when you're on a Web page.** When you move your mouse over an icon on the Active Desktop, the mouse pointer changes to a hand with a pointing finger. A single mouse-click will now activate the icon. You don't have to double-click anymore!

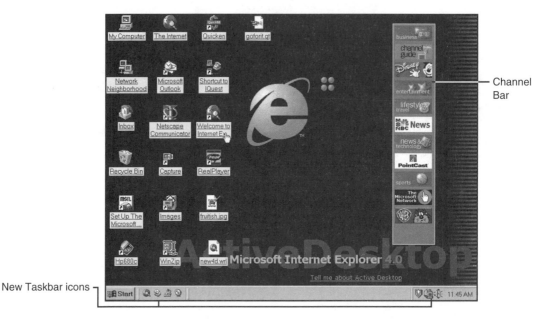

New Taskbar icons

Channel Bar

Figure 1.1   The Active Desktop.

- **The taskbar has more icons on it.** In addition to the buttons that represent your open and running programs, there are new icons that take you to new features, such as The Internet Explorer and Outlook Express.

- **Channel Bar.** This is a copy of the Channel Bar you encountered in Lesson 10. It allows you to tune in to high-quality Web sites with a click of the mouse.

For more information on The Internet Explorer, see Part IV, Lesson 2, "Installing Internet Explorer 4." To find out more about Outlook Express, see Part IV, Lesson 11, "Using Outlook Express Mail and News."

Using the Active Desktop

The Active Desktop performs two functions. It's an access point for the Internet, and it continues to perform its basic function as a site for the standard Windows icons and any program icons you place there as shortcuts. In addition, you can place active components, such as stock tickers and automatically updating news pages and weather maps right on the desktop! For more information on the Windows desktop icons, see Part I, Lesson 1, "Navigating the Windows 95 Desktop."

The Taskbar

The taskbar continues to display buttons for each of the programs you're using concurrently, but it also contains a new Quick Launch toolbar with the following button icons (see Figure 1.2):

- **Launch Internet Explorer Browser** takes you immediately to that program in its own window. If your Dial-up Networking or other Internet connection is set up, you will be taken directly to the Microsoft Home page.

- **Launch Outlook Express** takes you to a program for getting your Internet mail and news. This, too, is dependent on your successful setup of your Internet connection.

For more information on establishing your dial-up networking options and connecting to the Internet, see Part IV, Lesson 3, "Configuring for Internet Access."

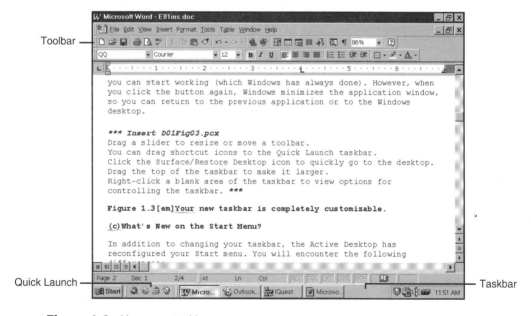

Figure 1.2 Your new taskbar.

- **Show Desktop** quickly returns you to the desktop when you have other applications running, so you don't have to close a bunch of windows.

- **View Channels** display the Internet Explorer Channels window full screen, with the Channels Bar on the left.

Taking Control of the Taskbar

You can take control of the Quick Launch toolbar and your new taskbar in several ways:

- Drag the slider (the double vertical lines) on the right side of the toolbar to make it take up more or less space on the taskbar.

- Drag the slider to the left or right of another toolbar's slider to move the toolbar.

- Drag document icons or shortcut icons onto the Quick Launch toolbar to create buttons for the applications you run most often.

- You can place additional toolbars on the taskbar. Right-click a blank area of the toolbar, point to **Toolbars**, and select any of the following options:

  Address places the Address text box on the taskbar. You can enter the address of a Web page into this text box to open a page.

  Links inserts a bar that contains buttons pointing to helpful Web pages. You can add buttons for your own favorite pages.

  Desktop displays a toolbar containing buttons for all the shortcuts on your Windows Desktop.

  New Toolbar lets you transform a folder into a toolbar. For example, you can select **New Toolbar**, and select **Control Panel**, to create a toolbar that contains icons for all the tools in the Windows Control Panel.

- To remove a toolbar, right-click on a blank area of the toolbar, and select **Close**.

- To view larger icons in the toolbar, right-click a blank area of the toolbar, point to **View**, and select **Large**.

- To turn text descriptions of the toolbar buttons on or off, right-click a blank area of the toolbar, and select **Show Text**.

You might also notice that the taskbar now toggles running applications. For instance, if you click the button for a running application, Windows moves the application's window to the front, so you can start working (which Windows has always done). However, when you click the button again, Windows minimizes the application window, so you can return to the previous application or to the Windows Desktop.

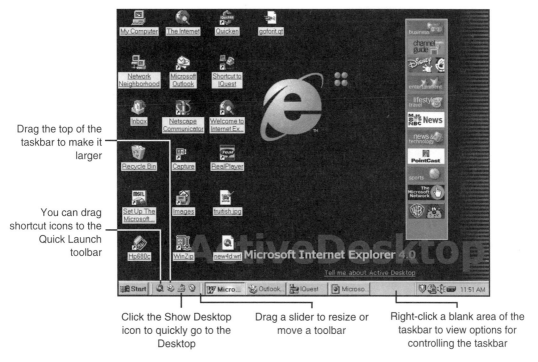

Drag the top of the taskbar to make it larger

You can drag shortcut icons to the Quick Launch toolbar

Click the Show Desktop icon to quickly go to the Desktop

Drag a slider to resize or move a toolbar

Right-click a blank area of the taskbar to view options for controlling the taskbar

Figure 1.3 Your new taskbar is completely customizable.

What's New on the Start Menu?

In addition to changing your taskbar, the Active Desktop has reconfigured your Start menu. You will encounter the following differences:

- The Start menu now has a Favorites submenu, which you can use to quickly open Web pages that you have marked as Favorites in Internet Explorer.

- The Find menu has a couple new options:

  Computer lets you search another computer on your network or intranet for files.

  People allows you to use Internet search tools to track down friends, family members, and business associates on the Web.

  On the Internet opens a Web page that helps you find Web sites and research topics on the Internet.

- You can rearrange applications and program groups on the Start menu simply by dragging them. As you drag, a black horizontal line appears, marking the new position of the application or group.

Using Active Desktop Components

One of the great new features of the Active Desktop is that it allows you to place components (*Desktop components*) of any size and dimensions on your Desktop. In other words, you can go beyond those small shortcut icons and add larger objects, such as stock tickers, scrolling news headlines, and e-mail notification boxes right on your Desktop. With Desktop components, you have complete control of their size and position. You can even set up Desktop components to receive automatic updates from the Web during the day.

  Desktop Components Desktop components are Web-friendly windows, applications, and other objects that you can place right on your Windows Desktop. You can set up subscriptions for these components, so they automatically download updated content during the day or night, giving you easy access to the latest information.

The following sections provide the instructions you need to start using the Active Desktop.

Adding Desktop Components

To add Desktop components, you must download them from the Web using Internet Explorer. Microsoft has set up a Desktop Component Gallery on the Web, where you can go to download some samples. The following steps show you how to access the gallery, download a Desktop component, and place it on your Windows Desktop:

1. Right-click a blank area of the Windows Desktop, select **Properties**, and click the **Web** tab. The Items on the Active Desktop list displays the names of any installed Desktop components.

2. Click **New**. The New Active Desktop Item dialog box appears, asking if you want to go to the Active Desktop Gallery.

3. Click **Yes**. This runs Internet Explorer and connects you to the Internet, if you are not already connected. Internet Explorer loads the Active Desktop Gallery Web page.

4. Click the link for the Desktop component you want. Another page appears, describing the component and displaying a link for downloading it.

5. Click the link to download it and place it on your Desktop. Internet Explorer displays a couple dialog boxes, asking for your confirmation and allowing you to specify how often you want your Desktop component to update information. Enter your preferences.

Figure 1.4 shows a Desktop component as it appears on my Active Desktop. Once a Desktop component is on the Desktop, you can move it or resize it. To move a component, point to its title bar to display a gray bar at the top of the window; drag the gray bar to move the component. To resize a component, drag one of the frame's corners. As these Desktop components become more popular, you will start to find Desktop components sprinkled all over Web pages.

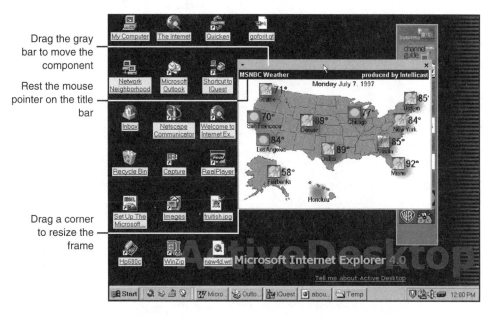

Figure 1.4 Desktop Components make your Desktop an active area, where you can receive the latest news and information.

Removing Desktop Components

Turning off or deleting a Desktop component is a little more difficult than adding one. Following these steps:

1. Right-click a blank area of the Desktop and select **Properties**. The Display Properties dialog box appears.

3. Click the **Web** tab. This tab contains a list of Desktop components, as shown in Figure 1.5, including the Channel Bar.

3. To turn off a component, click its check box to remove the check mark.

4. To completely remove a component, select it, and then click the **Delete** button.

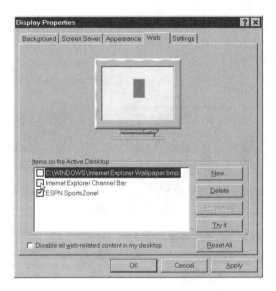

Figure 1.5 You can turn Desktop components on or off.

Also, the taskbar is now segmented. There are small pleated rectangles between the section containing your active application buttons and the section containing your Internet Explorer and Outlook Express icons. These segments can be expanded and collapsed by dragging these rectangles across the taskbar.

In this lesson, you learned about the Active Desktop and its use as a Web browser, as well as new features on the taskbar. In the next lesson, you'll learn about customizing the Active Desktop.

Customizing the Active Desktop

In this lesson, you'll learn to change the appearance of the Active Desktop.

Changing Your Desktop Appearance

If you installed Internet Explorer 4 on your computer and don't like the changes it made to the appearance of your desktop, you may decide to go back to the standard Windows Desktop. To remove the Internet Explorer 4 splash and Channel Bar:

1. Right-click your mouse on any empty portion of the Active Desktop. A pop-up menu appears. From the menu, choose **Active Desktop** to open the Active Desktop submenu.

2. Select **View as Web Page**. This removes the check mark and hides the Channel Bar and the Active Desktop Wallpaper.

Turning off the Active Desktop only hides the Web page background and any desktop components, including the Channel Bar. It does not affect the taskbar or single-click access to applications and files. To completely remove Active Desktop and all other Internet Explorer desktop integration features, you must uninstall the features, as explained in Part 4, Lesson 2, "Installing Internet Explorer 4."

Selecting Different Web Page Wallpaper

Internet Explorer comes with several Web page wallpaper designs that you can use in place of the default Microsoft wallpaper. To use one of these designs, follow these steps:

1. Right-click a blank area of the Desktop, point to **Active Desktop**, and select **Customize My Desktop**. The Display Properties dialog box appears with the Background tab in front.

2. Under Wallpaper, click **Browse**. The Browse dialog box appears.

3. Change to the **Windows\Web** folder.

4. Open the **Files of Type** drop-down list, and select **HTML Document**. A list of Web pages appears.

5. Select the desired wallpaper design, and click **Open**. The selected design appears in the Wallpaper list, as shown in Figure 2.1.

6. Make sure Disable All Web-Related Content in My Desktop is *not* checked. Click Apply to preview the selected wallpaper design.

7. Repeat steps 4–6 until you find the design you want, and then click **OK**.

Figure 2.1   You can use any of several Web wallpaper designs as your Windows background.

TIP   **Your Own Web Page Background**   You can download any Web page or create your own Web page and use it as a Windows background. Be sure you save the page and any graphic images that are embedded on the page. The best way to do this is to open the page in FrontPad and save it to your disk. If you save the page from Internet Explorer, graphics are not saved.

Refreshing Your Desktop

As you know from the previous lesson, your desktop components can automatically download updated content from the Web if you set up site subscriptions for them. However, if you want to make sure you are viewing the latest information, you can manually update your components:

1. Right-click a blank area of the Windows desktop, and point to **Active Desktop**. The Active Desktop submenu appears.

2. Click **Update Now**. The Active Desktop automatically downloads updated content for all of your desktop components.

Using the Channel Screen Saver

In addition to allowing you to pepper your screen with desktop components, Active Desktop allows you to use channels as screen savers. To use the Channel screen saver, you must first subscribe to channels, as explained in Lesson 1. Then, take the following steps to turn on the screen saver:

1. Right-click a blank area of the desktop, and select **Properties**.

2. Click the **Screen Saver** tab.

3. Open the **Screen Saver** drop-down list, and select **Channel Screen Saver** (see Figure 2.2).

4. Click the **Preview** button to see how the screen saver will appear when active. The preview shows the screen saver in action. Click the **X** in the upper-right corner of the screen to close the screen saver.

5. Click the **Settings** button. The General tab displays a list of desktop components that will appear when the screen saver kicks in.

6. You can prevent any of the desktop components from appearing by clicking their check boxes to remove the check marks.

7. By default, the screen saver displays the URL (address) of each desktop component for 30 seconds. Click the arrows next to **Display each URL for ___ seconds** to increase or decrease the time.

8. Click the **Advanced** tab.

9. Under **Closing the Screen Saver**, you can choose to have the screen saver close when you move the mouse. The default setting, Do Not Close the Screen Saver with Mouse Movement keeps the screen saver running even when you move the mouse.

10. Click the **OK** button to save your settings. This returns you to the Display Properties dialog box.

11. Enter any other screen saver preferences, such as password protection and the number of minutes of inactivity that will cause the screen saver to kick in. Click **OK** to save your changes.

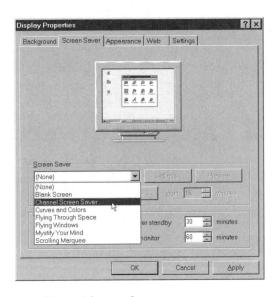

Figure 2.2 Turn on the Channel Screen Saver.

In this lesson, you learned to change the Active Desktop by both restoring the Standard desktop and changing the desktop settings. In the next lesson, you'll learn about the changes Internet Explorer has created in My Computer.

Using My Computer

In this lesson, you'll learn about the changes Internet Explorer 4 makes to the My Computer window and tools.

What's New with My Computer?

Click the **My Computer** icon in the upper-left corner of the Windows desktop, and keep an eye on the screen. You now see the new, improved My Computer, a two-paned window with a pretty background. As you can see in Figure 3.1, My Computer has a new toolbar that looks more like a toolbar you might find in a Web browser; in fact, you can use this toolbar to navigate the Web. If the toolbar is not displayed, select **View**, **Toolbar**, and select **Standard Buttons**.

When you point to a disk icon in My Computer or Windows Explorer, the left pane shows the amount of total and free disk space (see Figure 3.1). Click the **Control Panel** icon. When you rest the mouse pointer on an icon in the Control Panel, the right pane displays information about that icon and may display links for connecting to Microsoft technical support.

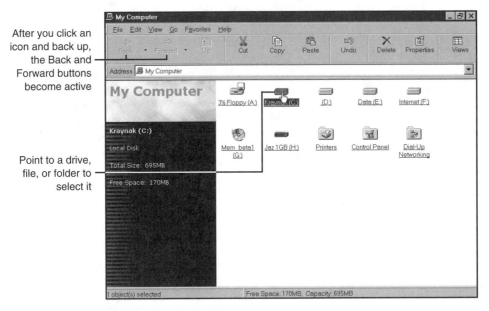

After you click an
icon and back up,
the Back and
Forward buttons
become active

Point to a drive,
file, or folder to
select it

Figure 3.1 My Computer helps you navigate your File system as if it were a Web page.

Selecting Icons

The first thing you'll notice when you move your mouse around in the My Computer window is that your mouse pointer turns into a hand when you're pointing to an icon (see Figure 3.2). This is all part of the Internet Explorer 4 influence—icons are treated like hypertext, so the mouse behaves as it would if you were at an actual Web site, pointing to a hypertext link.

To open My Computer from the Windows Desktop (Active or standard), click the **My Computer** icon. To select an icon, you only need to point to it with the mouse. To open the program, click once. Double-clicking is no longer necessary!

To Select multiple, non-neighboring files, hold down the Ctrl key while pointing. To select neighboring files, point to the first file in the group, and then hold down the shift key while pointing to the last file.

For more information about My Computer, see Part I, Lesson 10, "Using My Computer."

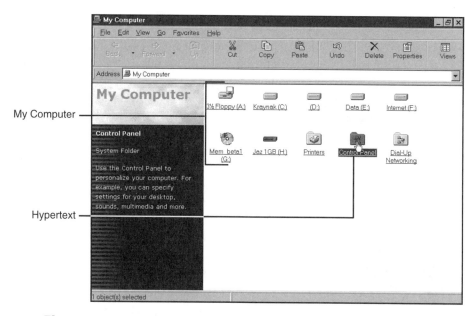

Figure 3.2 The My Computer window.

The My Computer Toolbar

Internet Explorer 4 has placed tools on the My Computer toolbar to assist you in going to a particular Web address, and for moving forward and backward between links on a Web page and between folders and drives on your computer or network. You can learn more about the features of My Computer in Part I, Lesson 12 "Managing Files with My Computer." The My Computer toolbar is shown in Figure 3.3.

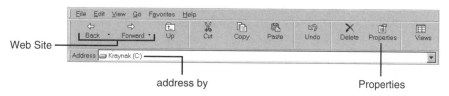

Figure 3.3 The My Computer toolbar.

Accessing a Web Site from the Toolbar

You can use the My Computer toolbar to go to a particular Web site. Click the **Address** drop-down list, and if Internet Explorer 4 is included in your Start menu, you can choose **The Internet** from the list. Internet Explorer 4 will connect to the Internet through your established connection method. See Part IV, Lesson 3, "Configuring for Internet Access" to learn about setting up your Internet connection. To access a specific Web site using the toolbar:

1. Type a specific URL (Web site address) into the Address box.

2. Internet Explorer 4 will access the site. As you follow hypertext links to other pages linked to the site, you can use the Back and Forward buttons on the toolbar to move backward and forward through the sites and pages you've accessed.

Disk, File, and Folder

The Properties button found on the toolbar opens a dialog box that allows you to view and change settings for your drives, folders, and files. Figure 3.4 displays the Properties dialog box for a hard drive.

To view a drive's Properties, point to (don't click) that drive in the group of My Computer icons (hold it there a second or two until the drive is highlighted to be sure it's selected), and click the **Properties** button. You can also choose **File, Properties** from the menu or right click the icon and select **Properties**.

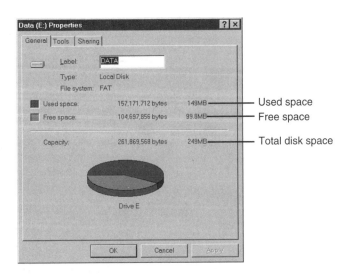

Figure 3.4   My Computer Properties.

The Tools tab (shown in Figure 3.5) in the Properties dialog box shows the last time three maintenance programs were run. By clicking the buttons in each of the three sections, you can start that particular maintenance program:

- **Error-Checking**   The ScanDisk program checks for errors on your disk drive. You can run a Standard check that looks only at files and folders, or a Thorough check which also scans the surface of the disk. Click **Check Now**.

- **Backup**   This option will run Microsoft's Backup program. For more information about using Backup, see Part I, Lesson 16, "Using Backup."

- **Defragmentation**   The Disk Defragmenter program checks your drive for fragmented files, and makes more efficient use of your drive's free space.

> **Defragment**   When a file becomes too large, your computer can't always find one big free space in which to store it. As a result, large files can end up stored in many separate pieces. This slows down disk access when you open and save files. Defragmenting reorganizes your disk's space so that each file is stored in one contiguous area.

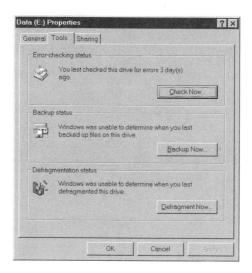

Figure 3.5 The Tools tab.

The My Computer Menus

Another way that the Internet Explorer 4 shell or Active Desktop affects My Computer is through the addition of two new menus:

- **The Go menu** (see Figure 3.6) offers choices for moving backward and forward between Web sites and links, going to the Microsoft Home page, searching the Web, or going to a list of the Web sites Microsoft rates "Best of the Web." There are also commands for accessing Internet Mail and News.
- **The Favorites menu** is developed by you. The menu offers commands for adding to the list of Favorites, accessing Web site subscriptions, and selecting a Favorite site. Figure 3.7 shows the Favorites menu with some Favorite sites listed.

For more information on Web concepts and HTML, see Part IV, Lesson 1, "Understanding the Internet and Web".

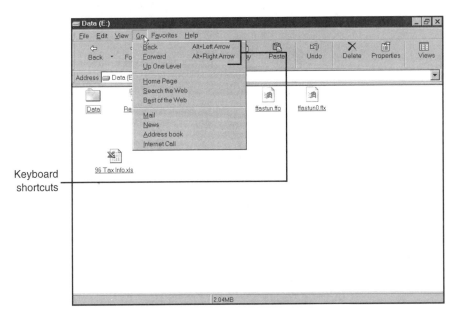

Figure 3.6   The Go menu.

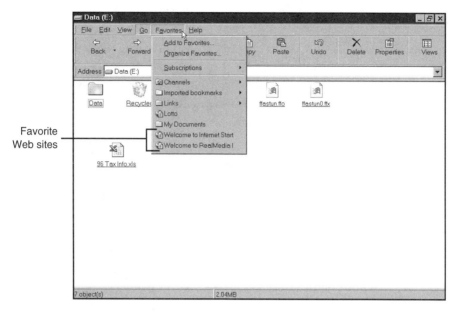

Favorite
Web sites

Figure 3.7 The Favorites menu.

Adding a Favorite for a File or Folder

Web site access is made simpler and faster by adding Web sites to your Favorites list. (More information about accessing a Web site is found in Part IV, Lesson 6, "Visiting a Web site.") You can use Favorites to make it easier to access your drives and folders, as well:

1. Open the drive or folder you want to add to the Favorites list.

2. Choose **Favorites**, **Add to Favorites**. The currently displayed drive or folder will be added to your list (see Figure 3.8).

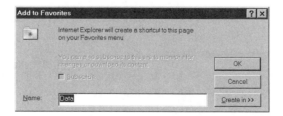

Figure 3.8 The Add to Favorites dialog box.

Customizing My Computer

My Computer is fully customizable. It offers options to return My Computer to its previous condition, add toolbars and buttons for navigating the Web, and even use Web pages and graphics as backgrounds for specific folders. The following sections explain the most popular customization options for My Computer.

Selecting the Integration Mode

If you don't like the new look and behavior of My Computer, you can change it. The biggest change you can make is to return My Computer to its previous condition. Take the following steps:

1. Select **View**, **Options**. The Options dialog box appears, with the General tab up front.

2. Select one of the following options, as shown in Figure 3.9:

   Web Style is the default. My Computer uses an HTML background for any folders that are appropriately set up. You point to icons to select them, click icons to open folders, run applications, or open files.

   Classic Style returns My Computer to mint condition. No Web page backgrounds are used. You click icons to select them, double-click icons to open folders, run applications, or open files.

   Custom lets you enter settings to control the look and behavior of My Computer.

3. If you select **Custom**, click the **Settings** button, and enter your preferences:

   Browse Folders lets you display the contents of each folder in the same window or in separate windows. If you choose to use one window, when you click a folder icon, My Computer does not open a new window for displaying the folder's contents.

   Show Folders as Web Pages tells My Computer to use Web pages as backgrounds for the My Computer window whenever they are available or only when you choose to use a Web page background.

   File and Folder Icons provides several options for controlling the appearance of selected icons and turning single-click access on or off.

4. Click **OK** to return to the Options dialog box.

5. Click **OK** to save your settings.

In addition, you can display any of the Internet Explorer Bars as a pane in the My Computer Window. Open the **View**, **Explorer Bar** menu, and select any of the following options:

- **Search** displays a panel which allows you to search for specific information on the Web. See Part 4, Lesson 7, "Web, Document and Site Searching."

- **Favorites** displays a list of pages and drive or folder icons which you have added to the Favorites list.

- **History** displays a list of pages you have recently visited, grouped by day or week.

- **Channels** displays the Channel Bar, which allows you to quickly tune in to premium Web sites.

- **None** turns off any bar that is currently displayed.

Figure 3.9 You can change the overall look and behavior of My Computer.

Customizing a Folder's Appearance

You may have noticed that when you click a drive or folder icon, the page background of the My Computer opening window disappears, and you no longer see a two-paneled window. My Computer allows you to use an image as the folder background or create a Web page background with FrontPad. Take the following steps to create a new Web page background for a folder:

1. Open the folder for which you wan to create a background.

2. Select **View**, **Customize This Folder**. The Customize This Folder Wizard appears.

3. Select **Create or Edit an HTML Document** and click **Next**. The Wizard displays information describing what it is about to do.

4. Click **Next**. The Wizard starts FrontPad, and displays a new Web View folder document, as shown in Figure 3.10. Don't panic, it's supposed to look funny in FrontPad.

5. (Optional) You can edit the page and change its formatting, as explained in Part 4, Lesson 12, "Understanding FrontPad."

6. Exit FrontPad. You are returned to the Wizard dialog box, which congratulates you on the changes you have made.

7. Click **Finish**. You are returned to My Computer, where the new background appears for the selected folder.

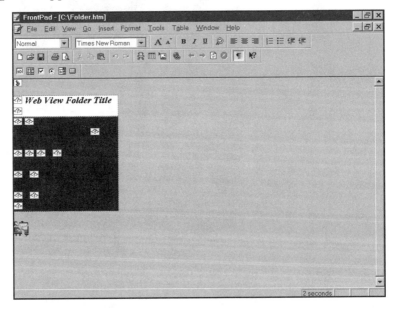

Figure 3.10   FrontPad automatically creates a Web View background for the selected folder.

Adding Web Navigation Toolbars and Buttons

Earlier in this lesson, you learned how to use the new Standard Buttons toolbar in My Computer to navigate Web pages and your own system resources. You can turn on additional toolbars and buttons to enhance navigation.

The View, Toolbar menu contains the same options for turning toolbars on and off as are available in Internet Explorer. Open the **View**, **Toolbar** menu, and select any of the following options: **Standard Buttons**, **Address Bar**, **Links**, or **Text Labels**.

In this lesson, you learned about new features in My Computer's menus and toolbar. In the next lesson, you'll learn about the new features of the Windows Explorer.

Using Windows Explorer

In this lesson, you learn about the changes that Internet Explorer 4 brings to the general appearance, menus, and toolbars in Windows Explorer.

Internet Explorer versus Windows Explorer

Due to the similarity between their names—Internet Explorer and Windows Explorer—it's important to distinguish these two programs. The *Internet Explorer* is an interface that turns your Windows 95 environment into a Web browser. Windows Explorer is a file management program. The Explorer window is shown in Figure 4.1. To get to the Windows Explorer:

1. From the **Start** menu, choose **Programs**.
2. Choose **Windows Explorer** from the submenu.

For more information on using Windows Explorer, see Part I, Lesson 14, "Navigating Explorer."

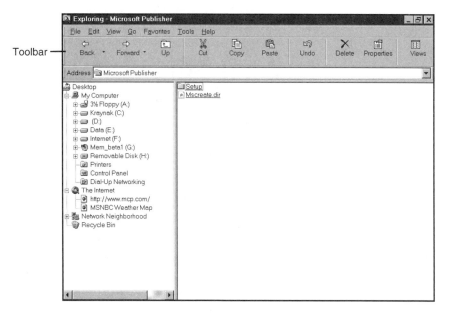

Toolbar

Figure 4.1   The new navigation toolbar.

As you can see from the Figure, Internet Explorer has not made many changes to the appearance and structure of the Windows Explorer Window. The window still consists of two panes. The left pane displays a list of drives and folders on your computer, and the right pane displays the contents of the currently selected drive or folder.

Internet Explorer 4 has placed new tools on the Windows Explorer toolbar to assist you in going to a particular Web address. You can use these same tools for navigating drives and folders on your system. The remaining tools on the toolbar pertain exclusively to your computer's drives and folders. You can learn more about these features of Windows Explorer in Part I, Lesson 15 "Managing Files with Explorer."

Windows Explorer Reorientation

Although Windows Explorer hasn't changed much in appearance, it has revamped the way you select and open files and programs. If you worked with My Computer in Lesson 3, the following list of tips will be review material:

- Click a file to run an application or open a document.

- Click a folder to open it.

- Don't click a file to select it; clicking opens the file or runs it (if it is a program file). To select a file, rest the mouse pointer on the file (point to the file). Windows Explorer highlights it.

- To select additional files, hold down the **Ctrl** key while pointing to other files you want to select.

- To select a group of neighboring files, point to the first file, and then hold down the **Shift** key while pointing to the last file in the group.

- To deselect a file, hold down the **Ctrl** key and point to it.

- You can still right-click a selected file to display a shortcut menu with commands for opening, cutting, copying, and pasting files.

- To rename a file, right-click it and select **Rename**.

- You can click the **Back** button to return to the folder you previously opened. If you backed up, you can click the **Forward** button to move ahead.

- The **Up** button moves you up one level in the folder tree.

- The **File** menu keeps track of which folders (and Web pages) you have opened, so you can quickly return to a folder by selecting it from the File menu.

- The **View** menu is nearly the same as the old Windows Explorer View menu; it contains options for arranging icons in the window.

The **Address** text box, the **Links** toolbar, the **Go** menu, and the **Favorites** menu perform the same tasks as they do in Internet Explorer. You can use these controls to navigate both the Web and your hard drive or company intranet.

Similarities Between My Computer and Windows Explorer

The changes that Internet Explorer makes to Windows Explorer are nearly identical to the changes made to My Computer. For instance, Windows Explorer offers single-click access to files and now sports two new menus: Go and Favorites, which you can use in tandem with Internet Explorer to access Web pages. Refer to Lesson 3 for details.

However, there are some important differences you should be aware of:

- Windows Explorer provides a two-paned window (which it has always had), which gives you a better interface for folder and file management tasks.

- In Windows Explorer, you can display a file list in the left pane and navigate Web pages in the right pane. In My Computer, when you enter a Web page address, My Computer runs Internet Explorer which opens the page in its own window.

- Windows Explorer has a Tools menu, not included in My Computer. Select **Tools**, **Find** to view a list of options for searching your local resources and for searching the Web for pages and people.

- You can't change integration modes (such as single-click access) in Windows Explorer using the **View**, **Options** command. To change integration modes, use My Computer, as explained in Lesson 3. This changes the mode for both My Computer and Windows Explorer.

Accessing Web Sites from Internet Explorer

The major improvement to Windows Explorer is that you can now use it not only to access your system resources, but also to open Web pages and navigate the Web or your company intranet. To open a Web page, scroll down the folder list in the left pane, and click **The Internet**. (You can also select **The Internet** from the **Address** drop-down list.)

Windows Explorer runs Internet Explorer in the right pane, which then opens your Internet Explorer start page (see Figure 4.2). You can now click links or enter page addresses to skip from page to page on the Web.

When you open a Web page in Windows Explorer, Internet Explorer takes over the window, displaying its own menu options and toolbars. For instance, when you open a Web page, Internet Explorer displays the following buttons in the toolbar: Search, Favorites, History, and Channels.

To return to the Windows Explorer toolbar and menus, you must select a drive or folder.

Use the Back and
Forward buttons to
return to pages

You can enter page
addresses in the
Address text box

Internet Explorer
displays Web pages
in this pane

Click The Internet

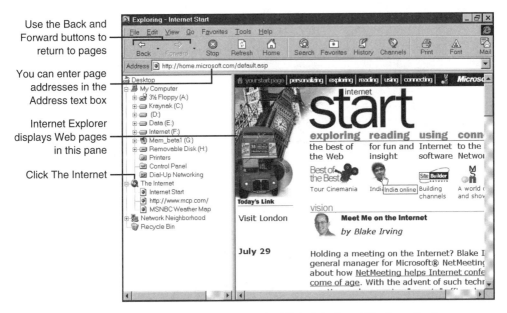

Figure 4.2   You can now browse the Web right from Windows Explorer.

The Windows Explorer Menus

The changes in Windows Explorer affect the menu bar as well. Two new menus
have been added to assist you in accessing Web sites:

- **Go menu** (see Figure 4.3) offers choices for moving backward and forward
  between accessed Web sites and links, going to the Microsoft Home Page,
  searching the Web, or going to a list of the Web sites Microsoft rates "Best
  of the Web." There are also commands for accessing Internet Mail and
  News.

- **Favorites menu** is developed by you. The menu offers commands for
  adding to the list of Favorites, accessing Web site subscriptions, and
  selecting Favorite Web sites. (To add a drive or folder to the Favorites
  menu, see Lesson 3, "Using My Computer," in the section named "Adding
  a Favorite for a File or Folder."

In this lesson, you learned what's new and different in The Windows Explorer,
and how Internet Explorer 4 has changed the appearance and function of the
menus, toolbars, and panes. In the next lesson, you'll learn about how Internet
Explorer 4 has influenced the Network Neighborhood.

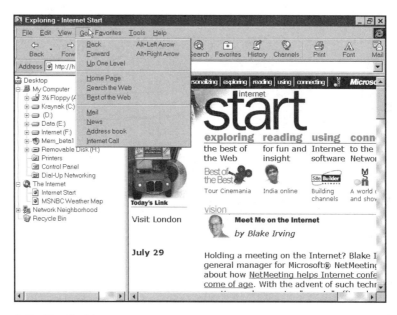

Figure 4.3 The Go Menu.

Using the Network Neighborhood

5

In this lesson, you'll learn to navigate the new features in the Network Neighborhood.

What's New in the Network Neighborhood

The change you'll notice immediately in the Network Neighborhood is that your mouse behaves as it would if it were in a Web site, pointing to hypertext links. Due to the influence of Internet Explorer 4, the Network Neighborhood now functions as a Web browser in addition to its network management functions. The Network Neighborhood is shown in Figure 5.1. (For more information on the Network Neighborhood, see Part III, Lesson 1, "Using Network Neighborhood.")

To access Network Neighborhood click the **Network Neighborhood** icon found on your Windows desktop (Active or Standard). You can also access Network Neighborhood from My Computer or Windows Explorer. Open the **Address** drop-down list and select **Network Neighborhood**. In Windows Explorer, you can click **Network Neighborhood** in the Folder list displayed in the left pane.

TIP **You Don't Need to Double-Click Anymore!** To select an icon, you only need to point to it with the mouse. To open the program, click once.

TIP **What If I Prefer Double-Clicking?** If you don't like the new single-click method for opening files—you may find it confusing if you're accustomed to double-clicking—you can turn the double-click method back on. From the **View** menu, choose **Options**, and in the **General** tab, click the button next to **Classic Style**. Click **OK**.

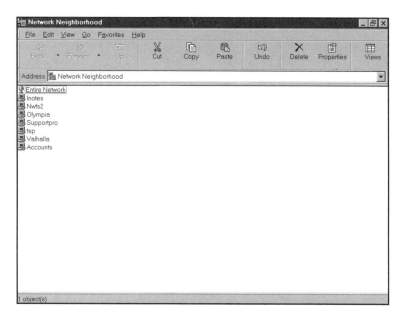

Figure 5.1 The Network Neighborhood.

The Explorer Toolbar

Internet Explorer 4 has placed new tools on the Network Neighborhood toolbar. The Address, Back, and Forward buttons assist you in going to a particular Web address, and moving between links on a Web page. The remaining tools on the toolbar pertain to your network drives. You can learn more about the network file management functions of Network Neighborhood in Part III, Lesson 3 "Managing Files and Folders with Network Neighborhood." The Network Neighborhood toolbar is shown in Figure 5.2.

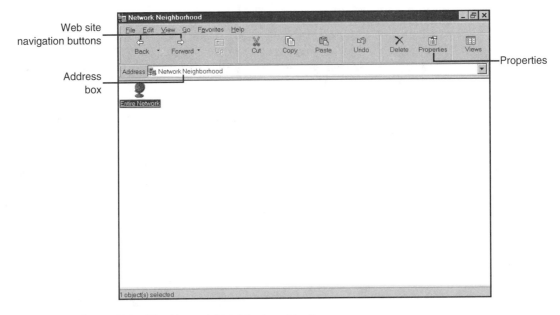

Figure 5.2   The Network Neighborhood toolbar.

Accessing a Web Site from the Toolbar

You can use the Network Neighborhood toolbar to go to a particular Web site. Click the Address drop-list, and choose **The Internet** from the list. Internet Explorer 4 will connect to the Internet through your established connection method. See Part IV, Lesson 3, "Configuring for Internet Access" to learn about setting up your Internet connection. To access a specific Web site using the toolbar:

1. Type a specific URL into the Address box and press **Enter**.

2. Internet Explorer 4 will access the site. As you follow hypertext links to other pages linked to the site, you can use the **Back** and **Forward** buttons on the toolbar to move backward and forward through the sites and pages you've accessed.

Network Drive Properties

The **Properties** button on the toolbar opens a dialog box that displays two tabs—**General** and **Tools**. The **General** tab (see Figure 5.3) displays a graphic illustration of a drive's capacities and available drive space.

To view a drive's Properties, point to that drive icon, and click the **Properties** button. You can also choose **File**, **Properties** from the menu or right-click the drive and select **Properties** from the pop-up menu.

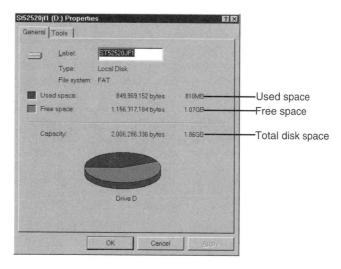

Figure 5.3 Network Neighborhood Properties.

The Tools tab (shown in Figure 5.4) in the Properties dialog box shows the last time three maintenance programs were run. By clicking the buttons in each of the three sections, you can start that particular maintenance program:

- **Error-Checking** The ScanDisk program checks for errors on your disk drive. You can run a Standard check that looks only at files and folders, or a Thorough check which also scans the surface of the disk.

- **Backup** This option will run Microsoft's Backup program. For more information about using Backup, see Part I, Lesson 16, "Using Backup."

- **Defragmentation** The Disk Defragmenter program checks your drive for fragmented files, and makes more efficient use of your drive's free space.

 TERM **Defragment** When a file becomes too large, your computer can't always find one big free space in which to store it. As a result, large files can end up stored in many separate pieces. This slows down disk access when you open and save files. Defragmenting reorganizes your disk's space so that each file is stored in one contiguous area.

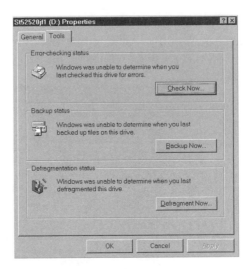

Figure 5.4   The Tools tab.

The Network Neighborhood Menus

There are two new menus, **Go** and **Favorites**, added to the Network Neighborhood menu bar. These menus allow you to seek out Web sites, and store the addresses of the ones you like.

- **Go menu** offers choices for moving backward and forward between accessed Web sites and links, going to the Microsoft Home Page, searching the Web, or going to a list of the Web sites Microsoft rates "Best of the Web." There are also commands for accessing Internet Mail and News (see Figure 5.5).
- **Favorites menu** is developed by you. The menu offers commands for adding a Web site to the list of Favorites, accessing Web site subscriptions, and selecting a Favorite site (see Figure 5.6).

Keyboard shortcuts

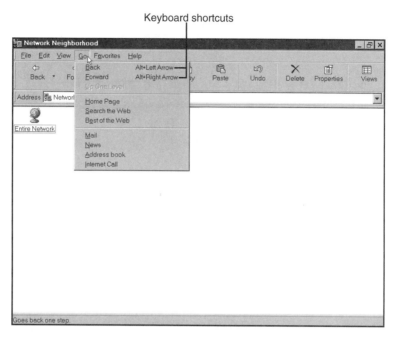

Figure 5.5 The Go menu.

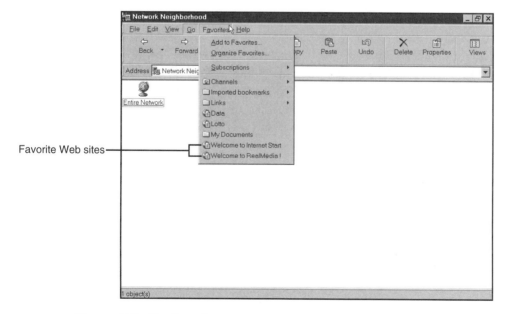

Favorite Web sites

Figure 5.6 The Favorites menu.

For more information on Web concepts and HTML, see Part IV, Lesson 1, "Understanding the Internet and Web".

Adding a Favorite Web Site

If there are Web sites you visit often, you may want to add them to the Favorites menu. More information about accessing a Web site is found in Part IV, Lesson 5, "Visiting a Web Site." To add a Favorite site to your list:

1. Go to the Web site or linked page within the site that you want to add.

2. Choose **Favorites**, **Add to Favorites**. The currently displayed site and page will be added to your list (see Figure 5.7).

3. Click **OK**.

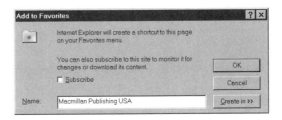

Figure 5.7   The Add to Favorites dialog box.

Organizing and Removing Favorites

If your list of Favorites has become long, you may want to categorize them. Figure 5.8 shows the Organize Favorites dialog box. To categorize them, you can place them in existing folders or create new folders to group them. To create a new folder:

1. From the **Favorites** menu, choose **Organize Favorites**.

2. Click the **New Folder** icon at the top of the dialog box.

3. A New Folder appears, with its name box selected. Type the folder name in the box, and press the **Enter** key.

To categorize your Favorite sites:

1. With the Organize Favorites dialog box open, click the Web site you wish to categorize.

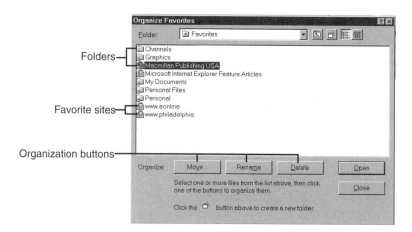

Figure 5.8 The Organize Favorites dialog box.

> **2.** Click the **Move** button. A second dialog box opens, showing a list of your folders. Click the folder you want to place your Web site in, and click **OK**.

After you've accumulated a lot of Favorite Web sites, you may want to delete some of them. To remove a Favorite site listing:

> **1.** Choose **Favorites**, **Organize Favorites**. A dialog box opens.
>
> **2.** Click the site you want to remove (you may have to double-click a folder to expose the site you're looking for), and click the **Delete** button.
>
> **3.** You'll be asked to confirm your intention to send the item to the Recycle bin. Click **Yes**.
>
> **4.** Continue to delete any unwanted sites, and then click **Close** to close the dialog box.

Mapping Network Drives to Your Computer

You can easily map any network drive to your computer, so it appears as a local drive. The easiest way to map a network drive to your computer is to add the Map Network Drive button to your toolbar. Follow these steps:

> **1.** Open the **View** menu and select **Options**. The Options dialog box appears.
>
> **2.** Click the **Advanced** tab.

3. Select **Show Map Network Drive Button in Toolbar** to turn it on.

4. Click **OK**. Two new buttons appear in the toolbar: **Map Network...** and **Disconnect Network...**(see Figure 5.9).

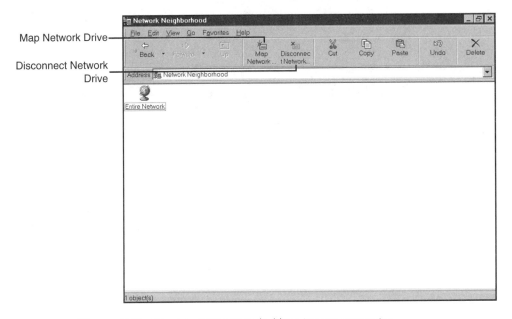

Figure 5.9 You can map network drives to your computer.

Once the buttons are displayed, you can quickly map network drives to your computer. Take the following steps:

1. Click the **Map Network Drive** button. The Map Network Drive dialog box appears, prompting you to select a drive letter and specify a location of the drive on your network.

2. Open the **Drive** drop-down list, and select a letter for the drive, as it will appear on your computer. This list contains letters starting at the first available drive letter for your computer. For instance, if you have a drive D:, the list starts with E:.

3. Type the path to the network drive in the **Path** box, or select a path from the drop-down list.

   4. To have the drive appear automatically on your computer whenever you
   log on to the network, place a check in the **Reconnect at Logon** check box.

   5. Click **OK**.

In this lesson, you learned about the Network Neighborhood's new menus and
toolbar features. In the next lesson, you'll learn about new features in the
Control Panel.

Understanding the Control Panel

In this lesson, you learn about the changes that Internet Explorer 4 has made to the Windows Control Panel.

What's New with Windows Control Panel

You have used the Windows Control Panel to manage your system resources, change printer settings, add and remove programs, and install new hardware. Internet Explorer has not changed any of that. The Control Panel is still the central control system for your computer.

However, with Internet Explorer's redesign of My Computer, the Control Panel has taken on a new look and offers a couple of additional features, including links that allow you to quickly access Microsoft online help for items in the Control Panel.

Running the Control Panel

The procedure for running the Control Panel is the same as it was before you installed Internet Explorer. Do one of the following:

- Open the **Start** menu, point to **Settings**, and click **Control Panel**.
- Start **My Computer** and click the **Control Panel** icon.
- Run Windows Explorer and click the **Control Panel** icon in the Folder list displayed in the left pane.

The Control Panel appears, as shown in Figure 6.1. Note that the left pane now displays links for accessing Microsoft's Home Page and a Technical Support page, where you can find help files for the various items in the control panel. See Lesson 7, "Connecting to Microsoft Support," for details.

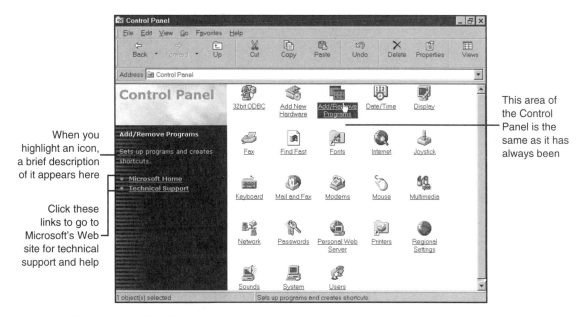

When you highlight an icon, a brief description of it appears here

Click these links to go to Microsoft's Web site for technical support and help

This area of the Control Panel is the same as it has always been

Figure 6.1   The Control Panel sports a new look.

Turning Off Web View

You learned in Lesson 3 how to turn off Web View for My Computer using the **View**, **Options** command. By selecting the Classic Style integration mode, you turn off single-click access and hide any Web page backgrounds that My Computer uses for drives and folders.

You can take the same steps to turn off Web View when the Control Panel is displayed. However, you can also turn off Web View for only the Control Panel. Open the **View** menu and select **As Web Page** to remove the check mark next to the option (see Figure 6.2). This hides the Web page background, including the links to Microsoft's Web site and Technical Support page, but leaves single-click access on.

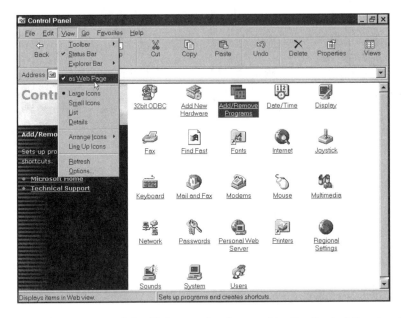

Figure 6.2   You can turn off the Web page background for the Control Panel or for any folder that uses a Web page background.

If you turn off Web View, you can no longer view a description of the high-lighted icon in the left pane. However, you can display descriptions in the main viewing area. Click the **Views** button in the toolbar three times, or open the **View** menu and select **Details**. The names and descriptions of the Control Panel icons appear, as shown in Figure 6.3.

Navigating the Control Panel

The Control Panel was never very difficult to navigate. You click the icon for the setting or device you want to change, and then respond to whatever dialog box appears. Internet Explorer has not changed the way you use the Control Panel.

However, the toolbar offers several controls to help you exit the Control Panel when you are done and use the My Computer window to view drives, folders, files, or Web pages (see Figure 6.4). The following list explains your options:

- Click the **Up** button to move up to My Computer, where you can access your drives and the Printers, Control Panel, and Dial-Up Networking folders.

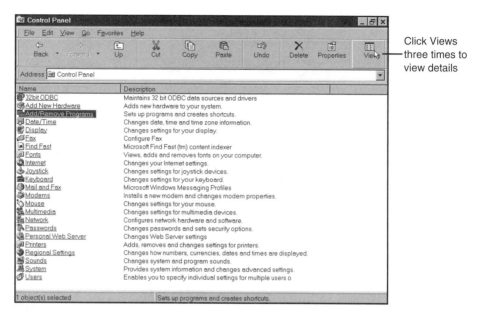

Click Views
three times to
view details

Figure 6.3   You can display details to see Control Panel icon
descriptions.

- If you started with My Computer and clicked the Control Panel icon, you
  can click **Back** to back up to My Computer.

- Open the **Address** drop-down list and select a drive, folder, or Web page
  that you have recently accessed during this session.

- Type a Web page address in the **Address** text box and press **Enter** to open
  a page in Internet Explorer.

- Select the desired drive, folder, Web page, or resource from the **File** menu.
  (The File Menu contains a list of recently accessed drives, folders, Web
  pages, and other resources.)

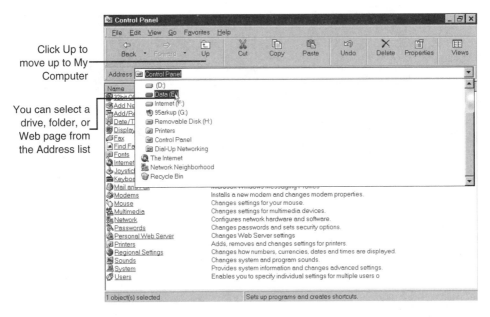

Figure 6.4   You can easily return to your drives and folders or open a Web page when Control Panel is displayed.

In this lesson, you learned about the Control Panel's new menus and features. In the next lesson, you'll learn about connecting to Microsoft Support on the Web.

Connecting to Microsoft Support

In this lesson, you will learn to use the Connect button found in the Windows Control Panel to access the Microsoft Support Web site.

Viewing the Microsoft Support Web Site

To access the Microsoft Support Web site, you can employ any method you currently have of connecting to the Internet and finding a particular Web address. The various options for doing this are covered in Part IV, Lesson 5, "Understanding a Web site" and Lesson 6, "Understanding Links." An easier and more direct method, however, is to access this useful site from within the Windows Control Panel:

1. Open the Windows Control Panel by clicking the **Start** button and choosing **Settings** from the Start menu. From the fly-out menu, choose **Control Panel**.

2. From within the Control Panel window, click the **Technical Support** line on the left side of the window (see Figure 7.1).

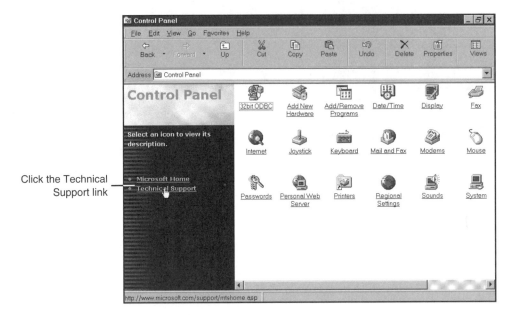

Click the Technical
Support link

Figure 7.1   The Control Panel window.

3. If you are currently online, you will go immediately to the Microsoft
Support Web site. If you connect to the Internet via modem, your modem
will automatically dial your ISP and connect you to the Web site as soon as
a physical connection can be made.

For more information about establishing an Internet connection, see Part III,
Lesson 7, "Connecting to an Internet Service Provider." You can also find more
information about Internet connections in Part IV, Lesson 3, "Configuring for
Internet Access."

Searching for Support by Topic

Within the Support Web page, there are many links to support topics. The best
way to find your topic is to choose a topic from the drop-list in the **Go** box (see
Figure 7.2).

Select a topic from
the drop-down list

The Go
button

Figure 7.2 The Microsoft Support Web site.

To search for a particular support topic:

1. In the **Go** box, click the drop-down arrow to view the list of topics, and choose the name of the product or area for which you need support, such as Internet Explorer (see Figure 7.3).

2. When the topic you need appears in the box, click the **Go** button.

TIP **Quick Search** To move quickly to an item in the list, type the first letter of the word you're looking for, and the list will move to the first item beginning with that letter.

Figure 7.3   A support topic is selected.

Following Hypertext Links

Within the Web page there is text and graphics that are links to other pages.
You'll know you're on a link if your mouse turns into a hand when you're
pointing to the text or graphic item. To go to the linked page, click the mouse
once.

Adding a Site to Favorites

As you move from topic to topic, following the links, you'll notice the address
changes in the Address box on the toolbar. This tells you the name of your link.
If you want to come back to a site again, choose **Favorites**, **Add to Favorites** (see
Figure 7.4). Click **OK**. The exact site you're on at the time will be added to your
list of Favorites. For more information about adding a Web site to your Favorites
menu, see Part IV, Lesson 8, "Working with Web Pages."

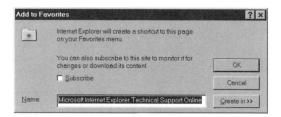

Figure 7.4   Adding a Web Site to Favorites.

Downloading a Web Site for Viewing Offline

Within the dialog box that appears to confirm your Favorite addition, you can also choose to keep a site available for viewing offline. This means that the graphic and text content will be saved in a file (in a location you choose) for viewing even when you're not logged on to the Internet, which can be especially useful when the site contains technical support and information. To save a site for viewing offline:

1. In the Add to Favorites confirming dialog box, click the **Subscribe** check box.

2. To choose a location (folder) for your downloaded site, click the **Create In** button, and choose a folder. Click **OK**.

3. In the Subscribe dialog box (see Figure 7.5), click **OK** to accept the download. For more information about Subscriptions, see Part IV, Lesson 10, "Subscriptions and Working Offline."

Moving Forward and Backward

As you go from linked page to linked page, you may want to move back and forth between pages you've already opened. To do this, click the **Forward** and **Back** buttons on the toolbar. To go all the way back to the to the Microsoft Home page, click the **Home** button on the toolbar, as shown in Figure 7.6.

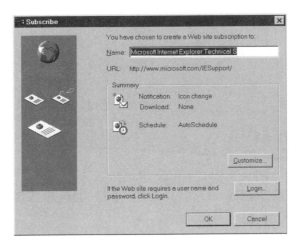

Figure 7.5 The Subscribe dialog box.

Figure 7.6 The Internet Explorer toolbar.

Printing Support Content

Once you've found the help you need, you'll probably want to print out the help text for future reference. To print the support content:

1. From the **File** menu, choose **Print**.

2. Enter any settings you need, such as number of copies, into the appropriate fields in the Print dialog box, and click the **OK** button.

In this lesson, you learned to access Microsoft's Support Web site from the Control Panel, and to search for help by topic and follow links within the Web pages.

Real World Solutions

How to Organize a Hard Drive

In this lesson, you'll find out how to organize your files and folders on the hard drive, just as you would organize your paperwork in a file cabinet.

Categorizing Your Files

When you install Windows-based software, the installation program creates a directory (folder) for the program to reside in on your hard drive. Microsoft Office, for example, is automatically placed in a folder called "MSOffice." This is done to keep the software separate from other programs you may have loaded on your computer. Figure 1.1 shows the contents of the MSOffice folder as viewed in the Windows Explorer. For more information on using Windows Explorer, see Part I, Lesson 15 "Managing Files with Explorer."

When you create a document, spreadsheet, database, or any other type of file, you determine where it will reside on your hard drive when you save it. Windows 95 has a default location called "My Documents," but you may want to create more categories for your files, to make it easier to find them later. Some examples:

- **Categorize your files by software**. You can create folders to store your files based on the software used to create them. For example, a folder called "Documents" to store files created with your word processor, "Spreadsheets" for files created with your spreadsheet software, and so forth. Figure 1.2 shows an example of this categorization method.

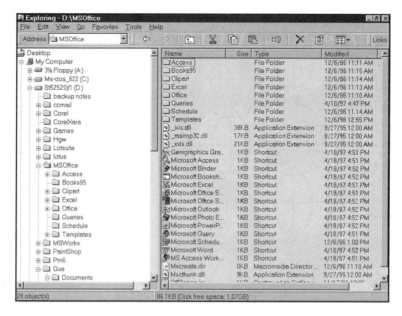

Figure 1.1   The Microsoft Office Folder.

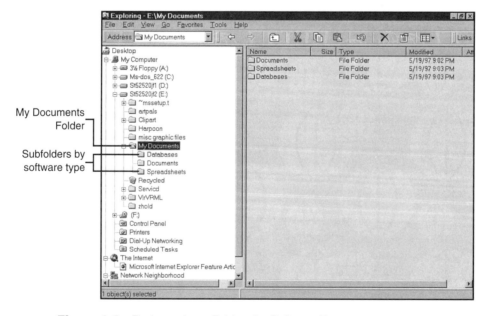

Figure 1.2   Explorer view—Folders by Software Type.

- **Categorize your files by date**. If you track your sales and general business activity by Quarter, you can create folders for all four quarters of the year, and place subfolders inside them, for each month in the quarter (see Figure 1.3).

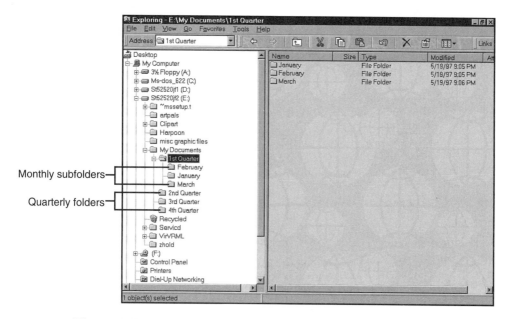

Figure 1.3   Explorer view—Folders by Date.

- **Categorize your files by client name**. If you sell to a few major customers, create a folder for each one, and then store any documents, spreadsheets, and other files for a particular client in that client's folder. Figure 1.4 shows a set of 4 client folders. If you have a group of less-active clients, you can store all the files pertaining to them in a "catch-all" folder entitled "Misc Clients," for example.

Subfolders by type of file

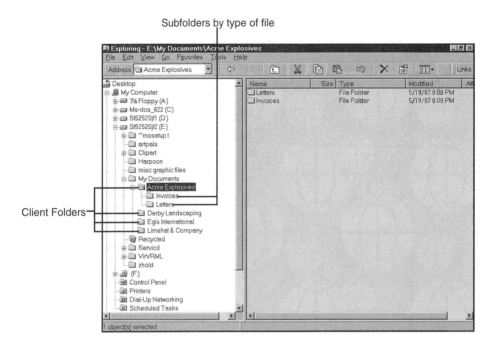

Figure 1.4   Explorer View—folders by client name.

Creating Folders

If you were creating a new folder for your paperwork in a file cabinet, you'd write a name or phrase on the tab of a manila folder, and put the papers in it. You might write "1st Quarter" or "Letters" on the tab, and that would tell you what to put in it, and help you find your paperwork later.

Use either My Computer or Explorer to create a new folder:

1. Be sure that you're in the folder that will contain your new folder. You can check the title bar, **Address** box, or the folder icon in the Folder pane to determine which folder is open.

2. From the **File** menu, choose **New**, **Folder**. A box appears in the window (or in the Contents [right] pane in Explorer) with a box around it and the text highlighted.

3. Type the name you want for your new folder. The text you type replaces the text "New Folder." You can use up to 255 characters, including spaces,

for your folder's name. You may *not* use any of the following characters, which have special meaning to the operating system: \ / : * ? " < > |.

4. Press **Enter**. Your new folder, with the name you assigned it, now appears in the window.

 TIP **What if I Put the Folder in the Wrong Place?** That's easy to fix! Click and hold the mouse on the folder you want to move, and drag it to the folder that you want to place it in. When the target folder highlights, release the mouse. If the mistake was just made and the new folder is still empty, you can also delete the new folder and recreate it in the right place.

For more information on moving, copying, and deleting folders, see Part I, Lesson 11, "Managing Files with My Computer," and Lesson 15, "Managing Files with Explorer."

In this lesson, you learned about organizing your hard drive through creating folders to categorize your files. In the next lesson, you'll learn about protecting your files and computer at home.

Working Safely at Home

In this lesson, you will learn precautions you can take to help prevent data loss or equipment failure during a power outage. You'll also learn some steps you can take that might help prevent carpal tunnel syndrome, backaches, and headaches when working at your computer.

Preparing for Power Failures

Your computer is a finely tuned electronic instrument that depends on a steady supply of electricity to function properly. Mostly it gets this and it functions just fine. However, occasionally the power fails. More than occasionally the power sags—as in a brown-out— or it surges. All of these things—black-outs, brown-outs, and power surges—can have a potentially devastating effect on your computer and your data.

Blackouts have the most impact. We have all experienced sudden power failures. Life is going on as usual, when the lights go out. Until the lights come back on, life goes on in a very unusual manner—usually in an inconvenient and disruptive manner. If you happen to be working at your computer when the lights go out, life can become extraordinarily difficult even if the lights come back on three seconds later. That is because the blackout may not only damage your computer but will almost surely cause you to lose data.

While sags and surges will rarely cause you to lose data, they too can make your life difficult because they have the insidious effect of gradually attacking the fine electronic components inside your computer. Over time, sags and surges can damage your computer in subtle ways. You may find that your computer occasionally crashes for no apparent reason. Oops! There goes all the work you did since you last saved. You may one day discover that your computer refuses to start normally. Oops! Now how are you going to meet that pressing deadline?

There are several ways to protect your computer and your data from the effects of blackouts, brownouts, and power surges:

- Get in the habit of saving frequently
- Back up any data files that you would not care to lose
- Get a surge protector
- Get an Uninterruptible Power Supply (UPS)

Save Early and Often

The first suggestion—get in the habit of saving frequently—is cheap and relatively easy to implement. Just keep reminding yourself to hit the Ctrl+S key-combination every few minutes. Put a Post-It note on your monitor. Tie a string around your finger. Do whatever it takes, but develop this habit.

Ctrl+S is the standard key-combination under Windows 95 for saving your work; it works in virtually every program that runs under Windows 95. It takes no time. It costs you no money. The first time you lose an hour's work or more, you will regret not having developed this habit. So do it now.

Backing Up Your Data

The second suggestion—back up your data files—is a much harder habit to develop. By *back up* we mean make a second copy of your data files (and maybe a third, fourth, and fifth copy), in case something happens to your working copy. Most people don't bother to back up their data files. It takes time and effort to do backups. It may cost money. The rewards are much less immediate than are the rewards for, say, remembering to hit Ctrl+S frequently.

But the first time you discover that an important file won't open, you will be thankful you made a backup. The first time you discover that you erased an important file by mistake, you will be thankful you made a backup. The first time you realize that you just wiped out important data by overwriting it then hitting Ctrl+S, you will be thankful you made a backup.

Part I, Windows 95 Essentials, Lesson 16, "Using Backup," teaches you how to back up your files in Windows 95. You might also consider the following advice:

Back up only what you would really regret losing. Backing up is hassle enough. Don't make it worse by backing up stuff that you know you won't ever need again. Also, the more you would regret losing a file, the more backup copies you should have. One backup copy may not be enough.

Develop a plan for backing up your important files. The plan should call for keeping redundant backups of your data, because by the time you realize you wiped out important data, you may have also wiped out the last backup copy of the wiped out data.

Figure out the easiest, most painless way of creating backups. The more effort it takes to do backups, the less likely it is that you will actually make the effort.

If it is necessary to spend money to make doing backups effortless, then it is money very well spent, and you should find a way to spend it. That may mean buying a tape drive to avoid backing up to floppy disk. It may mean hiring a computer whiz to develop your backup plan, because you either don't have the time to do it yourself or you don't feel you have the expertise to do it well.

The question isn't if you will ever need to fall back to a backup copy of a file; it is when. Someday you will need that backup copy.

Using Surge Protectors

You should absolutely buy a surge protector for your computer. Surge protectors protect your computer from power surges by absorbing the surges themselves. Many small power surges over time can gradually degrade the electronic components in your computer and cause it to fail gradually over time. The rare massive power surge can fry your computer in one hit.

Power surges can invade your computer through the power line, the phone line, or the network cable. Surge protectors fit between your computer and these lines. You plug your computer into the surge protector, and the surge protector into the power outlet. You run a phone line from your modem to the surge protector, then another phone line from the surge protector to the telephone wall socket.

When buying a surge protector, don't shop on price alone. Spend a little more money to get a high quality surge protector. The cheapest surge protectors use a protection method which deteriorates a little bit with each surge absorbed. Eventually, the surge protector will stop absorbing surges. However, the surge protector itself will not signal you in any way that it is no longer working. Your only way of knowing that will be when a surge turns your computer into a doorstop.

Uninterruptible Power Supplies (UPSes)

Surge protectors won't protect you from blackouts, but UPSes will. A *UPS* is a battery for your computer. As long as the power doesn't fail, the UPS keeps the battery at full charge. If the power fails, the battery in the UPS will keep your computer running long enough for you to save your files, close your programs, and shut down your computer.

The smallest UPSes will keep a standard desktop computer running for from five to ten minutes on battery power. An UPS with this much power will cost you around $100. If you need more running time, you can buy bigger, more powerful UPSes.

While UPSes are a lot more expensive than any surge protector, they provide all the protection a surge protector provides plus a whole lot more. If you need to protect your unsaved data and you can afford a UPS, it is a good investment.

Preventative Medicine

There is a lot of information available in books and on the Web regarding the health hazards of working long hours at a computer. From backaches and headaches to carpal tunnel syndrome, someone somewhere has an opinion, scientific or otherwise, and has written about the subject.

Buy a Good Chair

Save your back by purchasing a sound, ergonomically correct chair. We can share with you first hand that a good chair is a good investment. Undoubtedly we spend more hours at our PC than most people. Although it may be difficult to measure the effects of a "good" chair, we guarantee you will feel the effects of a "bad" chair in a very short amount of time. Invest in a chair that is comfortable, strong and can adjust to the height you need.

Consider a "Natural" or "Ergonomic" Keyboard

Ergonomic keyboards claim to position your hands in a relaxed posture and have a built-in rest for your palm. Ergonomic keyboards take some period of adjustment, as many of the keyboards split the keys into two parts, one for your left hand one for your right. Whether or not it has been scientifically proven that these keyboards prevent stress injuries such as Carpal Tunnel Syndrome, we're not sure. But we are sure that one of these authors has suffered from carpal tunnel and does feel that the ergonomic keyboard helps to keep her CP problems at a minimum.

When you Wear Bifocals

This may sound silly, but a lot of people who wear bifocals complain about working at a computer because they suffer from neck pain. As trainers, we see students who work at the computer with their heads tilted back in order to read the monitor through the bottom half of their lenses.

If you wear bifocals, pay particular attention to the positioning of your monitor. Place your monitor at a distance and height that eliminate the need to tilt your head. Once you do this, you will find working at the computer much more comfortable.

Better yet (although here, again, we are recommending that you spend money—sorry about that), buy a large monitor—17" or larger. The larger the monitor, the larger you can make the characters on the screen, and the further away you can place the monitor. Place it far enough away, and you may be able to stop using your bifocals entirely.

In this lesson, you learned about some preventative steps you can take to make working at your computer a comfortable and safe experience. You also learned how you can prevent data loss and equipment failure during a power outage. In the next lesson, you learn about e-mail etiquette.

Using E-Mail Etiquette

*In this lesson, you will learn some guidelines for writing
e-mail messages. This lesson does not address any specific
e-mail programs, but discusses things you should take into consideration
when using any e-mail program.*

What Is E-Mail Etiquette?

E-mail etiquette is the accepted practices and writing procedures for sending
e-mail messages. Because so many people use e-mail, it's necessary to have
certain "rules" that all users follow. E-mail began in corporations and businesses
whose employees needed to communicate with each other quickly and efficiently. Since e-mail was originally a business program, the people who used it
developed business rules and guidelines: What's proper; what's not; what's
acceptable; and what's grounds for getting in trouble. This is *e-mail etiquette*.
Some of these ideas and concepts will make perfect sense to you; with others,
you may ask "Why?"

Read these points of etiquette so you can responsibly and effectively communicate using e-mail. Remember that many large corporations have company
policies regarding e-mail; so if you're using e-mail at work, ask your company
for a copy of these policies. Breaking of company policies can, in some situations, result in losing your job. These points of etiquette also apply to e-mail that
you send from home, no matter how informal or unstructured.

Always Include Information in the Subject Line

Don't send any e-mail message without including something in the **Subject** line.
Why not? When you look in your inbox to see your list of mail, you'll see a list
that includes who the mail is from, the date of the mail, and the subject. If you
leave your subject line blank, that will be blank in the recipient's inbox.

Do you have voice mail? Or an answering machine? Say you've been out of the office for a day or so. You return to find 10 voice mails waiting for you, and somewhere in the middle is a message from someone saying "Hi, it's me; give me a call." You don't know the time, date, or subject of the call—or the name or phone number of the caller. So, how can you return this call? When you leave telephone or e-mail messages, be thoughtful and efficient; avoid leaving meaningless messages. When you send messages by e-mail, fill in the e-mail Subject line. Provide a clear and concise explanation of the contents of your e-mail, such as "Can you attend this meeting?"

Beware of the Written Word

If you're not willing to post your message by the water cooler, maybe you should think twice about e-mailing it. Although e-mail is fairly private, it's not entirely so. Someone might forward your message to others.

Also, sarcasm and humor don't always translate well from the spoken word to the written word. You might offend someone when you were only joking, because the reader may not realize you were joking and may take your remark seriously. If you do need to be funny, make it obvious that you are trying to be funny by inserting some clue to that effect. Some people follow wisecracks with the word "smile" or "grin" in parentheses. Other people use *emoticons*, which are strings of characters which, when looked at sideways, resemble faces. For example:

- :-) means "smile"
- :-(means "frown"
- :-O means "surprise!"
- ;-) means "wink"

Finally, get in the habit of spell checking and proofreading your messages before sending them. Otherwise, your reader may think of you as something less than the brilliant person you know you are.

Send E-Mail That Has Meaning

Some companies do not allow any personal use of e-mail. Maybe your company doesn't mind you using e-mail to ask someone to join you for lunch or to ask if she's going to the company softball game. Be thoughtful, however, about the number of messages you send people and the importance of those messages. People who use e-mail extensively for work might not appreciate unsolicited jokes, thoughts for the day, gossip, and cartoons. E-mail is a tool to help people work more productively.

Even if your e-mail is personal, not work-related, and sent from home to someone who will be receiving it at their home, be considerate in the information and number of messages you send. E-mail may be new and exciting to you. But many people receive so much e-mail that they don't have time to read it all, and they don't appreciate people adding to their burden for trivial reasons.

Don't Print Out Your Inbox

This is not exactly an etiquette issue, it's more a common sense issue. If you print your e-mail for reading purposes, aren't you defeating the purpose? Why not have people send everything to you on paper to begin with? Avoid being counterproductive. Printing off e-mail messages will cost you (or your employer) for paper and toner or ink cartridges.

Before You Send Attachments

You can send attachments of other files from other programs within most e-mail programs. This is a fantastic tool, but don't forget that within Windows products you can cut, copy, and paste information from one program to another.

If you attach a file, then the recipient has to start another program to read that file. That can take time out of his day. Send an attachment only if the recipient needs to make changes to or have a copy of that file for his records. Also send an attachment if the information you are distributing is a large amount of information. For paragraphs, small tables, small amounts of text, use cut, copy, and paste to put that information directly into the body of your Mail Memo. For more information on cut, copy and paste, see Part I, "Windows 95 Essentials."

When sending attachments, include information so the receiver knows what the file contains *before* he opens it. A simple line such as "Please read the attached" is not descriptive enough. A line such as "This is the spreadsheet for the third quarter budget" is much more descriptive and helpful.

DON'T USE ALL CAPS

This section title seems a bit too strong, doesn't it? Many e-mail programs don't provide a way to format text. They don't allow you to apply <u>underlining</u>, **boldface**, or *italics*, so people have to use ALL CAPS for emphasis. When you type in all uppercase letters, it implies that you're shouting. Most computer users and Internet mail users think shouting is impolite.

Even more importantly, though, all caps is harder to read than standard text. It is inconsiderate to type your messages in all caps. If you just can't bring yourself to use the Shift key to capitalize the appropriate characters, then type in all lowercase. At least people will be able to read it.

Use Reply to All

Depending on your e-mail software, when you answer an e-mail message, you can reply to the sender, or you can reply to the sender and all of the people that the sender included in the original mail. Maybe the sender cc'd (copied) several people or had several names in the **To:** field. If your answer would be of use to the others in the original list, remember to use the **Reply to All** feature. Otherwise, the poor person who sent you the e-mail may have to take your reply and resend it to the others he was including from the start.

Keep Your Messages Short

The shorter the better. Some people often skip over an e-mail when the message contains more than a screen full of information. They might think, "I'll read this later, when I have more time." E-mail is often forgotten because of exactly that thought, so keep it short and your message has a better change of being read. Short is not considered rude to the frequent e-mail user—it is appreciated.

If You Are Using Company Property

Your company purchased the computer on which you are working. Your company purchased the software you are using to send mail. And your company is paying you (generously, we hope) during the time you spend to write your mail messages. Sounds as if this is company property, doesn't it? It *is*. The company owns every word you write, and it has the right to read your messages and re-use them in any way it sees fit. Therefore, it's a good idea to treat your e-mail like company property. If your topic is too personal, not work related, or highly confidential, it might not be an appropriate piece of e-mail.

In this lesson, you learned some pointers for proper use of e-mail. You also learned not to "shout" and to keep your messages short, but meaningful. In the next lesson, you'll about computer viruses.

Computer Viruses

In this lesson, you learn what a computer virus is and what steps you can take to prevent and cure viruses.

What Is a Computer Virus?

A computer virus is a lot like a virus in a human. It is an incomplete piece of programming that can do nothing on its own but, if attached to another program, can take over the other program and carry out its own mission instead of that of the host program. So, when you run the host program, it does something wholly unexpected and usually unwelcome. It may do something benign, like popping a message up on your screen. Or it may do something malicious, like deleting files or reformatting your hard disk.

Part of the programming built in to every virus is the ability to spread itself to other programs. When you run a program that is infected with a virus, the virus loads into your computer's memory and waits for opportunities to install copies of itself into other programs on your computer. Then, when you send a newly infected program to someone else, their programs become infected too. Because programs reside everywhere in modern computers—in the boot record of every disk, in .com, .exe, and .dll files, and even in data files—you can pass computer viruses around with ease, and you must take extraordinary measures to avoid passing them around.

There are, in general, three kinds of viruses:

- **Boot sector viruses** These infect the program that resides in the boot sector of every hard and floppy disk. They load themselves into your computer's memory when you boot up your computer (which is when the boot sector program runs). Your computer becomes infected when you receive an infected floppy disk, forget to remove it from your disk drive when you turn off your computer, then re-boot with it in the drive the next time you turn on your computer. This loads the virus into your computer's memory. From there, it infects your hard disk and every other floppy disk that you may put into the floppy disk drive.

- **Program file viruses**   These infect executable program files, such as .exe and .com files, and the library (.dll) and overlay (.ovl) files that the executables call into memory from time to time. Your computer becomes infected when you run the infected program. Then the virus infects other programs on your computer.

- **Macro viruses**   These infect specific kinds of data files. For example, Microsoft Word data files (.doc and .dot files) can store programming in the form of Word macros. A Word macro can be programmed to act like a virus, in the sense that, when you run Word and load the data file containing the macro into memory, the macro writes a copy of itself into your *Normal* template. From there it can write itself into every other Word file that you load into memory. And, sooner or later, you will send one of those files to a co-worker.

The statistics on the number of new computer viruses being created every day are staggering—there are a lot of programmers out there with way too much time on their hands. While it's bad enough if your home computer gets infected (only you are inconvenienced), if a virus hits your computer at work, the ramifications can be much more far-reaching.

When a virus makes its way into an office computer, the chances of it "spreading" are good, as people in an office often share files. Just like spreading germs that make everyone get the flu, sharing infected disks spreads a virus through an entire company's computer system in very little time.

Curing and Preventing Computer Viruses

Obviously, prevention is better than a cure. Not downloading files or bringing disks from home will make it much less likely that your office PC will contract a virus. But there will be times that you have to accept a file from someone. What can you do? That's where Virus Protection software comes in.

Virus Protection software reads files and disks looking for viruses and "cures" them by removing the virus or by alerting you that it doesn't have the "cure" for your virus. If the virus protection software can remove the virus, you can then safely open the file. If the virus protection software cannot remove the virus, it's best not to use the file and you should consider deleting it.

Most virus protection software will run at all times that your computer is running and it will check all new programs as you install them. You can also run a check of a disk if someone gives you a file you must load on your PC.

It's a good idea to upgrade your virus protection software at least every six to eight months. You can usually download upgrades from the software company's Web site. Virus software programs will cost around $50. Since viruses have been known to completely incapacitate a computer, resulting in hours of work to rebuild the operating system and programs, virus protection is an inexpensive type of insurance. Better safe than sorry!

You can learn more about viruses on the Web. Search for "virus" or stop by the sites of virus protection software companies. Two of the largest (though hardly the only) companies who make virus protection software are McAfee Associates, Inc. and Symantec Corporation. McAfee makes a product called ViruScan and their Web site is **www.McAfee.com**. Symantec is the maker of Norton Antivirus products and can be found at **www.symantec.com**. See Part IV, "Communications and the Internet," for more information on using the Internet Explorer Web browser and downloading files from the Web.

In this lesson, you learned what a computer virus is and what you can do to help prevent viruses. In the next lesson, you learn who to call and how to prepare for the call when you need help with your computer hardware or software.

Calling for Help

In this lesson, you will learn what information you should gather before you call for assistance with your computer or computer programs.

Preparing For the Day You'll Need Help

A little preventative medicine can go a long way and, take it from the voice(s) of experience, so can a little planning. If you are using a computer at home, you should have a special place or filing system where you can keep the following:

- Warranty information on your hardware and peripheral devices.
- Software licenses that contain "keys" or "ID" product identification numbers.
- Books and pamphlets supplied with your hardware and software that contain telephone numbers to call when you need help or warranty information.
- Any service contracts you have purchased with information on who to call, telephone numbers and hours of operation, as well as Web site addresses to visit when you need technical or product assistance.

By keeping these documents in one location, your life will be made much easier when you have a problem and need to call for help. Easy access to the documents listed above will allow you to concentrate on the problem at hand, saving you from digging through the attic for these documents.

Depending on where you purchased your computer and from whom, you may some day have to ship it back to the seller or manufacturer via the US Post Office or a shipper. You may need to ship equipment due to failure or to have it upgraded. Some manufacturers require that the equipment be shipped in its original box to insure that the equipment is not damaged during shipping. Whether or not you keep the box around for these purposes is, of course, up to you.

When Do You Need To Call?

No one person can possibly know every "fix" to every problem that can be encountered when using a computer, and there will be times you'll need some help.

In seeking help, you want to be certain that you've first done everything to help yourself. By checking a few simple things before you call, you could save yourself time and embarrassment. Most support professionals are accustomed to helping novice, nervous, panic-stricken and, yes, even experienced users on the telephone. But some support professionals have their series of "war stories" about users who call only to discover that their equipment is not plugged in! You should strive to keep from being included in those stories!

Don't expect that a support professional is capable of or willing to help you with learning how to use software. The exception to this expectation may be your employer's Help Desk. Many large companies maintain a staff dedicated to taking your calls and instructing you, over the telephone, in how to use your software.

Other than your employer, you'll find that learning how to do something is not generally the purpose of technical support. Examples of when to call for help are when your equipment is not operating properly, your computer is crashing, your new software program does not install properly, or your modem fails to work.

Whether you are calling a friend, a Help Desk at work, or a software company help desk, you should first check the following:

- All hardware is properly connected and has electrical power to it. Check surge protectors to be certain they are turned on.
- If your problem is with software recognizing a modem, check to see if the modem operates with any other software on your computer.
- If you have a dedicated or second telephone line for the computer, be certain to call the help desk on the line that is not used by the computer. This way, if the support person wants you to test anything that requires the use of your modem, the telephone line for the computer is free.
- If your problem is with a peripheral device (mouse, monitor, keyboard, printer) try replacing the peripheral device with another and test it before you call. This, of course, will only work if you have two computers or extra peripheral devices.

What Will You Need When You Call?

At a minimum and regardless of the nature of your problem, you should have available:

- Your computer hardware configuration. What kind of processor you have (Pentium, 486, 386) how much RAM you have, and what operating system you are running. If you are calling your employer Help Desk, you may or may not need this information, so it's best to know before you call.

- The purpose of your call, using proper terms. A Help Desk can't help you if you call to say your "thingie" doesn't work. Know the name for the "thingie."

- Write down or be prepared to tell the Help Desk details about any recent changes that have been made to your system. For example, if you can't get old software to run that was running before you installed your new antivirus software, be sure to tell the Help Desk that you have installed new software.

- If you are at work, you may need to supply a serial or ID number from a plate located on your PC. You may also need to tell the help desk your location. "At my desk" is usually not a sufficient description of your location. "Building B, room 105" is a clear description of your location.

- If you are calling from home about your personal PC, the support person may ask you for your telephone number and zip code. We're sure you know your phone number and zip code, but we just wanted you to know that it's not unusual to be asked that information when you call for technical support.

If your monitor displays an error message due to a hardware or software problem:

- Try to call when the message is displayed on the screen so that you can provide the Help Desk with the exact contents of the message. If that isn't possible, write down the message before you call.

- Write down the steps you took leading up to the error message. For example, if you receive the message when you click on x, but not if you click on y before you click x, be prepared to give that information to the Help Desk.

If you're experiencing a software installation or operation problem, you may need to provide a key or ID number found on the original disk label or CD-ROM case.

If you have a service or support contract, you will need that contract number.

Who Should You Call?

If you are at work and your company has a Help or Support Desk, call them first. Do not call outside of the company unless your company has specifically instructed you to do so. In order to maintain hardware and software properly, a company needs to track the problems that their employees encounter. Calling outside of the company without the company's knowledge could be counterproductive. Additionally, "outsiders" aren't as familiar with your hardware, networking configuration and software—they could inadvertently steer you in the wrong direction when trying to help you.

If you are experiencing problems with your PC at home, *who* to call depends upon your problem. If it's a hardware problem and you have a warranty, call the store where you purchased your PC or follow the instructions on your warranty or service agreement. Do not call the salesman who sold you the computer. The salesman is undoubtedly busy selling more computers, and if he were inclined to help you he would be working at a Help Desk somewhere. If you have a hardware problem and no service warranty, check the product information that came with the hardware for instructions on getting service or support.

If you are experiencing a software problem, check the manual or pamphlet that came with the software. You should find a telephone number to call for technical support. Most support numbers are not toll-free so be aware that it's "your nickel" when you call. Some companies charge for technical support and they will tell you so, as they need to get your credit card number. Allow sufficient time from your day to make the support call. Since some software companies are inundated with calls, you could be on hold for a very long time. Many companies utilize programs that will notify you of where your call sits in the pool, and a recording might tell you that you are number 6 of 8, and that you can expect to be on hold at least 20 minutes. As your call moves up, you will then be notified of the expected wait time.

Finally, many companies maintain automated help resources in the form of fax-back services, bulletin board systems, and World Wide Web sites. And you can almost find an online discussion forum on a CompuServe forum, a UseNet News Group, an Internet mailing list, or a discussion at a Web site—where users and possibly company representatives talk about the problems they encounter with a hardware or software product, and how to solve them. Before you call the help line, you might want to check out these resources. You could save yourself the time, frustration, and expense of trying to get through to the "live" help representatives on the help lines.

In this lesson, you learned how to prepare when you need to call for technical assistance. In the next lesson, you learn about uninstalling software.

Uninstalling Software

In this lesson, you'll learn how to remove software from your system correctly.

Why You Must Uninstall Software

Back in the early days of PCs, when DOS was the only disk operating system, removing programs was an easy business. You simply deleted all the files in that program's directory. Removing software is one thing that Windows 95 has made more complicated if the program you're removing was not designed for Windows 95.

With a program designed to run under Windows 3.x or Windows 95, you cannot simply delete the folder that holds the application files. During installation, additional files may have been copied to the Windows folder, the Windows\System folder, the Windows\System32 folder, or any number of other folders. It is very hard to determine which files in these folders were put there by specific applications, so it's easy to leave some application files behind. Or, you may delete some files you shouldn't, and then some of your applications will not run properly. Check the software documentation before attempting to remove a program; it may tell you what files to remove and where they're located. Delete those files using My Computer or the Windows Explorer. Remember to also remove the shortcuts from the Start menu and the desktop.

Many applications designed for Windows 95 have an uninstall utility built into them to make them easier to remove. You can remove them using the Add/Remove Programs option from the Control Panel. You may need to insert the installation disk or CD, because the uninstall utility may be on that disk or CD (Windows 95 will ask you for the disk or CD if it's needed).

When you install software designed to run under Windows 95, the application's components are tracked through the Windows 95 Registry. Therefore, using the Add/Remove Programs option, you can remove all the files associated with an application, unless they're being shared by another program.

For more information on installing new programs, refer to Part II, "Customizing Windows 95," Lesson 6; "Installing New Software (Programs)."

Using Add/Remove Programs

To remove a Windows 95 program:

1. Click the **Start** button on the taskbar.

2. Choose **Settings**, **Control Panel** from the Start menu.

3. Double-click the **Add/Remove Programs** icon. The Add/Remove Programs Properties dialog box appears (see Figure 6.1).

Figure 6.1 The Add/Remove Programs Properties box.

4. From the list box in the lower half of the dialog box, select the program you want to remove.

5. Click **Add/Remove**.

6. Windows 95 asks for confirmation that you want to completely remove the application and all of its components. Click **Yes**.

7. When all the files are removed, Windows 95 alerts you that the task is complete. Click **OK**.

8. Click **OK** to close the properties box.

In this lesson, you learned how to properly uninstall applications from your system. In the next lesson, you'll learn more about computer hardware.

Understanding Computer Hardware

In this lesson, you'll get an overview of computer hardware so you'll understand the basics of a computer system and a network.

What's Inside the Computer Case?

Inside the computer case is the *Central Processing Unit* (CPU). This is the main chip of the computer system. It processes instructions, calculates, and manages information within the computer. You often refer to your computer by a shortened version of the model number of this chip ("386" for an 80386 chip, "486" for an 80486 chip). After 80486, Intel changed the model number to a name— "Pentium"—instead of calling it the 80586 chip.

As the model numbers increased, the capacity and speed of the processors increased. The speed of the processor, measured in MegaHertz (MHz), is the number of clock cycles the processor can perform per second. The higher the number, the faster the processor. So even if you have a Pentium processor, its speed may be only 90 MHz while your neighbor's Pentium is 133 MHz. This means your neighbor's computer will perform operations more quickly.

The CPU is attached to a *motherboard*, which is the main circuit board of the computer. All the electrical components of the computer plug into the motherboard.

The motherboard has several *expansion slots*. These are sockets in the motherboard. You plug expansion cards into these slots (see Figure 7.1). *Expansion cards* contain the circuits and chips to provide additional capabilities to the computer, such as sound, video, modem, or networking.

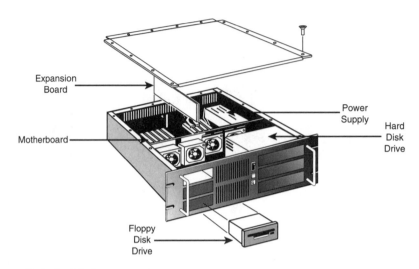

Figure 7.1 Inside the computer case.

There are several memory chips attached to the motherboard. They may be soldered directly on to the motherboard or they may be mounted on small circuit boards of their own—called SIMMs or Single In-line Memory Modules—which are themselves inserted into special expansion slots designed specifically to accept them. These chips are the *Random Access Memory* (RAM) of the computer, the memory that temporarily holds copies of the applications you're working on and the documents you are creating. When the power is turned off, all data in the RAM memory disappears. That's why you should save your documents to a disk. RAM is measured in megabytes (MB). A byte is approximately one character, 1096 bytes (or approximately 1000) is a kilobyte, and 1,048,576 bytes (or approximately 1,000,000) is a megabyte. You can increase the RAM memory of your computer by adding more memory chips.

Your computer case also holds several types of storage media that permanently store data for you. The *hard disk* is internal and is the primary storage device. Its size is measured in megabytes or gigabytes (GB). A gigabyte is a billion bytes.

The other memory storage devices are attached to the motherboard with connectors but have a "door" that allows you to insert portable media into them. One is the *floppy disk drive*, into which you insert a floppy disk (generally a $3^1/_2$ inch disk). Another is a *tape drive*, which holds a cassette tape for storing several megabytes of memory. You generally use tape drives to back up your hard disk. You may also have a *CD-ROM drive* that may accept music or data CDs. You can read from a CD but you can't store your own data there because these drives are Read-Only Memory (ROM) devices. However, a CD can hold several hundred megabytes of data or programs.

Also inside the case is a *power supply* that converts the normal electricity from your house or office outlet into electricity that the computer can use—lower voltage and direct current instead of your house's alternating current. Because the power supply generates a lot of heat, it has a fan inside to prevent overheating.

Inside every computer, on the motherboard, is a *bus*, which is the electronic highway inside the computer that carries information between devices. There are different types of buses (VL-Bus, ISA Bus, PCI Bus), and your computer may have more than one type for sending different types of information to different parts of the computer. The difference between the buses is defined by the width and the speed of the bus. An ISA (Industry Standard Architecture) bus, for example, has a width of 16 bits and a speed of 8 MHz. On the other hand, the VL-bus has a width of 32 bits and a speed of 33 MHz. Because the VL-bus is wider it can handle more traffic, and that traffic goes faster than with the ISA bus, so the VL-bus transfer information much faster than the ISA bus. The VL-bus primarily works with monitors, for fast updates of graphic displays. If you have a 486 computer, you probably have both an ISA and a VL-bus. A Pentium may combine an ISA bus with a PCI (Peripheral Component Interconnect) bus or one of its more recent descendants. The original PCI bus was 32 bits wide with a speed of 33 MHz, but though it has the same specifications as the VL-bus it has the ability to connect to more devices.

What Are Ports?

In the back of your computer case are several "plugs" where you connect outside devices to your computer (see Figure 7.2). These "plugs" are called *ports*. There are different ports for different purposes. You plug the mouse into a *mouse port* or, on some computers, a *serial port*, and the keyboard into a *keyboard port*. (On some computer models the mouse and the keyboard ports may be in the front of the computer case.) The monitor connects to a *monitor port* and a joystick connects to a *game port*. (You may not have a game port unless you purchased a joystick.) Your printer connects to the *parallel port*.

Some expansion cards provide additional ports. An internal modem—one that plugs into an expansion slot—will provide one or more ports into which you will have to plug a telephone line. Sound cards provide ports for your speakers, microphone, and such. Network adapters provide ports for connecting network cables.

On most computers, the ports are all labeled. However, even if they are not clearly marked, you probably won't plug your device into the wrong port, since most of the connectors are different. There are two possible problems that you can encounter. First, the mouse and keyboard ports on many computers use the same kind of connector, so you must be careful to connect to the correct port. Also, most computers have two serial ports, so you have to know which one you are using.

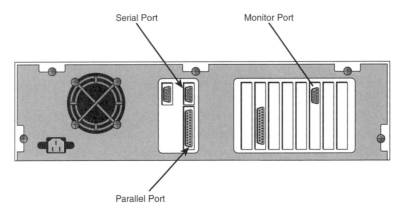

Figure 7.2   The ports are located in the back of the computer case.

CAUTION

My Mouse and Keyboard Don't Work   On some computer models, it is possible to plug the mouse or the keyboard into the wrong port. If you've changed the connections recently (maybe you moved your computer), you may have accidentally switched them. Their ports look almost exactly alike. Just reverse the connectors to switch the ports and reboot the machine.

TERM

Boot (Start) and Reboot (Restart)   When you start up the computer, you "boot it up." Starting the computer is doing a "cold boot." Sometimes, to re-adjust hardware settings, you have to reboot the computer to accept the modifications. Click the **Start** button and choose **Shut Down** from the menu. Select **Restart Your Computer** and click **OK** to restart the computer (hold down the **Shift** key as you make these choices and only Windows will restart). This restarting of your computer is a "warm boot."

Serial Ports

There are two types of ports: serial ports and parallel ports. *Serial ports* connect to your mouse, modem, scanner, and sometimes a printer. Only one *bit* of data (one-eighth of a character or *byte*) goes through a serial cable at a time. Data can travel reliably through more than 20 feet of cable.

A serial port has either 9 or 25 pins (small metal projections), and the cable that connects to the port has 9 or 25 holes. Because the number of pins or holes is uneven, the port has one side that's longer than the other—it's shaped like the letter "D". When plugging in the cable, you have to line up the connector so that the longer side on the connector matches the longer side on the port.

Your computer identifies each serial port as a COM (COMmunications) port, with the number attached to it. The first serial port is COM1, the second is COM2, and so forth. Therefore, when you're connecting devices to your computer you have to note the correct COM port in the hardware settings. Only one device is assigned to each port. A standard PC can accommodate up to four COM ports, but, without reconfiguration of the peripherals attached to the COM ports, you can normally only use two of them at a time. You can either use COM1 or COM3, and you can either use COM2 or COM4. That is because COM1 and COM3 share IRQ4 (Interrupt Request Line 4) and COM2 and COM4 share IRQ3, and they can't both use the same interrupt at the same time.

For an example of specifying a COM port for a hardware device, see Part II; "Customizing Windows 95," Lesson 9: "Installing and Configuring a Modem."

Parallel Ports

Parallel ports connect to printers and tape drives. Eight bits of data (one character or *byte*) goes through a parallel cable at a time, so a parallel port is faster than a serial port. However, data cannot travel reliably through more than 20 feet of cable.

A parallel port has 25 holes, and the cable that connects to the port has 25 pins (small metal projections). Because the number of pins or holes is uneven, the port has one side that's longer than the other. When plugging in the cable, you have to line up the connector so that's the longer side on the connector matches the longer side on the port.

Your computer identifies each parallel port as a LPT (Line Printer) port, with the number attached to it. The first parallel port is LPT1, the second is LPT2, and so forth. Therefore, when you're connecting devices to your computer you have to note the correct LPT port in the hardware settings. Only one device is assigned to each port. Windows 95 recognizes up to nine LPT ports, but most computers only actually have one.

For an example of specifying an LPT port, see Part I, "Windows 95 Essentials;" Lesson 20, "Printing with Windows 95."

Input and Output Devices

Information enters your computer through input devices: the keyboard, the mouse or trackball, modem, or scanner. The computer uses output devices to send information out: modem, monitor, printer, or sound card. *Peripherals* is a generic name for all these devices because they are external to the essential components of the computer (see Figure 7.3).

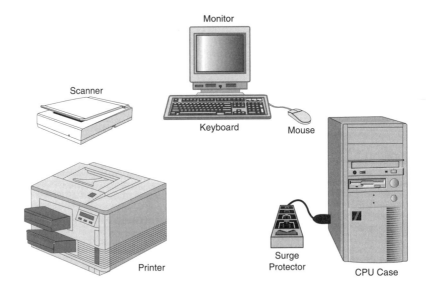

Figure 7.3 Input and output devices.

Use the keyboard to enter text-based commands and data into the computer. Use a mouse, trackball, or glide pad to move the mouse pointer on the screen and, with it, to point to and select items on the screen. The modem allows you to send and receive data via the telephone lines. In conjunction with a character-recognition program that translates images into text, the scanner transfers data from printed documents into the computer. You can input graphics too by scanning pictures or drawings.

The computer responds to you via the monitor, where you can see it acting on your commands or data input. You can output your data in written form using the printer or in electronic form via the telephones lines using the modem. The sound card makes it possible for Windows 95 to alert you to specific events by making sounds, such as a beep when you hit the wrong key.

Networks

A network involves two or more computers that share information and equipment. A Local Area Network (LAN) connects computers in a small area such as an office or building, and the computers are usually connected by cables. A Wide Area Network (WAN) connects computers across larger areas, such as cities or countries and may make use of telephone lines, microwave, or satellite to make the connections.

In a peer-to-peer network, each computer in the network can access files on any other computer in the network (see Figure 7.4). All the people using the network store their files on their own computers, which makes file management difficult. Peer-to-peer networks should be limited to 10 people.

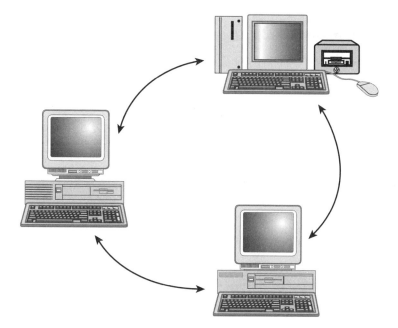

Figure 7.4 A peer-to-peer network.

A client-server network (see Figure 7.5) stores information more efficiently, using one main computer as the file server where everyone stores their data. Because the files are in one location they're easier to manage, backup, and protect. The client is a computer that can access information from the server; each user's workstation is a client. The file server is usually a stand-alone computer that nobody uses as a personal workstation. The server may be located in a locked back room.

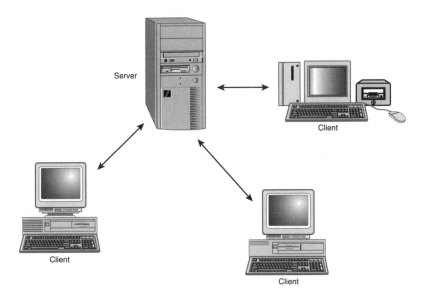

Figure 7.5   A client-server network.

What additional hardware do you need for a network? Each computer in the network must have a network adapter card, which controls the flow of data to and from the network. Network cables connect the computers to each other; data is transmitted along these cables.

In this lesson, you learned about your computer's hardware. In the next lesson, you learn about traveling with your computer.

Traveling with Laptops and Notebooks

In this lesson, you will learn some considerations for traveling with your laptop or notebook computer. You also learn how to secure your laptop and what to expect at airport security checks.

Preparing for Travel

If you've never traveled with your computer, you'll find some basic and essential information here on how to do so with as little pain as possible. If you're a seasoned computer traveler, you might still find a few tips to make traveling with your computer safe and comfortable.

Think Twice About Disk Compression

Consider that a laptop or notebook will be knocked around a lot more than a desktop, you might want to think twice about using a disk doubler or disk compression software on your laptop. Compressed data is more vulnerable to permanent loss. At least, that's what we've always been told. On the other hand, any rough handling that could damage the hard disk drive will smash your computer's LCD panel to smithereens. But, if you don't absolutely have to compress data on your hard drive, we advise you not to do so.

Obtain Local Access Numbers

Obtain local access numbers for your ISP or commercial online service provider and plug them into your program before you leave home. Hotels can charge as much as $1.00 for local phone calls. Why not save the cost for the call to obtain the local access number by obtaining it before you leave home?

Buy the Right Case

The number one priority for traveling with a laptop (or notebook) computer is a good case. "Good" should take into consideration size (not too big, not too heavy), padding (to protect your computer) and straps (good, strong straps). The next consideration is the manner in which you will carry this case; on the shoulder, like a briefcase, or on your back. Laptop cases are expensive ($40 to $200) and you should consider all of these factors before you buy.

Generally, cases with shoulder straps seem to be extremely popular. Be warned, however that if you also own and carry a shoulder strap briefcase and a shoulder strap purse, adding a shoulder strap laptop leaves you one shoulder short!

If your travel involves extensive flying and running through airports, you might want to use a backpack computer case. This leaves your hands and shoulders free for your briefcase or other items.

Whatever you do, don't even think about packing the computer inside a suitcase or checking it as baggage. Packing it inside a suitcase, even nested among lots of clothes for padding, is a guarantee for breakage.

If your travel takes you by automobile, you might want to consider a short handled or shoulder strap case that can fit on the passenger seat of the car. This way, when you're tied up in traffic, you can read your e-mail.

Charge the Batteries

It may sound silly to remind you to charge the computer battery. But, no sillier than admitting how many times we've left home without doing so. If you travel extensively, consider buying a second or long life battery for your computer.

If your computer uses PC cards, be aware that some PC cards (such as modems) stored in their slot while the computer is in a power down state may suck the battery dry in as little as two hours. Consider removing the cards when the computer is turned off and storing them in your case.

Remember the Supplies and Peripherals

We're not suggesting that you take the kitchen sink, but we do suggest that you think about how you will be using your computer before you leave for a trip. For example, if you plan to log on to your client's network, do you need to take a network cable? Here's a list of a few items you might want to pack in your computer case:

- **Phone cord**   You'll need to dial out to pick up your mail. Don't assume that the hotel will have a phone cord for you.

- **Extension cord**   Don't leave home without an extension cord! It's not unusual to find that the bathroom has the only available outlet in a hotel room. Beyond the obvious, working in the bathroom can make it difficult to reach the telephone jack.

- **Network cable**   This, of course, is necessary only if you have networking capabilities.

- **Map software**   If you have map software, why not take it with you? Many people plan a trip using their map software and then leave the CD at home when they are on the road.

Protect Yourself From Theft

Laptop computers are very, very popular with thieves. We've read statistics that claim one in every 14 laptops will be stolen in 1997. That is an increase of 20 percent over 1996. Laptops are being stolen off airport security conveyor belts, out of parked cars, from locked office buildings at night, and from hotel rooms.

Here are some safety measures you should consider:

- Never check your laptop as luggage at the airport. If you do and it's not stolen, it's still likely to end up damaged.

- If you decide to place it on the security conveyor belt, don't do so until you are the next in line to pass through the metal detector. Better yet: hand it to the security guard.

- Carry it in a nondescript case. Don't use a carrying case that has the manufacturer's name plastered all over it.

- Lock up the PC when you are away. If the hotel has a safe in the room and the PC fits in the safe, use it. Don't leave it in a drawer or, worse yet, on the desk in your hotel room, and don't check it with the bellhop.

- When you must walk away from the PC in a public place such as your client's office, remove the PC cards and secure the PC with a cable lock.

- Encrypt sensitive data stored on your laptop.

- Protect valuable data by using removable hard drives, if possible.

- Buy theft insurance.

Understand and Respect Airport Security and FAA Regulations

Expect that you will be asked to remove your PC from it's case and boot it up at airport security. This is another reason for leaving home with a charged battery. Security will look to see that you are actually carrying a working PC, not some type of plastic explosive or something like that. It may seem an inconvenience to have to do this, but it is for your safety and the safety of others. Remove your PC and place the case on the belt for the X-ray machine.

Although many people believe that the PC cannot be harmed by traveling through the X-ray machine, you will undoubtedly have to remove it and boot it up anyhow, so why not remove it first?

There will be periods just before takeoff and landing when the pilot or crew will request that all electronic devices be shut down. There are some people who might advise you that this practice by the airlines is unnecessary—that your computer could not possibly interfere with signals and transmissions used for takeoff and landing. Despite what others say, it is our understanding that it is an FAA requirement to turn your equipment off when asked. So do it.

In this lesson, you learned how to prepare for traveling with your laptop. You also learned some precautions you can take to reduce the chance your laptop will be stolen while you are traveling. In the next lesson, you learn about sharing information between applications using Object Linking and Embedding.

Understanding OLE (Linking & Embedding)

In this lesson, you'll explore two concepts: linking and embedding. You'll learn how these concepts help you work with more than one application.

Sharing Information Between Applications

You can incorporate data in one application that you created in another application such as a spreadsheet, a word processing document, a graph, a drawing, or a scanned image. Rather than keying in the information from the other application, you can "capture" it from its original application and place it in the document you're creating at the moment.

For example, you're writing a report. Data you need to incorporate in that report is contained in a spreadsheet. You want to capture that spreadsheet data and put it into your report document.

You can share information between applications using several methods:

- **Importing** converts data from its "native" program so you can include it in your current document. Generally, users import data when they can't open the source document. For instance, if you need a picture in your document, you import the picture from a clip art library into your document. Once you place the picture you can't open the clip art file and change that picture, and if someone updates the original picture file those updates do not automatically appear in your document. Your picture remains the same as it was when you imported it.

- **Edit, Cut and Edit, Copy commands** allow you to store data temporarily in the Clipboard (a memory holding area created by Windows) and then place it into your document with the Edit, Paste command. To learn more about cutting and pasting, see Part I, "Windows 95 Essentials;" Lesson 8, "Copying and Moving Information Between Windows."

- **Linking** utilizes the Clipboard (via the Cut and Copy commands) to bring data from a source document and place it into your document. Any updates to the source information will also appear in your document. All users of the document must have access to the source file, and the location of that source file cannot change or the link will fail.

- **Embedding** places an "object" created by another program directly into your document. You can edit the object contents by activating the source application directly from your document (all you have to do is double-click on the object). Changing an embedded object does not change the source document.

Object   An object is a single piece of data such as text, graphics, sound, or animation created by an OLE-supported application.

Programs that let you share data use one of two methods to share that information:

Dynamic Data Exchange (DDE) is a communications protocol that lets you share data between two open applications. DDE is an older technology, so most programs in Windows support it.

Object Linking and Embedding (OLE) extends your ability to dynamically share information between programs and program files. Because of OLE, you can embed or link files from another application into a document; or you can embed a new object and use the object's application to enter data into your document. Not all applications support OLE (especially older ones), so you may not be able to embed files from all your applications.

As a user, you don't have to know if an application supports DDE or OLE. Your application will automatically employ OLE if the originating application supports it and DDE if it doesn't. If a program supports neither DDE nor OLE, its menu simply won't offer you the option of linking or embedding pasted data.

Understanding Linking

When you link data from an application to your document, the linked object maintains a reference or pointer back to the originating file. Then, when the original file changes, the modifications also appear in your document.

For example, if you copy data from a spreadsheet file containing your yearly budget into a word processing document and link the data to its source spreadsheet, any new data you add to the spreadsheet file at the end of the first quarter will also show up in your word processing document. Likewise, anyone else who also linked the spreadsheet data to their own documents will also receive the updates to the spreadsheet.

As a user, you can't edit or update linked data without using the source application program. You would also need access to the source file and find the file at the same drive and directory or folder as listed in the reference pointer to the source file. In other words, if the file the data came from was on the server's drive F in the Import directory, you need to specify F:\Import as the source location to access the file from your computer.

What are the advantages of linking files?

- You can link files between older Windows programs that don't support embedding.
- You can change the source file and automatically update any documents you linked to it.
- Linked files require less memory than embedded objects.

What are the disadvantages?

- You can't change the location of the source file or delete it entirely because you'll break the link between documents.
- The linked document must be in a shared location.
- Lines that update automatically may slow down operations.

Creating Links

To create a link from a source document to the document you have open:

1. Start the application that created the source file.

2. Open the source file.

3. Select the data you want to copy.

4. Switch to the document to which you want to add the linked data.

5. Position your cursor (insertion point) where you want to place the data or item.

6. Choose **Edit**, **Paste Special**. The Paste Special dialog box appears (see Figure 9.1).

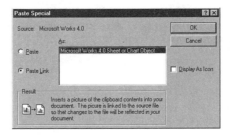

Figure 9.1   The Paste Special dialog box.

7. Select **Paste Link**.

8. Choose a display format in the **As** box.

9. If you'd rather see an icon in your document instead of the linked data, select **Display as Icon**. Figure 9.2 shows an example of an icon in a document.

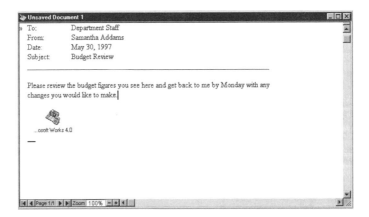

Figure 9.2   The data displayed as an icon.

10. Click **OK**. If you didn't choose **Display as Icon** in step 9, above, the linked object appears in your document, similar to Figure 9.3.

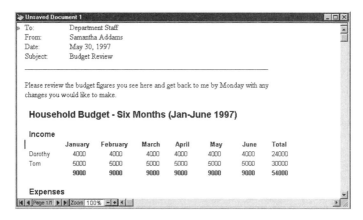

Figure 9.3 The linked data shown in the document.

Some applications support the newer OLE 2.0 technology, which lets you link data by using drag-and-drop. To do this:

1. Start up both applications—the application where you want to put the data (the destination application) and the application that created the data (the source application).

2. In the source application, open the file that contains the data you want to copy. In the destination application, open the document where you want to put the data.

3. Point to an empty space on the taskbar and click your right mouse button.

4. Choose **Tile Vertically** or **Tile Horizontally** from the pop-up menu to make both windows show at the same time.

5. Starting in the source application window, select the data you want to link.

6. Hold down the **Control** and **Shift** keys, and drag the selected data to your destination document.

7. Release the mouse button to drop the data where you want it to appear in the document.

Once your linked data appears in a document, your application tries to update that information each time you open that document. A dialog box appears asking if you want to refresh the information. Answer **Yes**.

Understanding Embedding

When you embed a file or object, a copy appears in your document. An embedded file maintains no connection to the source application file, so updates to the source file don't change your document.

What are the advantages of embedding?

- Since the document and the data are stored together in the same file, you don't need to maintain links, path names, and source files.
- You don't even have to keep the source data because it becomes part of the document.
- To update the embedded object, you can stay right in your document. You don't have to go out to the source application.

What are the disadvantages?

- The documents that contain embedded objects are larger than other documents, so they may take longer to open and they take up more storage space.
- If you update an embedded graphic, you may end up with a file that prints at a lower resolution than the original (not as clear a copy).
- The embedded document has no relationship to the original document. You have to update each document individually, instead of updating only the source document.

Embedding Objects

To embed a file:

1. Open the document where you want to store the embedded file.
2. Position your cursor where you want the object to appear.
3. Depending on the application you're using, the menu command may be **Insert, Object** or **Insert, Picture**.
4. A dialog box appears asking what type of object or what object file you want to embed. Figure 9.4 shows an Insert Object dialog box. Choose **Create New** to embed an empty object that you can complete from within your document.

Choose **Create from File** from the Insert Object dialog box (as shown in Figure 9.5) to select a file that you want to incorporate in your document.

5. Select the type of object or the name of the file and then click **OK**.

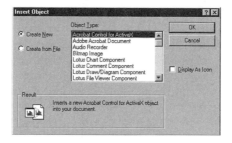

Figure 9.4   An Insert Object dialog box with Create New selected.

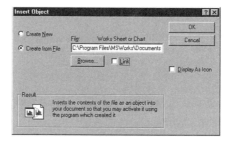

Figure 9.5   An Insert Object dialog box with Create From File selected.

To edit the data in an embedded object, double-click it to open the file in the source application, as shown in Figure 9.6. Make your changes and click the document outside the embedded object selection border.

You can also paste data to embed it in your document:

1. In the source application, select the data you want.

2. Choose **Edit, Copy** to copy it to the Clipboard.

3. Switch to the destination application and open the document where you want to place the embedded object.

4. Position your cursor in the document where you want the embedded object to appear.

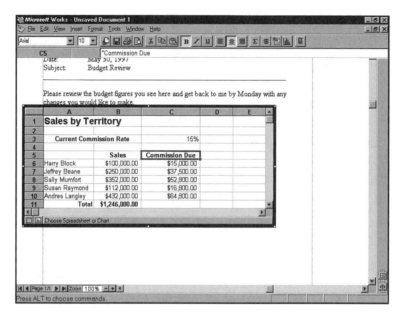

Figure 9.6   Editing the embedded object.

5. Choose **Edit, Paste Special**. The Paste Special dialog box appears (see Figure 9.7).

Figure 9.7   The Paste Special dialog box with Paste selected.

6. Select **Paste**.

7. From the **As** box, pick the source from which you copied the data.

8. If you want to display and icon instead of showing the embedded data, check **Display as Icon**.

9. Click **OK**.

TIP **Drag-and-Drop** In Windows 95 you can drag-and-drop a file to embed it in a document. Open the application and the document where you want to put the data. Then click the **Start** button on the taskbar and choose **Programs, Windows Explorer**. In the Explorer, locate the file you want to embed. Drag that file icon onto your open document window and drop it where you want the embedded file to appear.

In this lesson, you learned about linking and embedding and how to place linked data and embedded objects into your application documents. In the next lesson, you learn to plan for crashing computers and other mishaps.

Rebooting, Restarting, and Disaster Planning

In this lesson, you learn what to do if a program stops responding or hangs up your system. You also learn what Windows Safe Mode is and how to prepare for operating systems problems by creating a boot disk.

Using Ctrl+Alt+Del

If you have used previous versions of Windows, or are a tried and true DOS aficionado, you may find that Ctrl+Alt+Del is a hard habit to break. It is a habit you *should break*, however, as Microsoft does not recommend rebooting a Windows 95 machine in this way.

Ctrl+Alt+Del restarts the computer without regard to open programs. In previous versions of Windows and DOS, it was the recommended "catch all" action you take if your computer or program stops responding. But Windows 95 needs to save information about programs and files *before* they shut down and pressing Ctrl+Alt+Del prevents that from happening. In Windows 95, Ctrl+Alt+Del must be pressed twice before it reboots the PC. This keeps you from shutting down "illegally" and activates the Close Program dialog box which will allow you to end a task legally.

If a program has stopped responding and you receive an error message in Windows 95 to that affect, you should:

1. Press **Ctrl+Alt+Del**.

2. The **Close Program** dialog box appears. If a program has stopped responding, the words "not responding" will appear next to the program name in this dialog box.

3. Select the program you want to close and click the **End Task** button.

This closes down the program and you can restart the program by selecting it from the Start menu, reinstall the program if it continues to fail or call technical support for that program.

Restarting Windows 95

Correctly restarting and shutting down Windows 95 is very important. If you need to restart the computer, doing so correctly assures that people connected to shared resources such as printers or files do not lose data because you are restarting or shutting down Windows 95.

If you close a program using Ctrl+Alt+Del and then choose End Task in the Close Program dialog box, other programs that you have running at that time are not affected. But, what happens if Windows 95 itself stops responding and you can't shut down legally? Then you might have to reboot the computer by pressing Ctrl+Alt+Del a second time.

Doing so may cause Windows to start up in Safe Mode. Safe Mode is a sort of stripped down mode of Windows 95, it is the operating system running in default mode, without loading network connections, CD-ROM drivers, or printer drivers. It is designed to help the Windows administrator or consultant in diagnosing operating system problems and is beyond the scope of this book. However, if you shut down Windows illegally by pressing Ctrl+Alt+Del twice, you may find yourself in Safe Mode when you restart.

You'll know you are in Safe Mode as it is written all over the Windows Screen. To exit Safe mode and start up Windows 95 in Standard mode:

1. Select **Start**, **Shut Down** from the taskbar.

2. The Shut Down Windows dialog box appears. Select Restart the Computer.

3. Click **Yes** to restart Windows.

Disaster Planning

The better prepared you are for a disaster, the less likely the disaster will happen. Why? Well, if you are prepared for a disaster, then your potential disasters are merely inconveniences!

Two very important steps you can take in disaster preparation are to back up your new PC hard drive and create a system boot disk.

Back Up Entire Hard Drive

Throughout this book, we talk about the importance of backing up your data. But there is one more type of backup you might want to consider. That is to back up the entire hard drive.

There was a time, as computer professionals, when we would not have suggested that anyone back up an entire hard drive. After all, if your data was backed up and your hard drive failed, you could simply reinstall the operating system and software programs and then restore your data. Time consuming, perhaps, but straightforward.

These days, you can't reinstall your operating system and programs because manufacturers don't always provide you with the CDs when you buy your computer. What would you do if your hard drive failed? Or, what would you do if you decided to upgrade or change your operating system and your computer failed to run? Without the original software CDs you could not reinstall software or your original operating system.

Therefore, it's a good idea to back up the entire drive of a new PC shortly after you bring it home. Do this once, and you don't really need to back it up again. Put the backup tape or disk in some secure place and, hopefully, you'll never have to use them again. For more information on backing up, see Part I, "Windows Essentials," Lesson 16 "Using Backup."

 TIP   **An Alternative to Backing Up the Hard Drive**   Some computer manufacturers offer the CDs containing your operating system through their ordering department for an additional charge. You may want to purchase the CDs instead of using backup. Contact your computer manufacturer for more information.

Creating a Startup Disk

You should have a startup disk to start your computer if you are experiencing problems starting Windows. Create the startup disk and keep it in a safe place. Use it only when your computer hangs when it starts windows. Place the startup disk in the floppy disk drive before you reboot or start the computer.

If you are experiencing problems which require you to use the start up disk, you might need the help of a professional or a very experienced Windows/DOS guru. These kinds of problems and their fixes are beyond the scope of this book, but creating a start up disk will assist the person helping you when they are troubleshooting your PC.

To make a startup disk, you need a floppy disk. It should contain no other files, and we recommend you store this disk in a safe place, label it "startup disk" and hopefully, never have to use it.

To create a startup disk:

1. Click **Start**, **Settings**, **Control Panel** on the taskbar.
2. In the Control Panel, select **Add/Remove Programs**.
3. The **Add/Remove Programs** Properties box appears. Click the **Startup Disk** tab.
4. Click **Create Disk** and follow the instructions for creating the startup disk.

Store your startup disk in a safe place.

In this lesson, you learned about rebooting, restarting and disaster planning.

Appendixes

Installing and Using Microsoft Plus!

This appendix describes Microsoft Plus!, tells you how to use it, and gives you instructions to install it.

What Is Microsoft Plus?

Microsoft Plus! is a companion program to Windows 95 that you purchase separately. Plus! makes it easier to maintain Windows 95 on your system and enhances the look of your desktop. It offers several features:

- **System Agent** monitors your system and performs disk maintenance tasks, like checking disk space and starting scheduled programs.

- **Disk Compression** is improved with the addition of DriveSpace 3.

- **Desktop Enhancements** such as animated mouse pointers, font smoothing, desktop themes, improved window dragging, new desktop icons, wallpaper stretching, and the new Pinball game are included.

- **Network and Internet features** improve Internet setup and provide Internet mail support, Internet Explorer, Internet security, automatic dial-up, server capabilities for dial-up networking, and scripting support for dial-up networking.

Installing Microsoft Plus!

To install Microsoft Plus on your hard disk:

1. Locate the CD code on your CD case. Write it down. You'll need to enter it later in the installation.

2. Insert the CD with the Microsoft Plus! program into your CD-ROM drive (or the installation disk in your floppy disk drive). The opening window of the installation program should automatically appear (see Figure A.1).

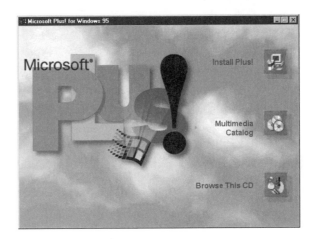

Figure A.1   The opening window of the Installation program.

If the installation program doesn't automatically start, click **Start** and choose **Run** from the Start menu. Enter the drive name for your CD-ROM drive and the name of the file that starts the program (**D:setup.exe**) and click **OK**.

3. Click the **Install Plus!** button.

4. A warning will appear asking you to close all open windows. Right-click on any buttons on the taskbar that represent open windows and choose **Close** from the pop-up menu. Click **Continue** when you have finished closing the open windows.

5. When the Name and Organization dialog box appears, enter your name in the **Name** box and the name of your company or organization (if you have one) in the **Organization** box. These boxes may already be filled in if you entered this information in Windows 95, so correct any errors.

6. Click **OK**. The Confirm Name and Organization Information dialog box appears. If the information you entered for your name and organization is correct, click **OK**. If not, click **Change** to modify the information and then click **OK**.

7. Enter the 10-digit code that is on the sticker attached to your CD case (the one you looked for in step 1). Click **OK**.

8. The installation program displays the path and name of the folder where it's going to copy the program files. If you want it stored in another folder, click **Change Folder**. If it's acceptable, click **OK**.

9. Click **Typical** to have Microsoft Plus! installed with the most common options, or click **Custom** to control which options you want installed. Unless you feel comfortable in many program choices, select the typical installation.

10. Choose whether you want the System Agent to run certain system maintenance tasks at night by clicking **Yes**. If you don't leave your computer on at night, click **No** and the System Agent will run the tasks during the day when you aren't using the computer.

11. After the installation program copies all the files to your hard disk, it offers you the choice of selecting a desktop theme next. Click **OK** (click Cancel in the next window if you decide not to use a theme).

12. Choose a theme from the **Theme** drop-down list (see Figure A.2). In the **Previews** section click **Screen Saver** to test the screen saver or **Pointers, Sounds, etc.** to see the pointers and sounds that come with the theme. A sample desktop shows in the large window. Click **OK** when you've finalized your selection.

13. Click **Restart Windows** to reboot your computer and accept the Microsoft Plus! settings.

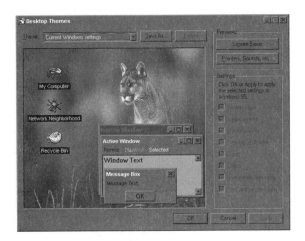

Figure A.2 The Desktop Themes dialog box.

Changing the Desktop Theme

Once you install Microsoft Plus!, you can access the Desktop Themes through the Control Panel to make any changes.

To open the dialog box and change your theme:

1. Click the **Start** button on the Taskbar.

2. Choose **Settings**, **Control Panel** from the Start menu.

3. Double-click the **Desktop Themes** icon in the Control Panel window (see Figure A.3).

4. The Desktop Themes dialog box opens (see Figure A.4). From the **Theme** drop-down list, select the desktop theme that you want to use. A preview of the desktop appears in the large box at the bottom left of the dialog box. In addition to showing the wallpaper for the theme you selected, it displays the new look for the desktop icons, active windows, inactive windows, and message boxes.

5. To see how your choice of theme affects your screen saver, click the **Screen Saver** button. Your screen blanks out and then the screen saver appears. Press any key or move the mouse to return to the dialog box.

Figure A.3   The Control Panel window.

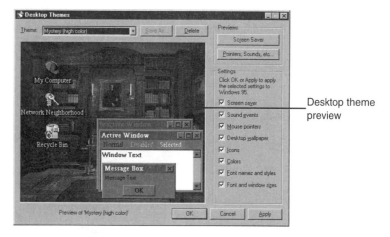

Figure A.4   The Desktop Themes dialog box.

6. To view the set of mouse pointers associated with your theme, hear the sounds attached to various system events, and look at visual elements changed by the theme, click the **Pointers**, **Sounds**, **Etc.** button. The Preview dialog box appears (see Figure A.5).

Figure A.5 The Preview dialog box with the Pointers tab selected.

7. Select the **Pointers** tab to see a list of Mouse pointer types associated with specific events. Click the mouse pointer type you want to view (such as **Busy**), and the pointer appears in the **Preview** window.

8. To investigate the sounds that are associated with your theme choice, select the **Sounds** tab (see Figure A.6). From the Sound event list box, click an event. A preview of the associated icon appears in the **Icon** box. Click the right arrow button next to the box to play the sound.

Click here to play sound

Figure A.6 The Preview dialog box with the Sounds tab selected.

9. To check the visual elements that your theme incorporates, select the **Visuals** tab (see Figure A.7). Click the Visual Element you want to check. If it's an icon, the element appears in the **Picture** box.

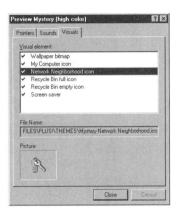

Figure A.7   The Preview dialog box with the Visuals tab selected.

10. When you have completed your survey of the pointers, sounds, and visual elements involved in your theme, click **Close** to close the Preview dialog box and return to the Desktop Themes dialog box.

11. In the **Settings** section of the Desktop Themes dialog box, click the theme settings you don't want to apply to Windows 95 to remove the check marks.

12. Click **Apply** to temporarily apply the theme settings to your desktop, so you can see what they look like. Click **OK** to accept the new settings.

Using Animated Mouse Pointers

Even if you don't change your desktop theme, you can use the animated mouse pointers available in Microsoft Plus!

To use an animated mouse pointer:

1. Click the **Start** button on the taskbar.

2. Choose **Settings**, **Control Panel** from the Start menu.

3. Double-click the **Mouse** icon in the Control Panel window.

4. The Mouse Properties box appears. Select the **Pointers** tab (see Figure A.8).

5. Click the pointer style you want to change (Working in Background or Busy work well as animated pointers).

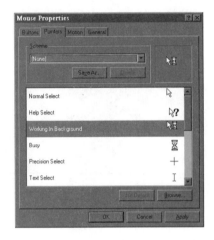

Figure A.8   The Mouse Properties box with the Pointers tab selected.

6. Click the **Browse** button to locate the file for the pointer you want to use. The Browse dialog box opens (see Figure A.9). Select the file you want (an example of it appears in the **Preview** box) and click **Open**.

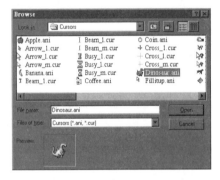

Figure A.9   The Browse dialog box.

7. Click **OK** to accept your new choice.

CAUTION

I Can't Find My Mouse Pointer Files   If you can't find the mouse pointers you want, try looking in the Windows\Cursors folder, the Program Files\Plus!\Themes folder, or the Microsoft Plus! folder.

Enhancing Your Display

Microsoft Plus! makes it possible for you to see the contents of a window while you're dragging it (instead of just an outline of the window), to change to large icons, to smooth the edges of screen fonts, to show icons using all possible colors, and to stretch the wallpaper to fit the entire screen (instead of tiling it).

To modify your display:

1. Click the **Start** button on the taskbar.

2. Choose **Settings**, **Control Panel** from the Start menu.

3. Double-click the **Display** icon in the Control Panel window.

4. The Display Properties box opens. Select the Plus! tab (see Figure A.10).

Figure A.10 The Display Properties box with the Plus! tab selected.

5. If you want to change your desktop icons, select the icon from the **Desktop icons** box and click the **Change Icon** button. The Change Icon dialog box appears (see Figure A.11).

6. In the **File Name** box, enter the file name and path of the icon you want to use (click **Browse** and select the file if you're not sure of the path or file name). Click **OK** to return to the Display Properties box.

Figure A.11   The Change Icon dialog box.

7. In the Visual Settings section, check the appropriate box:

- **Use Large Icons** enlarges the icons for files, folders, and shortcuts on the desktop. Large icons require more memory than smaller ones and may cause a decrease in performance.

- **Show Window Contents While Dragging** lets you see the contents of a window as you drag instead of just the border of the window. You may also see "trails" as you drag the window. Checking this item means you may not see what's behind a window as you move or size it.

- **Smooth Edges of Screen Fonts** smoothes the jagged edges of large fonts on your screen, making them more readable. You must have a video card and monitor that support 256-color or high-color for this feature to work properly.

- **Show Icons Using All Possible Colors** lets you use all the colors supported by your current display and color-palette settings. Using this feature involves up more computer memory, so it may take longer for your desktop to refresh.

- **Stretch Desktop Wallpaper to Fit the Screen** makes a centered wallpaper stretch to cover your entire screen, so you don't have to tile the image to cover your screen. To use this option, you must make sure to select **Center** as the **Display** choice for the wallpaper (on the **Background** tab).

8. Click **OK** to accept your modifications.

Starting the 3D Pinball Game

Microsoft Plus! adds a new game to your system: 3D Pinball. It looks like pinball games you see in arcades.

To start 3D Pinball:

1. Click the **Start** button on the taskbar.

2. Choose **Programs**, **Accessories**, **Games**, **Space Cadet Table** (see Figure A.12).

Figure A.12   The 3D Pinball window.

3. Choose **Help** to find out how to play the game.

Using the System Agent

On the more serious side, Microsoft Plus! contains several components that deal with system monitoring and maintenance. One such component is the System Agent. It checks your disk drives for available space and starts scheduled programs. To have System Agent continually monitor your system, you must leave your computer on and running, whether you're using it or not, although you can turn your monitor off.

The System Agent lets you schedule programs at times you specify. Disk Defragmenter, ScanDisk, and a low-disk space notification program run at regular intervals once you set up Microsoft Plus!

To schedule any other programs or adjust the settings of already-scheduled programs:

1. Click **Start** on the taskbar.

2. Choose **Programs**, **Accessories**, **System Tools**, **System Agent** (see Figure A.13).

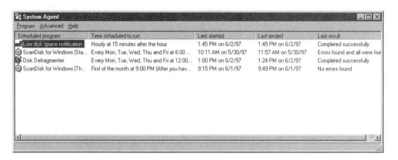

Figure A.13   The System Agent window.

3. Choose **Program**, **Schedule a New Program** to set up a new program schedule. In the Schedule a New Program dialog box (see Figure A.14), enter the name of the **Program**, add a **Description**, type the path of the program folder in the **Start In** box, and choose to **Run** the program in a **Normal Window**, **Minimized**, or **Maximized**. Then click **When to Run** to set the schedule. Set the time interval specifications and click **OK**.

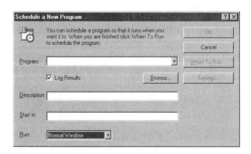

Figure A.14   Schedule a New Program dialog box.

Choose **Program**, **Change Schedule** to adjust the schedule of a program that's already scheduled (see Figure A.15). Specify the **Run** interval, the **Start At** time, and what to do **If the Program is Running and I Start Using My Computer**. Click **OK**.

TIP **How Much Warning Do You Want?** Set how much free space should be left on your drive before the low disk space reminder appears. In the System Agent window, select **Low Disk Space Notification** and then click **Properties**.

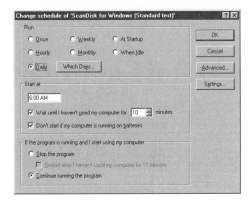

Figure A.15 Adjusting the program schedule.

Using Disk Compression

DriveSpace 3 is part of Microsoft Plus! It's an enhanced version of DriveSpace and supports an improved compression technology for creating compressed drives of up to 2 gigabytes.

Why would you create a compressed drive? The answer is that you're running out of space on your current hard drive. If you can't afford to install a new hard drive, DriveSpace 3 gives you a way around the problem by squeezing more space out of your current drive. DriveSpace compresses your files so they take up less room, but decompresses a file when you want to use it. It creates a second "drive" on your hard disk, which is not a real disk drive but is a large file (a compressed volume file, or CVF).

Using compressed drives can slow down your system when reading and writing files to the compressed drive. There are also some programs that cannot use compressed files, and sometimes you can't save large files to the compressed

disk. Therefore, you should talk to your system administrator if you're consider-
ing doing this at work or to someone who is knowledgeable in Windows 95
before tackling this yourself at home.

To create a compressed drive:

1. Click **Start** on the taskbar.

2. Choose **Programs**, **Accessories**, **System Tools**, **DriveSpace**.

3. Select the drive you want to compress from the list in the DriveSpace3
   window.

4. Choose **Drive**, **Compress** from the menu.

Internet and Network Tools

Microsoft Plus! includes several features to help you connect to and browse the
Internet, as well as tools to set up your computer so others can dial into it.

- **Internet Setup Wizard**   Plus! helps you set up an Internet connection
  using The Microsoft Network or another Internet access provider.

- **Internet Mail Support**   Plus! helps configure Microsoft Exchange if
  you're not using The Microsoft Network (already has mail set up) so you
  can send mail to and receive mail from other Internet users.

- **Internet Security**   Plus! provides support for "proxy" servers, which act
  as barriers between the Internet and your local area network (LAN). Proxy
  servers protect your network from being accessed by outsiders. All requests to and from the Internet are filtered through the proxy server, so
  your company information is not readily available to the Internet.

- **Automatic Internet Dial-Up**   Plus! includes automatic dialing capabilities
  to connect you to the Internet or disconnect you if you haven't actively
  used the Internet for a specified time.

- **Server Capabilities**   Plus! offers an addition to Dial-Up Networking that
  lets you dial in to your computer from a remote location and use its
  network resources. This feature includes password protection.

- **Scripting Support**   Because your Internet access provider requires
  information such as your user name and password to establish your
  connection, Plus! helps you create a Dial-Up Networking script to supply
  this information automatically when you dial in.

Installing Windows 95 OSR2

What's New in Windows 95 OSR2

OSR2 is the OEM Service Release 2 version of Windows 95. It is a version of Windows 95 which you can only get if you buy a new computer on which Windows 95 was installed by the OEM, the Original Equipment Manufacturer. This is because Microsoft has made OSR2 available only to computer makers for installation on their new computers. If you buy Windows 95 in the store, intending to upgrade an existing computer with it, you can only get the original version of Windows 95.

OSR2 includes a host of enhancements over the original version of Windows 95, and a lot of people covet some of those improvements. But Microsoft has made OSR2 available only to computer makers because most of the enhancements included in OSR2 support new hardware features that only new computers sport. That older computer of yours probably could not benefit from many of those new features in OSR2.

Still, there are some features in OSR2 that would benefit even us owners of older computers. Most of these are available from Microsoft's Web site. Downloadable enhancements, as set forth in Microsoft's Web site, include those listed in Table B.1. Some of these were not quite available yet, but merely "available soon" as of the time we wrote this.

Table B.1   Windows 95 Enhancements Available at www.microsoft.com

Enhancements	Description
Internet Explorer 3.0	Upgraded Internet browser.
Internet Connection Wizard	Upgraded wizard for setting up Internet connections.
Internet Mail and News	SMTP and POP3 mail client, and NNTP News reader.
NetMeeting	Make telephone calls over the Internet. Remotely view and control any program; share a whiteboard, chat; transfer files.
Personal Web Server	Set up your own, low-volume Web site.
DirectX 2.0 (including Direct 3D)	Graphics, sound, input, and communications enhancements for game players.
ActiveMovie	Video enhancements.
OpenGL	Support libraries for OpenGL graphics standard.
Dial-Up Networking Improvements	User interface enhancements, support for scripting, and hands-free dial-up.
Voice Modem Support	Support for VoiceView and AT+V modems to allow switching between voice and data transmission, and to allow the modem to answer voice calls.
Service for NetWare Directory Services	Client support for Novell NetWare 4.x, including NetWare Directory Services.
32-bit DLC	32 bit support for the Data Link Control protocol for SNA host connectivity.
Infrared Support	Support for Infrared Data Association (IrDA) 2.0 compliant devices—includes Infrared LAN connectivity.
Desktop Management	Support for Desktop Management Interface (DMI) 1.1—allows a desktop management application to monitor devices on the PC.
Display enhancements	Support for dynamically changing screen resolution and color depth. Adapter refresh rate can also be set with most newer display driver chipsets.
Wang Imaging for Windows 95	View image data from a variety of different file formats, including JPG, XIF, TIFF, BMP, and FAX. Scan and annotate images with built-in TWAIN scanner support and Imaging applet.

Fonts	Support for HP LaserJet 4 grayscale fonts.
Microsoft Network client 1.3	Performance improvements.
Fixes/updates	Various Windows 95 updates including: updated OLE components, enhanced Windows Messaging client with improved performance, and fixes to Microsoft Fax.

You can download the above-listed enhancements at **http:// www.microsoft.com/windows95/info/updates.htm**. Note: you may have to have a frame-compatible Internet browser to get to this page. If you are still using Internet Explorer 2.0, the version that comes with standard Windows 95, you will first have to download and install Internet Explorer 3.x or later or Netscape Navigator 3.x or later. Download Internet Explorer from Microsoft's World Wide Web site at **http://www.microsoft.com/ie/default.asp**. Download Netscape Navigator from Netscape's Web site at **http://www.netscape.com**.

Other features of OSR2, only available with new computers, are listed in Table B.2

Table B.2   Windows 95 Enhancements Only Available with a New Computer

Enhancements	Description
FAT32	Enhancements to the Windows 95 FAT file system designed to efficiently support large hard disks, up to 2 terabytes (1 terabyte = about 1 trillion bytes) in size. Includes updates to fdisk, format, scandisk, and defrag disk utilities to support FAT32 partitions.
DriveSpace Update	Updated version of the Windows 95 drivespace compression utility that supports compressed volumes up to 2 GB in size. (Note: drivespace compression is not supported on FAT32 volumes.)
Power Management Improvements	Support for Advanced Power Management (APM) 1.2 BIOS, wake-on-ring for modems, multi-battery PC's, drive spin down, and powering down of inactive PCMCIA modems.
Storage Enhancements	Support for IDE Bus Mastering, 120M optical/ floppy disk drives, removable IDE media, Zip® drives, and CD-ROM jukeboxes. Also adds the SMART predictive disk failure APIs.

continues

Table B.2 Continued

Enhancements	Description
PCMCIA Enhancements	Adds support for new PC Card 32 (CardBus) bridges, PCMCIA cards that operate at 3.3 volts rather than 5 volts, multifunction PCMCIA network/modem cards, and PCMCIA Global Positioning Satellite (GPS) devices.
CDFS Enhancements	Support for ISO 9660 CD-ROMs up to 4 GB in size, and CD-I format CD-ROMs.
PCI Bridging/Docking	Support for PCI devices used in PCI docking stations.
IRQ Routing	Support for PCI interrupt routers.
Intel MMX Support	Support for the Intel Pentium Multimedia Extensions (MMX) for improved audio and video support on Intel Pentium MMX and Pentium II and later processors.
NDIS 4.0	Support for NDIS 4.0 network interface card drivers.
Automatic scandisk on boot	If a PC was not shut down normally, scandisk automatically runs at the next reboot in order to check for damaged files.
Online Services Folder	Client software for America Online 3.0, CompuServe 3.0, CompuServe WOW!, and AT&T Worldnet.

Of the features listed in Table B.2, many would be welcome additions to our older computers. The foremost example of such a feature is the FAT32 file system. The original FAT16 (File Allocation Table — 16-bit) file system supported by DOS- and Windows-based computers did not anticipate that we would all be packing hard drives of one gigabyte capacity and higher. FAT16 is very wasteful of disk space on these large hard drives.

All computer file systems allocate disk space in blocks of some minimum size—say, for example, 4096 bytes. This means that, no matter how small a file is, it will occupy at least 4096 bytes of space on disk. Thus, a batch file storing only 100 bytes of actual data would waste 3996 bytes of disk space. This wasted space is known as *slack space*.

The design of the FAT16 file system permits the disk drive to be divided up into a maximum of 65,536 allocation units. On a one-gigabyte drive, this means that each file, no matter how small, must occupy at least 16,384 bytes of disk space.

On a two-gigabyte drive, each file must occupy at least 32,768 bytes of space. On a four-gigabyte drive, each file must occupy at least 65,536 bytes of space. A 100-byte batch file on one of these disks wastes ridiculous amounts of slack space.

The FAT32 file system increases the potential number of file allocation units on a disk to over 4 billion. This in turn makes it possible for us to reduce the size of an allocation unit on our 4-gigabyte disk to the 4096 bytes or so that we used to enjoy with our 80-megabyte disks of yore. This is a vast increase in efficiency. If you are pushing the limits of your hard drive and are trying to figure out how to avoid laying out several hundred dollars for yet more disk capacity, the prospect of recovering thousands of bytes of slack space per file is very tempting.

Trouble is, you can't do it, because Microsoft won't sell you the version of Windows 95 that allows you to do it. However, if you can get your hands on a properly licensed copy of the OSR2 version of Windows 95, then there is a way to upgrade your computer to it and, in so doing, gain the benefit of, among other features, the FAT32 file system. The trouble here is that, since Microsoft didn't intend you and me to be upgrading our computers in this way, it can't be done. The best you can do is blow away your current Windows installation entirely, then install OSR2 from scratch, then re-install all of your software and restore all your data files from backup.

To do this *and* install the FAT32 file system, we have to use a tedious manual process which involves two separate installations of Windows 95 OSR2 edition on your hard disk, as well as two reformattings and one repartitioning of your hard disk with the format and fdisk commands. If you are not familiar with these commands, stop reading right now, cart your computer over to a computer store, and pay them to install additional hard disk capacity in your computer. If you are not familiar with these commands but want to become so, then you need to learn about DOS. Stop reading right now, run over to your nearest well-stocked computer book store, and buy a book about DOS and start reading and learning.

If you are knowledgeable about DOS and the Windows 95 install process, you are adventurous, and you are still game to upgrade your computer to FAT32, the steps you must follow appear below. These steps are from the readme file included with the copy of OSR2 that comes on the Microsoft Developer Network (MSDN) CD-ROMs. This is the only version of OSR2 that Microsoft distributes except to OEMs themselves. The MSDN version is intended for software developers to use in testing their software.

The steps below also include extra information gleaned from our experience with the OSR2 installation process. Read these steps carefully and make sure you understand what is going on before actually performing the process. The general idea is that you will install OSR2 once, use it to make a bootable floppy that includes the FAT32-compatible version of fdisk that comes with OSR2, then repartition your hard drive to FAT32, reformat the partition, and re-install OSR2 onto this new partition. If, of course, you already have OSR2 installed on a computer—say, because you recently bought a new computer that had OSR2 installed at the factory—then you could skip over step 4 and the first cycle through steps 5 through 11. You could jump from step 3 to step 12, and save yourself from the first installation of OSR2.

1. Back up every important file on your hard disk.

2. Make sure you have a valid Certificate of Authenticity for the copy of OSR2 that you are installing. You will need the number from it when installing OSR2. If you are using the version of OSR2 that comes on the MSDN CD-ROMs, the number is included in the readme file, and is for use only on software test systems.

3. Examine the config.sys and autoexec.bat files on the hard disk to determine what files are necessary to make your CD-ROM drive operable from a plain DOS command prompt.

4. Prepare a bootable floppy disk that includes the drivers for your CD-ROM drive identified in step 3, above. The disk should also include mscdex.exe, xcopy.exe, format.com, and, optionally, sys.com, edit.com and qbasic.exe. The versions of these programs should be the same as the version of DOS that the floppy disk boots up into. If the bootable floppy boots to the Windows 95 version of DOS, you can copy these files from the c:\windows\command folder. If the floppy boots to an earlier version of MS-DOS, you can copy the files from the c:\dos directory.

5. Reboot the computer with the disk you made in step 4.

6. Using the format program on the boot floppy disk, reformat your hard disk. Either use the /s switch to make the new hard disk bootable, or use sys.com to add the operating system files to the hard disk after formatting it. Reformatting the hard drive will, of course, wipe out all information on it, so we hope you didn't neglect step 1, above.

7. Copy the CD-ROM drivers, mscdex.exe, and xcopy.exe from the floppy disk to the hard disk.

8. Set up a config.sys file and autoexec.bat file on the newly formatted hard drive that will cause the system to load the CD-ROM device drivers and run mscdex.exe at system startup.

9. Reboot the system from the newly formatted drive C:.

10. Copy the Windows 95 installation files from the OSR2 directory on the MSDN CD-ROM into a temporary subdirectory on the new drive C:.

11. Install Windows 95 from the copy in the temporary directory. You can do a minimal install if you want, since, in step 12, you will only be using this installation of Windows 95 to create a FAT32-compatible version of the floppy disk you created in step 4.

12. When the OSR2 version of Windows 95 is installed and running, make yet another bootable floppy disk, this time containing the OSR2 version of DOS, the same CD-ROM drivers as in step 4, above, and the OSR2 versions of mscdex.exe, xcopy.exe, format.com, fdisk.com, and, optionally, sys.com, edit.com, and qbasic.exe.

13. Reboot the system using this new boot floppy disk.

14. Use fdisk to delete the partition from the hard disk, then create a new partition. If the partition is larger than 528 MB, fdisk will automatically create a FAT32 partition. When you exit from fdisk, it will force a reboot of your system.

15. After your system reboots, follow steps 5 through 10, above, to reformat drive c: and re-install Windows 95 OSR2 edition. This time, when you re-install Windows 95, do a full install, since this will be your final working version of Windows 95.

16. After Windows 95 is installed and running, re-install all of the software that was previously installed on your system and restore any backed up data files that you will need.

Again, don't take this upgrade lightly. If there is any doubt that you know your way around DOS or you don't understand all of the instructions you find in this chapter, wait to upgrade when the next release of Windows is available.

Index

U

Y-Z